Violence in Early Renaissance Venice

A Volume in the
Crime, Law, and Deviance
Series

Guido Ruggiero

Violence in Early Renaissance Venice

Rutgers University Press
New Brunswick, New Jersey

Felice Bradley Fund

Library of Congress Cataloging in Publication Data

Ruggiero, Guido, 1944–
  Violence in early Renaissance Venice.

  (Crime, law, and deviance series)
  Bibliography: p.
  Includes index.
  1. Crime and criminals—Italy—Venice—History.
2. Violence—Italy—Venice—History. 3. Venice—
Social conditions. 4. Venice—History—697–1508.
I. Title. II. Series.
HV6995.V45R84   364.1′5′094531   79–25650
ISBN 0–8135–0894–0

For Kris

CONTENTS

LIST OF FIGURES

LIST OF TABLES

ACKNOWLEDGMENTS

A number of outstanding teachers prepared the way for the writing of this book, foremost among them Henry Catalino, Paul Miller, Boyd Hill, Richard Rouse, and Lauro Martines. Lauro especially has overseen this project with a deft reading of the manuscript at several stages and by providing a great deal of valuable advice and support.

The people of Venice played a very important role in this book also. The staffs of the Archivio di Stato, the Marciana, Correr and Querini-Stampalia libraries, and the Fondazione Giorgio Cini were all helpful. Venetian friends, especially Fabio Barzellato and Federica Ravizza, frequently acted as a private foundation supporting this foreign scholar.

Fellow students of Venice provided both intellectual stimulation and many pleasant Venetian days, most notably Giorgio Ferrari, Gaetano Cozzi, Frederic Lane, Donald Queller, Felix Gilbert, Benjamin Kohl, Paul Grendler, John Law, John Manion, and especially Deborah Longair and Martin Lowry. At the University of Cincinnati students and colleagues have contributed as well; Gary Ness, Leonard Harding, Kathy Holwadel, Debra Norris, Elaine Carte, and Mary Lindemann were unusually helpful. A special note of thanks must go also to Marlie Wasserman, a very efficient and thoughtful editor. Both the Taft Foundation and the University of Cincinnati Research Council provided a series of much appreciated small grants which helped to finance this project.

Finally, I would like to thank the editors of the *Journal of Criminal Law and Criminology* and the *Journal of Social History* for permission to reprint from articles of mine that appeared in those journals. My thanks also for permission to use material from my article "The Church of State in the Bureaucratic State," © 1979 by The Regents of the University of California, reprinted from *Viator* 10 (1979) by permission of the Regents.

Of course writing a book has its trials along with its pleasures. One person more than any other carried me through the former while adding to the latter: Kris Ruggiero. This book is a better work because of the help of everyone mentioned here and many others as well, but especially for Kris's unfailing support. The errors, which I hope are few, of course remain mine.

INTRODUCTION

The current fascination among historians with violence has largely concentrated on revolutionary violence—the point at which violence threatens to rend, suddenly and irreparably, the fabric of society. This concentration reveals more about contemporary values and fears than it does about violence in a historical context. I prefer to focus on violence as a concept expanded to include the broad range of interactions that a given society—in this case fourteenth-century Venice—considered asocially aggressive. One limitation is immediately apparent. If we adopt the perspective of Venetian society, we are limited to a great extent to the vision the leaders of that society expressed in their own documents. In manipulating power and authority, leaders often create a private reality only poorly related to actual historical events. Nevertheless, to understand a society, we must first view it as its leaders perceived it and revealed it in the documents they left behind. Only after we have done so can we take a more detached, and perhaps more objective view.

The principal violent crimes one finds reported in the Venetian archives are murder, assault, sexual violence, and verbal violence. Clearly only a sample of Early Renaissance violence, the reports of these crimes nonetheless reflect the perception of violence by a broad spectrum of the Venetian ruling class. The nature of the perceptions revealed in the archival sources is central. Behind the irregularities of reportage and the biases of witnesses, judges, and record keepers lies a structure of social norms and values unencumbered by the accepted rhetorical and moral trappings of society. I use *perception* rather than *definition* because perception implies an awareness not limited to self-conscious reason. For example, although rape was legally and morally defined in Venice as a serious crime, the handling of cases and the minimal penalties imposed by the courts reveal that it was perceived to be unimportant.

This perception of violence, often unarticulated, was and remains a crucial factor in the development of political and social structures. During the Renaissance, the idea that violence was the primary danger threatening political and social organization was a crucial touchstone of civic rhetoric and myth—especially in Venice. Such rhetoric identified violence as an action that "disturbs the peace and honor of the state," that disrupts the inherent justice of the state, and that almost incidentally does damage to the victim. The priorities are significant. The primary perception of violence in relation to the state's view of itself provides a telling measure of the political and social self-awareness of the ruling class. It was seen only secondarily as an indicator of the value of justice, social defense, and order. The damage inflicted upon an individual was of only tertiary importance.

Understanding the perception of violence reveals much else as well. For a social historian, it is the key to an entire style of life—from minutiae to grand generalizations. On the one hand, it shows us that the crowd of vagabonds and displaced people sleeping under the Rialto bridge was so dense that a late arrival could be tossed without compunction into the Grand Canal to drown; it shows that a noble lady's light lunch of broth with bread floating in it might be liberally seasoned with arsenic by an unhappy husband; it shows that working-class mothers regularly slept with their young children—perhaps a form of birth control, but certainly an obstacle for rapists. On the other hand, the Venetian attitude toward violence gives us an insight into the consequences of hardening class perceptions, loosening sexual mores, and tense family relationships in a world caught between feudalism and capitalism, ritual and reason, violence and order.

For the study of violence in Venice, the years between 1290 and 1406 are particularly appropriate. The period began with the social definition and state reorganization initiated by Doge Pietro Gradenigo and best exemplified by the Serrata of the Major Council, which within a few decades created a hereditary nobility in charge of a sophisticated bureaucracy and state economy. In 1406, the permanent expansion of Venice onto the mainland significantly altered the problem of social defense and consequently altered the perception of violence, especially in such areas as speech and sedition.

This century saw the formation of a social order dominated by a hereditary elite—a ruling group aware of its uniqueness and importance, whose values tended to dominate society. A bureaucratic state also evolved in this period that engulfed and transformed the medieval commune without completely destroying it, much as the modern city has transformed the nineteenth-century city. The last major attempts to overthrow Venetian society by revolution took place; and the great war with Genoa, which had spanned two centuries, exhausted state finances, and secured Venice's predominant position in Mediterranean trade, came to an end. Finally, this was the century of the plague, of declining export markets, and of increasing Venetian investment in industry. In sum, this was the period that built the economic, political, and social foundations of Venice's golden days as a Renaissance power.

I have tried to approach the subject of violence and its perception in a straightforward manner. In the first section, I trace the steps by which Venice organized a bureaucracy to control violence. In the second, I explore the social context of violence both quantitatively and qualitatively. In the final section, I examine the perception of violence in the context of four major crimes: speech, assault, rape, and murder. By moving from the institutional to the social to the perceptual, I hope to unfold the layers of meaning implicit in violence and thereby enrich our understanding of Early Renaissance Venice, encourage similar studies in other cities, and supply some historical background for the modern study of violence.

The State and Violence

On July 10, 1355, the people of Venice witnessed the ritual execution of an assassin named Federico da Ferrara. Venetians were accustomed to such spectacles, recurring dramas that symbolized the state as protector and avenger. Although Federico was executed at the order of a complex bureaucracy, his execution was carried out with elaborate symbolic ritual. The bureaucracy responsible, though it had ritual moments, primarily reflected the rationalizing, order-seeking drives of a merchant-banker nobility. Similarly, although the ritual of execution had rational overtones, it reflected a tradition in which government, by modeling its public actions on religious ceremony, appropriated some of the transcendent qualities of religion for its secular ends.

Ritual action and bureaucratic action, emotional needs and rational needs form an uneasy partnership in a state; yet the strength of Venetian institutions lay precisely in the success with which these two traditions concomitantly created a subtle range of responses to the problems of urban life—especially violence—that threatened Venetian stability.

In Federico's case, the path to execution began with an orderly passage through the councils and committees responsible for controlling crime. He was tortured by a *collegio,* an ad hoc committee of high-ranking officials who oversaw torture. On the basis of evidence obtained in this manner and of other evidence collected, he was prosecuted by the Avogadori of the commune (loosely speaking, the state attorneys); and he was convicted and sentenced to death by the Forty, a council representative of the most important families of Venice. The sentence pronounced, Federico was taken immediately to a waiting boat to undergo the ceremony of execution. The penalty was to be far less businesslike than what preceded it. Federico had entered a different world, an older tradition, a ceremonial tradition where individuals became archetypes or mythic exemplars and where the purification of society was symbolized by the bloody removal of the violent disruptor.

The act of removing the offending member of society was so vivid that Jacobo Bertaldo, a state chancellor of the early fourteenth century, suggested that the concept of state justice be symbolized by having the doge always followed in public processions by an official displaying the ducal sword used to "cut off the offending member." This was hardly a perverse fascination with the bloodletting authority of the state. Rather, it expressed the deepest meaning of the state, in its promise of order and tranquility. The doge displayed the sword of justice in public ceremony much as the pope displayed the cross. Both objects were representations of the authority of the men who possessed them.[1]

For Federico, his initiation into this mystery of the state was deadly; for the Venetians who watched, it was a ritual of purification. Federico was first rowed up the Grand Canal to the far end of Venice, his guilt proclaimed by a communal herald. He was then led back over land, the chanting continuing, to the Rialto bridge, where the crime had taken place. There his right hand, the "offending member," was cut off and hung by a chain around his neck. Next he was led to the Fontico Frumenti, the communal grain office which also served as a treasury. Here he handed over to the state the forty-eight ducats paid for the assassination. Through these acts, the state was ritually undoing the crime: it eliminated the hand that carried out the deed; it reintegrated the blood money; and it would complete the renewal through one final action.

Federico was brought back to the main square of Venice, San Marco, and there in the piazzetta where land met sea, before the Ducal Palace and Cathedral of San Marco, between the columns of justice at the center of Venice, he was hanged. This execution of a simple leather worker purified the state and renewed its promise of order and stability. It also demonstrated the state's antipathy to paid assassins.[2]

It is not surprising that the political theorists of the Middle Ages saw important connections between the church and the state as administrative and spiritual entities. This was a natural association, not merely because the state copied many of its institutions from the church but because the state was and remains in many ways a secular church. The emotional context of the state, which if the state is to survive transcends its blunter legal and administrative powers with a spiritual mystique, is an aspect of political organization that cannot be overlooked. In the study of violence, this is especially apparent; and in Venice it is especially important, inasmuch as the ruling nobility responded to violence with a complex mixture of rational and ritual solutions. The result was a unique ability to apply state power to the control of extralegal violence.

Chapter I

THE CONTROL
OF VIOLENCE

The Destruction of the Falier Conspiracy

On Wednesday night, April 15, 1355, Venice was in grave danger from a plot to "cut to pieces" the members of the Major Council. In that by that date membership in the Major Council was synonymous with political and social nobility, the plot struck at the roots of established Venetian order. Worse, the plot was tied to the symbolic leader of the nobility: the Doge, Marin Falier.[1]

That night, informants revealed the plot to a few Venetian nobles, who quickly called together the ducal councilors: Giovanni Mocenigo, Ermolao Venier, Tomaso Viadro, Giovanni Sanuto, Pietro Trevisan, and Pantaleone Barbo. As the highest executive officers of the commune below the doge, they were the most prestigious group to whom the case could be taken; but they were not politically or legally strong enough to act without assistance. After assessing the extent of the danger to the state, they therefore called together the primary governmental bodies that oversaw public security in trecento Venice. Either at the Ducal Palace or at the church of San Salvatore, the councilors met with the heads of the Forty, the Avogadori (excepting Nicolo Falier, brother of the doge), the Signori di Notte, the Capi di Sestiere, the Cinque alla Pace, and most important, the Council of Ten. This larger group sent out a contingent to capture the principal suspected conspirators, who were then tortured in order to elicit the full extent of the danger to the commune.[2]

Their torture-extracted testimony finally identified the aged Doge Falier as leader of the conspiracy, although he had been implicated earlier. With the magnitude of the danger clear, the Ten, heart of this peacekeeping complex, took control of the situation. Swiftness, secrecy, and unlimited power were its characteristics. It put special patrols into the streets, armed the nobility, and called in troops from Chioggia. By the next evening, with the streets under their control, the Ten met with a *zonta*—an ad hoc committee of twenty of the most important communal leaders—to adjudicate the case of Marin Falier. Before morning, this enlarged Ten had interrogated the doge, secured his confession, voted for decapitation, and seen the sentence carried out in the Ducal Palace. By that time, the other main conspirators had also been taken. The streets of Venice were quiet, and the threat to order had been eliminated. In less than forty-eight hours, a conspiracy of grave potential danger led by the chief executive officer of the city had been destroyed. Its destruction was primarily a result of the efficiency of the Venetian bureaucracy.[3]

Little more than a half-century before, a conspiracy to "cut the Major Council to pieces" would have been unlikely. In 1290, the Major Council was merely an important representative council. By 1355, it had become the base of a state hierarchy. It acquired this position primarily because of the Serrata of 1297–1298. Within a short span of time, this Serrata defined the ruling class of Venice, made it hereditary, and allowed all adult male members automatically to sit on the Major Council. As a result, the Major Council in a sense became the state: virtually all offices were filled by it and virtually all officers drawn from its ranks. Furthermore, by 1310 membership in the Major Council was synonymous with noble status. Thus the Falier conspiracy to assassinate the members of the Major Council was essentially an attempt to overthrow the political and social order established by the Serrata. By that time, however, the state had developed an effective organization to counter just such a threat.[4]

More general social trends were taking place in northern Italy as well, from which Venice was by no means isolated. At the end of the thirteenth century, a merchant-banker elite that had already gained economic status was attempting to defend that position politically and legally. Within this context, the Serrata was parallel in general social terms to the Florentine Ordinances of Justice (1293) and variations adopted by other communes. The Ordinances of Justice attempted to limit the competition for elite status in Florence by barring from communal office those labeled magnates. This exclusion of a group of powerful families, most of whom were representative of an older set of dysfunctional social values, theoretically meant that the office-holding group would be drawn primarily from a monied group not unlike the Venetian nobility defined by the Serrata—though the wealth of the latter may have been generally older and more trade oriented. It is significant that those who defended the ordinances stressed that the magnates as a class were responsible for disrupting the orderly function of society. The ordinances were consequently justified as an attempt to control violence.

This argument was not entirely rhetoric: the merchant-banker elite, although they maintained much of the honor code and religious ideals of an older elite through a sort of inertia of values, required a more controlled environment. Socially acceptable levels of violence became much more narrowly defined throughout the cities of northern Italy at this time. The Florentine Ordinances of Justice are a fine example of this tendency. They were designed to restrict a set of class behaviors that interfered with the style and economic requirements of urban commercial life.

In Venice, the dominance of a merchant elite had a longer tradition than it enjoyed in many other cities. The Serrata was nevertheless the specific event that locked this elite into place at the top of society. First in the Major Council, then through the Venetian Senate, they imposed a system of state-controlled capitalism of rare sophistication for the period. Self-centered power so openly displayed required an even more careful form of public security than the Ordinances of Justice provided for the merchant-bankers of Florence. In Venice's geographically isolated urban environment, moreover, the technical problems of institutionalized peacekeeping were considerably lessened. These broad social trends, in combination with the Serrata and the need to protect a legally defined nobility, impelled Venice toward controlling society as it had not been controlled before through a complex organization of public power for public security.

The Traditional System

At the beginning of the fourteenth century, the linchpin of this organization—the Council of Ten—did not exist. The responsibility for maintaining the peace was dispersed through a number of councils limited by ritualistic traditions and confused lines of authority. Writing before the full meaning of the Serrata became apparent, Jacobo Bertaldo (in *Splendor venetorum civitatis consuetudinum*) placed the prime responsibility for maintaining order within Venice in the hands of the doge and his councilors.[5] Although Bertaldo described a period during which the dogeship enjoyed a renaissance under the forceful leadership of Pietro Gradenigo, these powers were nevertheless shared, primarily with the Forty—a council with both legislative and judicial authority. The Forty, in turn, was limited by its reliance on the Avogadori of the commune, who, rather like a modern grand jury, referred cases to it.[6]

In this system, the Avogadori were the central element. They investigated most criminal cases and many civil cases; and depending upon the results of their investigations, they chose the relevant council for adjudication. By 1300, this process, limited by a host of customs, had become too cumbersome to operate efficiently, especially in response to security problems.

More immediate in their response to disorder in this traditional system were the Cinque alla Pace and the Signori di Notte. The Cinque alla Pace was a patrolling body responsible for keeping the peace. It was aided by small groups of *custodi* who worked under each of the five noble members of the council. It also provided summary justice in the streets for minor violent crimes, carrying illegal weapons, or violating curfew. Unfortunately, no records of the Cinque are preserved from the trecento. The Five must have been busy, however, because the *Gratie* record thousands of adjustments to the jail sentences and fines they levied.[7]

The Signori di Notte comprised a more powerful group of peace-keepers. According to Bertaldo, as a council it had "extraordinary power." It could—on its own authority or by order of the doge—capture and imprison robbers, rapists, fornicators, and any other malefactors who threatened the order of the commune. To perform this policing function, each councilor had the help of a body of armed assistants. Together, the Cinque alla Pace and the Signori di Notte were the focus of active efforts to keep the peace in the streets of Venice.[8]

The Rise of the Ten, 1310–1355

Long before the 1350s, the Council of Ten began a radical reordering of the traditional network of peace-keeping bodies. The doge and his councilors, backed by the Major Council, were still theoretically the source of all power directed toward maintaining order; but in practice the Council of Ten had taken over most of this authority, especially in matters concerned with social stability, where it had the power to act independently and override all other councils.[9]

A little more than a decade after the Serrata, persistent popular unrest in conjunction with a growing awareness of the closed nature of Venetian society finally induced the elite to respond by establishing an institution—the Ten. This unrest was first indicated by the conspiracy of Marin Boccono. Early in 1300, Boccono, "who had a great following and was related to many popolari," attempted a forced entry to the Major Council to challenge the closed nature of that body.[10] While a large group of armed supporters strolled menacingly in the piazza of San Marco, Boccono and eleven associates, all secretly armed, presented themselves at the Ducal Palace and demanded entrance to the session of the Major Council then in progress. They planned to enter the council, where by law all were unarmed, to do a bit of pruning of their opponents and secure open admission again. Pietro Gradenigo was their main target because he was popularly held responsible for the Serrata.[11]

Luckily for Gradenigo, some word of the conspiracy was overheard at the church of the Servi. The doge's party sent a troop of its own followers to mingle in the square with Boccono's men. Council members were also ordered to come armed to the meeting. Deceived by the size of the crowd, Boccono was reportedly encouraged by the number of men in the square. When he presented himself at the door of the Major Council, he may have been even more encouraged, for he was greeted by a friendly doge who told him that he and his eleven henchmen had just been made members of the council. Once they entered the palace, however, they were quickly arrested and turned over to the Signori di Notte and the Avogadori, who had them tortured in the Camera del Tormento to discover all the particulars of the conspiracy. That night all twelve were executed, and their bodies were hung between the columns before the palace.[12]

This sight must have profoundly impressed Boccono's popular followers in the morning. When they peacefully left the piazza the day before, they believed their leaders were meeting with a humbled Gradenigo who was acceding to their demands. Meanwhile, the investigation by the Signori di Notte and the Avogadori identified more than forty others who were significantly involved. They were quickly banned from communal territory, and their property was confiscated.[13]

On the whole, the response to the conspiracy was restrained. Hanging the corpses of the executed between the columns of St. Mark's, though a bit rushed, was typical of the Venetian concept of exemplary punishment. Bodies hanging before the palace were always a forceful reminder about the dangers of revolutionary behavior. The banishment of lesser conspirators was a common expedient in most late medieval Italian communes. Exile eliminated the dissidents as a force in the city but avoided the potential turmoil and vendetta that could result from mass executions. But the commune took no radical steps to prevent future rebellions: no new councils were set up to meet the threat of popular unrest; no new police patrols were instituted to keep the people quiet.

Gradenigo and his followers apparently believed that they—along with the Signori di Notte and the Avogadori—had dealt effectively with the conspiracy. Few really important people were involved, so once the leaders and the element of surprise had been destroyed, they considered the danger over. In fact, with its leaders gone, the popular party went underground.[14]

By 1310, it was much more obvious that the Major Council (and through that body the government itself) was closed. In consequence, the Querini–Tiepolo conspiracy of that year posed a much more serious threat. The Major Council had become an unusually well defined ruling class. Those outside had a much clearer sense that governmental power was beyond their grasp. In later years, the commune developed more subtle ways to mask this harsh distinction; but in 1310, the distinction was perhaps as apparent as it ever was.[15]

Nicolo Trevisan, writing in his *Cronaca di Venezia* within a half-century of the Querini–Tiepolo conspiracy, gave three reasons for this threat to the established order: first, a rejection by the conspirators of the restricted political enfranchisement caused by the Serrata; second, the rise of a

Guelph faction, to which the conspirators belonged, which was opposed to the Ghibelline policy of Gradenigo and his supporters; and finally, a series of personal disputes between the two factions.[16]

The personal conflicts within the ruling class that Trevisan pointed out are well known.[17] A more important factor in the conspiracy was the opposition of a Guelph faction to the war for Ferrara, an expensive venture against the papacy that was proceeding badly for Venice. The Guelph label here cannot be taken in the limited sense of the word, for in fourteenth-century political nomenclature, *Guelph* had little generic value. In 1310, the Venetian Guelph faction was led by families like the Querini and Badoer, whose large land holdings in the Padovano had helped them to strike up close relations with mainland Guelphs.[18] These ties made them natural opponents to a war with the papacy. Even Baiamonte Tiepolo, the major personality of the conspiracy, had Guelph ties.[19] Both archival and chronicle records show that after the initial optimism about the war had passed these families led an increasingly insistent opposition. By 1310, Venice was suffering under papal interdict and excommunication. This theoretically entailed the confiscation of Venetian goods and property and the treatment of Venetian merchants as bandits throughout Europe. In sum, an unsuccessful war and a too successful interdict hardened the areas of disagreement that already existed and formed two factions clearly at odds.[20]

Although these events may seem to minimize the effect of dissatisfaction with the Serrata, the third reason given by Trevisan for conspiracy, that discontent played its part both in the Querini–Tiepolo conspiracy and in the growing realization of the nobility that the revolutionary potential of the lower classes had been heightened by the Serrata. That the conspirators understood this was shown by the prominent place given to Baiamonte Tiepolo in the conspiracy. The Tiepolo name—rightly or wrongly, given the aristocratic character of Baiamonte—evoked memories of the long-standing Tiepolo association with the lower classes that culminated in 1289 in an attempt by the people to proclaim Baiamonte's father, Jacopo, doge. In this they were thwarted, receiving instead the young Pietro Gradenigo, leader of the Ghibelline ruling faction, who was now held responsible for both the Serrata and the war with Ferrara. When the Querini began planning their conspiracy, they enlisted Tiepolo, who had been living on his Trevisan estates, mainly for the popular support they assumed his name would bring.[21]

In the end, Baiamonte's potential for leadership was never tested and there was no opportunity for the people to give him their support because of flaws in the conspiracy itself. In keeping the conspiracy secret until the last moment, its leaders undoubtedly hoped that the people of Venice would come to their aid if necessary when they made their rush on the

Ducal Palace and support them once in power. The doge's rapid rout of the Querini–Tiepolo forces and the quick deployment of special patrols to control the streets made open public support of the conspiracy minimal. The attempt to take the Ducal Palace by surprise was over before it really began. The doge's careful actions to maintain public order immediately following the rout of the conspirators were nevertheless clear signs that substantial popular support for the conspiracy was feared.[22]

The first legislation passed by the Major Council following the conspiracy reflects a significant hardening of social distinctions. For the first time, the ruling class made a definite "we–they" distinction between their status as nobles and that of the rest of society. First, the nebulous question of noble status was defined. A *nobiles* was a man "who was or could be a member of the Major Council."[23] Thus the Serrata came to control social as well as political status. But this *parte* went further; it offered pardon to non-nobles who confessed to participating in the conspiracy because "they did not understand what they were doing."[24] This act was intended to strip Tiepolo and his fellow conspirators of their lower-class support. Beyond immediate, practical concerns, however, the rhetoric implied that non-noble conspirators were led astray by noble conspirators because they lacked the political understanding to be responsible for their actions and had no legitimate grievances of their own. This was mercy at a price: acceptance of the political and social distinctions created by the Serrata. A fear that the masses could rise up clearly lay behind this patronizing mercy. Those who did not come forward to beg the pardon of the doge were treated as severely as nobles. They and all their heirs were to be perpetually banned from Venice and all territory subject to Venice, and their property was to be confiscated.[25] The non-noble population, however, remained restive. On June 30, fifteen days after the failure of the conspiracy, the Major Council in effect declared martial law, granting full authority to the doge, his councilors, and the heads of the Forty. With full power to spend money, pass or repeal legislation, try, and execute, they acted essentially as a substitute government. This the *parte* made perfectly clear: "Everything which this group decides is legal as if it were decided by the Major Council."[26]

By July 10, it was apparent that these expedients would not lessen the continuing tension. In typical Venetian style, a temporary committee of ten *sapientes* was elected by the Major Council to meet with the emergency group and oversee the maintenance of order and the elimination of further threats by the Querini–Tiepolo conspirators.[27] This was the first Council of Ten. Although these *sapientes* were to meet only until September 29, their mandate was renewed no fewer than eight times, for periods of two months each, until January 30, 1312, when they were confirmed for five more years.[28]

In 1314, the Major Council, realizing that the original duties of the Ten were essentially finished, questioned whether it should be dissolved. By that time, however, the Ten was considered to be filling a new need; and it was continued. In 1316, the Major Council, arguing that the Ten "is so useful and necessary as is known" gave it a ten-year continuation. On May 12, 1325, it was prematurely given another ten-year extension. Finally, in 1335, the Major Council decided to make the Ten permanent "because it is most useful both for the preservation and honor of the society." This was sealed in 1339 when the Ten was approved by an *arengo,* a gathering of all citizens, which was convoked only rarely in the trecento to approve decisions of the highest importance.[29]

The Ten controlled social order by exercising the complex powers authorized in its original mandate. Because the development of its control cannot be traced in detail here, a broad outline must suffice. The Ten controlled speech, potentially so dangerous for elites that monopolize power, through intentionally vague rulings that allowed prosecution for everything from insult and threat to conspiracy against the nobility. Association was restricted, especially among non-nobles. At first, this restriction was directed against conspiratorial association; but by mid-century the Ten was overseeing any association with a potential for disruption, even the popular religious confraternities. Carrying arms, already restricted, was further limited and licensed. Gambling and drinking were regulated, taverns and hostels watched. Special regulations were even devised for festivals and public events. The Ten's primary concern, however, remained speech or deeds directed against the commune. Most of its fourteenth-century convictions fell under this broad responsibility.[30]

To make its authority respected and feared, the Ten created a system of patrols in the 1320s and 1330s which, at least theoretically, ensured that its agents were regularly policing the commune and that there was a militia always ready to preserve order. All these measures were supplemented by a sense of showmanship in the penalties imposed, including regular public mutilations and executions, which demonstrated the unhealthiness of behavior that threatened the nobility and created a climate of submission. In sum, thanks to the Ten's careful investment in the techniques of control, the Serrata's definition of society was not open to question.

Despite the range of the Ten's powers, the older apparatus, as was customary in Venetian government, continued virtually untouched, which caused a confused blend of new and old, rational and ritualistic, unlimited power and carefully circumscribed power—ill defined but amazingly effective. The suppression of the Falier conspiracy provides one example of this blend at the height of its success. Individual nobles, hearing of a plot that possibly involved the doge, turned immediately to the traditional center of legal authority in the commune, the ducal councilors. When the councilors realized that they would require a wider base of support, they mobilized virtually the whole of the peacekeeping apparatus of the state. That group arrested the major suspects, used torture to verify (to their minds at least) the extent of the danger, and traced the case to the doge himself. At this point, the Council of Ten took over. Its asset was its ability to act swiftly and without restraints. If the Forty or the Major Council had attempted to try Falier, the case could have stretched over months, with the danger that the doge might mobilize considerable support; but the Ten could and did act immediately. Within a day, the doge was dead. The ability of the Venetian peacekeeping apparatus to switch from traditional modes of operation to the application of unfettered power had ended the conspiracy. Although this case was too important to be regarded as typical, it demonstrates the unique flexibility of the system in the face of emergency. The blend of old and new gave the commune a unique range of possibilities which, if judiciously gauged, could be most effective in maintaining the status quo.

Another example of this flexibility can be seen in the handling of an assault on Francesco Contarini, called Rizo, by Donato Vitturi in 1336. Both men were nobles of important families in the trecento. Donato's testimony against Francesco in a litigation apparently set off the ensuing incident. Francesco took exception to the testimony, and words rapidly led to blows. In this case, Donato, who was illegally armed, got the better of his assailant—he hit Francesco twice over the head, leaving him so seriously wounded that the attending physician believed death was imminent. In the case of a potential murder, the physician was required by law to report the matter to the Signori di Notte. Francesco survived, however, and thereby saved his assailant from a major penalty, disproved his doctor's prognosis, and thwarted the investigation of the Signori di Notte, who passed the matter back to the Cinque alla Pace. Assault was more typically the Five's responsibility. Utilizing the testimony gathered by the Signori di Notte, the Five convicted Donato and fined him 200 lire di piccoli.[31]

This was not the end of the matter. The Avogadori, responding to the fact that important families were involved, stepped in to reinvestigate the case. Satisfied that the matter required a new hearing, they brought it before the politically and socially more sensitive Council of Forty for yet another trial. The Forty finally settled the matter by fining Donato 300 lire di piccoli.[32] This new penalty, though not much more costly, demonstrates how carefully the commune could match penalty to crime. A fine from the Cinque alla Pace did not have the same impact as a fine from the Forty. The former was primarily the technical decision of a limited body; but the latter was, at least in appearance, a careful assessment of the crime by a sizable body of the most important peers of the Vitturi and Contarini families. Through the medium of the Forty, both families were thus placed on notice that their peers considered the matter settled with the payment of the fine. Faction and vendetta were thereby discouraged. In sum, the process matched the crime. This flexibility gave the Venetian system of justice an unusual ability to restrict violence efficiently and effectively.

The Ten Annexes a Police Force, 1319–1355

When the Ten was created, it was only one element of a complex governmental organization concerned with the maintenance of public order; but when it gained its own police and espionage subsidiaries, it was able to bypass the cumbersome old public security complex. With policing powers, the Ten could move from arrest to execution on any act it considered a threat to the security of the state, without submitting to external checks.

Even before 1320, the Council of Ten began to move in this direction. On August 10, 1319, the Ten voted to create its own private patrolling body, the Capi di Sestiere, by electing one noble to lead four patrollers in each of the six *sestieri,* the main political divisions of the city. These nobles, who had to be more than thirty years of age, were elected for six-month periods.[33] Less than a year later, however, the Ten voted to discontinue the Capi. No reason for this change was given.[34] Perhaps it was difficult to attract nobles to and keep them in posts that were both dangerous and tedious. Nevertheless, the government still believed that a new patrolling group was needed to work with the Signori di Notte and the Cinque alla Pace in preserving public order and to guard against the more dangerous but nebulous social crimes the Ten oversaw. Within three months, the Major Council resurrected the Capi di Sestiere, calling for the election of nobles between thirty and forty years of age, one from each sestiere. By establishing a penalty of 100 lire for renouncing the office, the Major Council also made it more difficult to escape the responsibility. To make the job a bit safer, they provided eight well-armed men for each noble patroller, doubling the earlier four.[35]

Almost immediately, the Ten began to utilize the services of this patrolling group. In August 1324, the Capi di Sestiere reported to the Ten that Tuscus da Lucca had said "in an evil manner," "awful and dishonest words" at the Rialto against the "doge and the whole land." The Ten's response—perpetual banishment—showed that the Capi had captured a worker whose "dishonest words" were considered a substantial threat to Venetian society.[36]

By 1328, the relationship between the Ten and the Capi had become less informal as the Ten sought to expand the group and establish direct control over it. The first fragmentary references reveal directives to increase again the number of patrollers of each sestiere up to twelve, depending upon need.[37] In December, the Ten ruled that there should be two noble capi for each sestiere, implying that there would be between sixteen and twenty-four patrollers working in each. This extensive enlargement was justified as ensuring the "order and security of the land." When any disturbance (*rumore*) occurred, the patrollers were to quell it, then investigate it and report their findings in writing to the Ten within five days.[38]

Four days later, the Ten issued directives that made its intentions clearer. With this patrolling body, the Ten intended to establish a tight and efficient control of the city through a pyramidal organization that extended downward from the Ten to every able-bodied man within the city. The structure was as follows: the Ten oversaw the newly enlarged Capi di Sestiere, who in turn appointed and oversaw two Capi di Contrata for each *contrata* or neighborhood within the sestiere. These *contrate* were centered on virtually every little square of Venice; and the Capi di Contrata, besides being responsible for keeping track of each neighborhood, oversaw the *duodenas,* or popular militia, which organized all able-bodied men in the commune into groups of twelve. With this support behind them, the Capi di Sestiere became the strongest patrolling body in Venice. Most important, the Ten had gained authority in the streets, where a government's ability to control unrest is ultimately tested.[39]

The Ten effected this reorganization at a time when the Venetian nobility had been given yet another reason to be alarmed. Just before creating this elaborate mechanism, the Ten had voted to cut off the heads of the brothers Jacopo and Marino Barozzi, who led another conspiracy against the nobility. Contributing to the insecurity of the situation was the imminent death of Doge Soranzo, who was old and seriously ill. These conditions required that any disorders be crushed quickly and efficiently. It was from fear of a new period of popular unrest and reluctance to rely on the older institutions that the Ten assumed control of the Capi di Sestiere and undertook the elaborate reorganization designed to protect the political and social order that had grown up after the Serrata.[40] This new organization was to undergo many minor modifications, but it continued to assure that the authority of the Ten extended from the streets of Venice to the highest levels of the state.

Public Order and Police Patrols

Aided by the insularity of the city, patrolling bodies created or continued in the trecento were able to blanket the neighborhoods. The capture of Nicolo da Vicenza in 1351 exemplifies the success of these patrols. Nicolo planned to abduct Flos da Milano with the purported intention of marriage. Accompanied by several co-workers from Padua, he came to Venice and began to carry her off "by force with threats and drawn weapons." Flos was a reluctant bride, and a boatman at the *traghetto* to Mestre—the boat service between Venice and the mainland—noticed her struggles and refused them passage. The resulting quarrel became a brawl in which the boatman was wounded. A cry was immediately sent up for the Signori di Notte and the Cinque alla Pace.

Nicolo Mocenigo, one of the Signori di Notte, along with a number of his patrollers and some men from the Five, arrived just in time to see a stolen boat carrying Flos up the Grand Canal toward the inner lagoon and Mestre. Commandeering another boat, Mocenigo and his men gained rapidly on the kidnappers, who abandoned their boat at Santa Sophia and tried to escape through the narrow alleys. The patrollers eventually cornered the criminals at the edge of the lagoon in Cannaregio. After a brief struggle, with superior numbers and perhaps superior training, they captured and subdued Nicolo and his henchmen with a minimum of injury.[41]

This is an ideal example of law enforcement. The citizenry observed that a crime of violence was occurring, intervened, and put out a cry for the police. The police arrived in considerable force almost immediately. Moreover, it was a cooperative effort. Patrols from both the Signori di Notte and the Cinque alla Pace worked together under Mocenigo, apparently the only noble peacekeeper in the area at the time. They pursued the culprits aggressively and, assisted by Venice's isolation in the lagoons, captured them.

The rapid appearance of both the Signori di Notte and the Cinque alla Pace raises a question. Was it an accident that patrols from each group were nearby at the time of the crime, or were there always a considerable number of patrols on duty? Although the number of officials in the streets of Venice is difficult to calculate because there were constant variations, it is clear that collectively they constituted an unusually large patrolling force. The total was basically determined by a tension between the cost of their pay and the desire for as many patrols as possible. Implicit in this tension was the confidence that patrols would be effective in controlling the level of violence and crime in the city. The rhetoric of a *parte* passed by the Major Council in 1360 provides a typical example of this assumption: special patrols at the Rialto and San Marco were increased from eight men to twelve "so that brawlers and other malefactors may be captured." A raise in their salary was also justified: "These patrollers did not earn as much as others and thus were not of high quality"; and as a result, "the said areas were not well patrolled." Investing money in patrols promised to control disruption.[42]

Although the total number of patrollers fluctuated, a good estimate can be worked out on the basis of their number in 1382, just after the War of Chioggia. This war placed a heavy burden upon state finances; and to reduce it the commune adopted economies designed to limit the operating expenses of the government, including a cut in the number of patrollers. Patrollers of the Signori di Notte were reduced from twenty for each noble to sixteen. Before the reduction there were 120 patrollers, afterwards 96. The Capi di Sestiere were simultaneously reduced from 96 patrollers to 72.[43] The Cinque alla Pace normally had from 8 to 12 patrollers per capi. In addition, the Signori di Notte had special patrols at the Rialto and in the San Marco area of 12 men each.[44] Thus before the reduction of 1382 there was an active patrolling force of approximately 310 men, not including the noble councilors who patrolled occasionally as well; about 1 patroller for every 250 Venetians.[45] Even after the reduction, the number of patrollers probably did not drop much below 230, about 1 patroller for every 350 people. In emergencies, the Capi di Contrata and the civil militia could be called up as well. Venice was clearly equipped with a considerable police force.

In theory at least, there was yet another resource for peacekeeping in the streets. After 1349, all officials of the commune licensed to carry arms were empowered to stop fights in the streets, confiscate illegal weapons, summarily impose penalties, and receive portions of the fines imposed. Thus a considerable number of communal officials, if they were brave enough or acquisitive enough, could become ad hoc patrollers.[46]

Numbers, however, are only one aspect of a police force. The kinds of men who made up the force are also important. Leadership positions were held by nobles; non-nobles were responsible for most of the actual patrolling. Occasionally the records of arrests reveal nobles actively participating in patrols, and the capitularies of the policing councils called for such action; but later in the century, most patrolling was carried out by non-noble *custodi* or *pueri*, leaving noble councilors free to oversee administration and investigation.

This shift was prompted by more than a need for organizational efficiency. Patrolling the streets of Venice was tiresome and dangerous, with little reward in either prestige or pay. It is not surprising that nobles preferred the more sedentary world of council chamber and debate. In fact, wealthier non-nobles were apparently not interested in such dangerous posts either, so the patrollers tended to be drawn from the lower strata of society. Thus contact between patrollers and populace, usually a source of tension, pitted similar social groups against one another. Much of the popular resentment engendered by police patrols, as is discussed later, was aimed not at the noble creators of the patrols but at the lower-class patrollers. The latter often served as buffers for their noble superiors.[47]

Among members of the various councils concerned with violence, the nobles of the Ten tended to be the most important. The Ten actually comprised seventeen council members—including the doge, the ducal councilors, and one of the Avogadori di Comun. Because of the council's extensive and relatively undefined powers, membership was highly prized; and by the later years of the century, there were frequent cases of nobles rotating between the office of ducal councilor and that of councilor of the Ten. Important men could thus serve on the council for several years in succession. Family ties made the dominance of important nobles even more pronounced. As few as twenty families controlled the council throughout the century.

For example, Giovanni Mocenigo served on the Ten for four years between 1392 and 1407. His brother Leonardo served for three; and another brother, Tomaso, served for one—eight years representation within one immediate family in a fifteen-year period. The closeness of the brothers is attested by the fact that the latter two were executors of Giovanni's will. Another relative mentioned in this will was a nephew, Pietro Mocenigo, who himself spent three years on the Ten. Broader family contacts suggest an even more powerful position. Giovanni's sister, Campagnola, married into the Donà family, whose members sat on the council for ten of these fifteen years. Giovanni's daughter Helena married into the Molin family, whose members served four times. Finally, Giovanni himself married Caterucia Loredan, whose family served seven years on the council.[48]

Giovanni was also a man of considerable wealth. At his death, he was a Procuratore di San Marco, holding the most prestigious office in the commune after the dogeship, a position that implied great economic power. In his will, he distributed the sum of 3624 ducats, much of which was tied up in loans. He also made a considerable number of modest charitable bequests, leaving dowries of 12 ducats each, for example, to twelve poor but deserving young girls. It is difficult to estimate Giovanni's total worth from his will because, as was customary, rather than enumerating all of his wealth he left instructions for dividing up the residuus of his patrimony—the unspecified amount of property that his executors would find remaining after they had doled out his specified bequests—which may have been considerable or negligible. Nonetheless, like most members of the Ten, Giovanni was a man of substance, both personally and through his family connections.[49]

The Signori di Notte, Capi di Sestiere, and Cinque alla Pace were normally drawn from nobles of lesser standing, either because they came from families with less prestige or because they were young men at earlier stages of their careers. Although the policing function was vital to the city, little wealth or power was to be garnered from these posts. They were a form of state service that might eventually lead to higher opportunities. For important nobles, they could serve as stepping stones during youth; for lesser men, they were the only posts available.

Thus the creation of the Ten, with its powerful membership virtually unlimited by older traditions or "constitutional" checks, added the elements of speed and efficiency in the control of violence. Tradition and ritual could be preserved, but the Ten organized itself to operate efficiently at all levels of society from the streets to the Ducal Palace itself and presented an alternative that could cut to the heart of truly dangerous matters. The execution of Doge Falier symbolized how far that power could reach. More common crime, in contrast, was handled by traditional councils like the Signori di Notte and Cinque alla Pace, supported by their extensive patrolling organizations. The result was a unique blend of tradition and innovation that seems to have functioned well in the fourteenth century.

Chapter II

THE PREPARATION
AND TRIAL OF
CRIMINAL CASES

Tradition and Innovation

In his *Splendor venetorum civitatis consuetudinum,* Jacobo Bertaldo praised the Venetian procedure for handling criminals, with its display of justice, for teaching the people to avoid evil and do good.[1] Given this acknowledged moral context of justice, it is significant to find a tendency toward ritualism in the judiciary process itself. Such associations were not limited to Venice; but in Venetian judicial procedure, *il rito* ("the rite") had many ritual overtones.

This ritualism may have been a natural outgrowth of the sacred nature of oath taking, which played a dominant role in early medieval judicial procedure. Nevertheless, the ritualistic nature of legal procedure, which is still evident, seems to arouse some basic human feelings about the need to free society, families, and individuals from guilt. The courtroom experience, to be successful in a psychological sense, seems to call for the Divine, whether it be in the form of a blind pagan goddess; a divinely judged ordeal; or the *vox populi* of the jury system.

Through an inner dynamic, however, the rite tends to become increasingly elaborate and formalized and to lose its ability to adapt to individual situations. This growth may be deeply satisfying as ritual, but concern with efficiency (perhaps in the bourgeois sense) or with the true ritual form encourages reform as a means to return to the simplicity and effectiveness of the original. Reform frequently fails to follow the rhetoric of return, however, and moves on to the new instead. Venetian judicial procedure or ritual underwent just such a reform in the early trecento; in retrospect, it was actually creating a new style of flexibility.

Bertaldo described a world of elaborate judicial procedures, replete with a highly developed symbolism and ritual. By the end of the thirteenth century, the system had tied most acts of the judiciary into a tight network of legal constraint. Only in the final decisions meting out penalties was much latitude built into the ritual—a significant exception because flexibility in sentencing ameliorated a host of earlier sins. The limited flexibility of the old system nevertheless became a liability in the fourteenth century; and following the Serrata, much of Venetian judicial procedure was reviewed and rationalized, ostensibly in the name of reform but also with the intent of effecting more efficient and flexible control.

Strong elements of tradition and ritual were retained in two procedures dealing with violent crimes: the preparation of cases by the Avogadori for trial before the Forty; and the preparation of cases by the Signori di Notte for trial by the Giudici di Proprio. In the legal sense, these bodies operated within tight restrictions; but in daily operation, personality and politics introduced a degree of flexibility. In contrast the Council of Ten, a creation of the fourteenth century, was considerably more flexible in its procedure. It acted swiftly, secretly, and virtually without restriction to protect Venetian society from violence through conspiracy or speech. The flexibility of the Ten, in contrast to the rigidity of the Avogadori and Signori di Notte, bespeaks more than their respective periods of creation; it is linked to the relative danger society saw in the types of violence with which each group dealt.

The Avogadori investigated heterosexual sex crimes (including rape) and certain kinds of nonsexual violence, ranging from brawls to murder. They presented the results of their investigations to the Forty and argued cases in the manner of state prosecutors. The Forty decided on guilt or innocence and voted on penalties. The Signori di Notte dealt with the whole range of interpersonal violence, excluding heterosexual sex crimes, in two separate ways: petty violence was handled summarily in the streets; murder and robbery cases were investigated and presented to the Giudici di Proprio who determined guilt and penalty. Finally, the Council of Ten dealt primarily with crimes against the state, and its authority was virtually unlimited.

From this division of responsibility, a rough hierarchy of the seriousness of these crimes—as it was perceived by influential Venetians—can be inferred. Petty violence was of little threat and occurred with great regularity. It was handled summarily, with no time wasted on ritual. Interpersonal violence of greater magnitude garnered an elaborate ritualistic response. The need to provide for expiation and the severe nature of the penalties required more than a perfunctory process. In crimes like conspiracy, however, which threatened society itself—the most serious of all crimes in the Venetian view of reality—all else was sacrificed to efficiency.

The Avogaria di Comun

One of the most ancient of Venetian governmental bodies, the Avogaria di Comun was also one of the most complex and, in criminal matters, powerful centers of authority in Venice. Unlike most of its counterparts, it had neither judicial nor legislative powers; but in the evolution of Venetian political organization, these defects were overcome by an accretion of responsibilities that assured it unusual authority in both determining and implementing the law. Central to this authority was the responsibility of the Avogaria for collecting and editing into one series of registers the major legislation of the commune, making it in effect Venice's collective legal memory.[2]

This task, turned over to the Avogaria so that it could derive some order from the chaos of the legislation passed by the wide variety of councils with legislative authority, gave its members the power to codify that legislation so as to reflect their own view of the law. Such power is difficult to evaluate because it is difficult to isolate; but Venetian government worked best within the interstices of responsibility and procedural requirements, where considerations of status, family, and power could be interposed despite "constitutional" limitations. The authority to determine which legislation would be used as a guide and which would disappear into a morass of unfindable records of individual councils gave just such a power. In the exercise of this power the members of the Avogaria had a basis for authority that transcended the more circumscribed duties of regular judicial procedure.

Accompanying this authority was the responsibility of the Avogaria to see to it that important communal legislation was implemented. The Avogadori sat in the central councils of state to verify that they followed the rules and procedures of the Venetian government—as recorded by the Avogadori. They also had the right to enforce the capitularies of the major councils of state. Finally, they suggested the penalties for a wide range of crimes. Thus although lacking direct power, they had considerable authority. This is one reason why the position of Avogador continued to attract the most important nobles of Venice.

When violence was involved, the Avogadori were the font of the law for the Ten, the Signori di Notte, and the Cinque alla Pace. Their primary responsibility, however, lay in their role as prosecuting attorneys before the Forty, the Senate, and the Major Council. Because by far the largest proportion of serious violent crimes were tried before the Forty, the Avogadori played a crucial role in the judicial procedure of the commune.[3]

To understand the Avogadori's authority and its limitations, one must look at their routine activities. Three in number, they were elected by the Major Council, and after 1318, they served for two years.[4] In the fourteenth century, even with assistance from several notaries and a varying number of *pueri*, the job placed demands upon so small a council. In 1308, the Avogadori met each Wednesday and Thursday from the ninth bell until vespers; but by 1314 they were meeting daily. This extension of the work week occurred, moreover, at a time when new councils like the Ten were reducing the Avogadori's sphere of operations. Such an increase in hours was a further indication of the nobility's heightened interest in public order, typical of the period of administrative and social adjustment following the Serrata.[5]

Judicial Procedures of the Avogaria di Comun

Reconstructing the actual judicial procedures of the Avogadori in the fourteenth century is extremely difficult. Surviving manuals of procedure reflect much later practice, and the contemporary records are fragmentary. Nonetheless, from the records of the Avogadori and the Forty and from their capitularies a procedure of six stages can be discerned: 1. accusation; 2. *inquisitio* and preparation of the *intromissio;* 3. *placitare* of the *intromissio* before the relevant council; 4. determination of guilt or innocence; 5. proposal of a penalty; and 6. determination of the penalty.

Perhaps the simplest way to comprehend this process is to follow one particular case. In 1343, Giovanni Andruzo da Lucca, who worked in Venice's nascent silk industry, came to the attention of the communal authorities when he was unjustly accused of stealing 100 ducats by his employer, a silk merchant named Federico Spira. For this false accusation, the Forty fined Federico 100 ducats. Federico actually had a real complaint against his employee: Giovanni had broken into Federico's house and stolen the virginity of his daughter.[6]

As soon as Federico's real complaint became known (the records do not explain how this came about), the Forty began regular penal proceedings against Giovanni. On September 10, the Forty referred the accusation of rape to the Avogadori, who sent Giovanni to jail while they made an *inquisitio* into his case.[7] After three weeks, the *intromissio* or summation of their findings was recorded in the *Raspe* registers of the Avogadori.[8] That same day, October 1, the Forty heard Giovanni's case and voted by a sizable majority to accept the Avogadori's accusations as they were pleaded (*placitare*). Doge Michael Giustinian, his councilors, and the captains of the Forty then proposed that Giovanni spend a year in jail, the Avogadori that he be given the choice of the jail sentence or a fine of 100 ducats. In the end, the Forty chose to follow the doge's suggestion by a vote of 29 to 6 (with 3 abstaining). This is a good example of the way in which Avogadori were intimately involved in every stage of judicial procedure. Even though their recommendation for the penalty was passed over, as it often was, they succeeded in defining the limits within which the penalty would fall.[9]

This case reveals the Avogadori's role in the penal process from the actual case records. Another perspective is provided by the statutes that originally defined the Avogadori's authority, but the significant statutes a historian culls from a capitulary or from the records of the Major Council may have had little significance for the working Avogador of the fourteenth century. In a bureaucracy without data retrieval systems beyond the most elementary forms of alphabetization, he was unlikely to refer to the statutes for instructions on how to proceed. Though the Avogadori, more than any others, should have been aware of their capitulary, they probably depended upon an orally inherited working procedure that was rarely matched against the legal requirements. This was the pattern for most governmental officials.[10]

The legal limits of the Avogadori nonetheless provide details about their activities and give some insight into what their judicial procedures should have been. Although Giovanni's case was first referred to the Avogadori by the Forty, it appears that all cases were originally referred to the Avogadori by the doge and his councilors, who were the primal font of judicial authority. As that authority was passed from the doge to various councils empowered to deal with specific problems, the right to bring matters to the attention of the Avogadori became more widespread. In 1308, although the practice was clearly older, a *parte* of the Major Council empowered the Forty—which included the doge and his councilors as voting members—to submit cases to the Avogadori for investigation by a simple majority vote.[11] Records of investigations show that by midcentury the Signori di Notte, the Cinque alla Pace, and the Ten were also referring cases. Because the Signori di Notte and the Cinque alla Pace were policing bodies, and through the Capi di Sestiere the Ten controlled an extensive policing organization, the Avogadori must have received a large proportion of their cases from such referrals.

The other major source of cases was the victims themselves, who brought accusations either directly to the Avogadori or to other councils that referred them to the Avogadori. Presumably, this was the way Giovanni's case came to their attention. In the early criminal registers of the Avogadori, there are frequent references to accusers, especially in sexual cases. As the recording of cases became more formulaic, however, the identification of accusers was omitted. The natural incentive to report a crime to the Avogadori was generally improved by the practice of paying one-quarter of the fine to the accuser, but this practice was not followed with crimes of violence. The reward of seeing justice served (or vengeance achieved) was deemed adequate to secure information.[12]

Actual referrals were contingent upon a number of factors. Crimes interrupted in progress or those in which the criminals were immediately apprehended by communal officials were regularly referred. Crimes occurring in public places with many witnesses were also well reported, depending on the level of the violence involved. But the reporting of private crimes of violence was to a degree contingent upon the level of violence of the crime and qualified by both the relative social positions of the victim and the criminal and the likelihood of successful prosecution. These factors are analyzed more closely in later chapters; in general, it appears that the principal factors in crime reporting were the public nature of the crime and the perceived seriousness of it.

Once accused, a suspect was usually placed in jail to be kept available for examination about his crime. Until 1378, the Avogadori theoretically received their authority to hold an accused criminal from the doge and his councilors, although the Forty regularly ruled on such matters as well. After 1378, the burden of remanding criminals to jail in routine cases was officially transferred to the Forty.[13] If the accused was not available for arrest, he could be prosecuted *in contumacia.* On the basis of evidence presented by the Avogadori, the Forty would declare a suspect *in contumacia* if he did not turn himself in within a prescribed period to defend himself against the charges. The amount of time could vary from three days to several months, but the normal period was eight to fifteen days. If he missed the deadline, the accused would be presumed guilty and placed under a ban, making him a man outside the law. A further grace period to return and pay the prescribed penalty was normally granted, but a stricter penalty was also imposed on those who did not surrender but later were apprehended by Venetian authorities.

Those accused of crimes often took advantage of this procedure to assess the seriousness of the penalties they faced. In 1351, Mafeo Polani, a noble, was accused of raping the wife of a lower-class worker, but he had disappeared. The Forty found him *in contumacia* and ordered that he surrender within four days. If he met the deadline, his penalty would be a fine of 100 lire di piccoli and one month in jail; if he did not, he would be placed under a ban, and the jail sentence and fine would both be doubled. Because the penalty was mild, Mafeo reported to jail to begin serving his sentence two days later. Not everyone was in such an enviable position; for the lower classes and the transient, to be *in contumacia* was often the equivalent of life banishment.[14]

After a crime was reported, the Avogadori began preparing an *intromissio*—the prosecution case—to present before the Forty or other relevant court. This consisted primarily of collecting testimony. At the beginning of the fourteenth century, the Major Council reformed the procedure for taking testimony. In 1300, it ruled that the Avogadori could collect testimony only with two ducal councilors present; but the difficulty of getting these important officials together for the routine business of criminal investigation soon forced a revision of procedure. In 1303, the Avogadori were given the authority to take testimony unassisted "in order to expedite the matter and to examine the witnesses more easily." [15]

Torture was relatively rare in examinations by the Avogadori. Cases involving sexual violence were either sufficiently public or too unimportant to require that kind of evidence. For robbery and treason—crimes of some threat—torture was used more frequently, though still with restraint. Such crimes were usually examined and tried by the Signori di Notte and Giudici di Proprio or, in the case of treason, by the Council of Ten. The Avogadori did not perform the torture themselves. They relied upon a *collegio* to oversee the process or upon evidence from torture ordered by another council before the case was referred to them.[16] A *collegio* was a special ad hoc group of about four officials. When torture was inflicted, a ducal councilor and a representative of the Avogadori were usually present to question the accused. The torture was actually inflicted by professionals hired by the Signori di Notte. This procedure, which was also used by the Council of Ten, imparted a legal tone to the proceedings. It could be applied even to powerful suspects, and the responsibility for the deed was carefully spread among important officials. Acquittal when torture failed to secure a confession was not unusual.[17]

Heavy reliance on testimony rather than confession in crimes of middle-range violence was an unusual aspect of Venetian procedure. Testimony reduced the need for torture and required more aggressive investigation. It also gave considerable discretion to those judging guilt or innocence. When testimony was not clear enough to prove guilt without question, Venetian practice allowed wide latitude in the imposition of penalties. In these circumstances, although justice retained its theoretical objectivity, the interpretation of testimony introduced a personal element that cannot be ignored.[18]

After testimony was taken and the *intromissio* prepared, the Avogadori had to inform the defendants which law or laws would be used as the basis for prosecution. Unfortunately, little other information survives from the fourteenth century about the preparation of defense cases. This requirement, which dates from 1327, reveals a sophisticated sense of due process. The defendant was to be informed of the charges against him "so that the thing comes out equally and justly for all concerned." The final result of this process was a written defense that would presumably attempt to answer the charges of the Avogadori's *intromissio*.[19]

After completion of their case, the Avogadori had one month to bring it before the Forty.[20] Eventually the stipulation was added that cases could not be continued beyond six months.[21] During the fourteenth century, the Avogadori disposed of most cases in about two months, although there are occasional references to defendants released because they had been in jail so long awaiting trial for minor offenses that a trial was no longer necessary.[22] Toward the end of the century, the capitularies of the Avogadori begin to refer to cases involving nobles carried over for so long that a considerable number of nobles had become ineligible for the office of Avogador—a pending case being sufficient for disqualification from holding office.[23] This phenomenon, however, probably had more to do with nobles who had escaped prosecution than with those who had waited an unnecessarily long time for trial. These men had not been awaiting justice in jail; they remained active in public life by somehow managing to avoid trial. That their number was large enough to be mentioned, even rhetorically, for causing difficulty in filling the offices of the Avogaria di Comun—considering the number of nobles actually tried for violent crimes—contradicts the myth of the peaceful Venetian noble merchant. In any event, most accused men came before the Forty much more rapidly. The case of Giovanni described earlier took only three weeks from referral to sentencing.

Once the Avogadori had prepared the *intromissio* and informed the defendant about the laws, they brought the case before the Forty for the *placitare*. (An echo of this can be found in Venetian dialect, where *"fare un placito"* means to speak evil of someone.) The *placitare* of an *intromissio* consisted of two parts: an *arrengare* or oral argument; and a *legere* or the reading of the brief and testimony compiled by the Avogadori. Before 1351, this process was spread out over four sittings of the Forty, two devoted to the *arrengare* and two to the *legere;* but councilors often came only to the last session to hear the final reading of the case. To avoid this and compel councilors to hear the *arrengare,* it was ordered that the *placitare* be accomplished in three meetings and that both the *arrengare* and the *legere* be done together in each.[24]

Prolonging a case in this way had a purpose beyond insuring that all members of the Forty could hear and consider it: it left considerable room for politics to become involved with judicial decisions. Despite the carefully ordered procedures of Venetian judicial ritual, it was still fully and deliberately intertwined with the political and social system. The Serrata made every judicial decision at least potentially a decision by a legally defined ruling class for its own ends.

The strong political forces sometimes applied can be seen in the requirement, first imposed in 1367, that the doge could not speak on a case brought by the Avogadori without the approval of four ducal councilors—a rule that could only have come from political motivation. It is significant that the doge was not entirely forbidden to speak against the Avogadori; he was merely required to speak from a broader political consensus. The *parte* obviously asserted that the doge use his political power not for private ends but only when it was deemed politically appropriate by a majority of his councilors.[25]

This confusion of the judicial and the political was not accidental. It was an important part of the wisdom that helped the Venetian system endure, a wisdom which held that order and control required that the political or social contexts of a case would be fully aired before decisions were made. That the law requiring cases to be heard over a number of meetings was intended to encourage this becomes more obvious when the social context of penalties imposed for violence is examined later.

At these same meetings, the accused's case, based upon written testimony presented in much the same manner as the *placitare,* was also heard. Information on defense presentations is limited. Only a few formal *parti* survive, apparently intended to protect defendants. The Avogadori, for example, were not allowed to put a defendant on trial before more than one council at a time.[26] Theoretically, this gave him a better chance to argue his defense. After 1361, moreover, the Avogadori were not allowed to introduce new evidence in a case unless the defendant was there to hear it.[27]

These safeguards, however, contained a typical bias: the lower-class criminal lacked the wealth or understanding to make them work for him. They therefore probably protected only the upper classes. It is difficult to imagine that the Avogadori were able to handle the volume of business brought before them if many defendants argued their cases according to these elaborate legal procedures. In daily practice—as in Giovanni's three-week case—there was little spirited defense; and the Forty tended to vote overwhelmingly against the accused, especially in cases involving the lower classes.[28] An elaborate defense capable of creating some doubt in the minds of the Forty was generally limited to the upper classes.

When the council found a defendant guilty, the Avogadori had one final responsibility: to suggest a penalty. Not only had they prepared the case and argued it, they were also the repository of the law. Their suggestion for a penalty represented an evaluation of what law and justice required. It is significant that their suggestions were seldom taken. This seems to symbolize the fact that although legal theory had its place in the ritual of justice, politics usually won out. In the Forty, the penalties suggested by the most politically potent group tended to prevail. Law and procedure merely defined the limits within which the more significant forces of politics, class, economics, and the perceptions of the nobility came into play.

The Signori di Notte

At the beginning of the fourteenth century, although the Avogadori enjoyed a legal and procedural advantage over other councils, the Signori di Notte had the advantage in the streets. Their principal responsibility was to organize and oversee the patrols of the city. Originally, these six nobles—one for each sestiere—were themselves the chief patrollers; but by the trecento, much of this duty had devolved onto subordinate *custodi*.

According to Marin Sanuto, there was only one Signore di Notte before the middle of the thirteenth century. Later there were two, one for either side of the Grand Canal. By 1281, all six were patrolling, with both *custodi* and the old medieval patrols of individual *contrate* under their control. In that year, the Major Council ruled that the Signori di Notte be elected three at a time for staggered six-month terms. Under this format, three experienced men were always working with three newcomers.[29] By 1314, their terms of office had been extended to one year and their small salaries taken away, presumably because they received a percentage of the fines collected.[30]

Their predominance did not endure too far into the fourteenth century. Although the Cinque alla Pace, another medieval patrolling body, remained subordinate because its responsibility was limited to petty violence, by 1330 the Council of Ten had seriously undercut the police authority of the Signori di Notte. Their loss of predominance in the streets did not entail a loss of all power; they acted regularly as the arm of the law, complementing the Avogadori, who acted as its recorder and interpreter. For example, the Signori were responsible for arresting criminals for a number of councils, for arresting certain officials and fining them when they broke the capitularies of their offices, and for supervising torture. They also oversaw the investigation of some of the crimes, including murder and robbery, considered most serious in the eyes of the commune.[31]

The Signori di Notte and Judicial Procedure

The Signori di Notte's procedure in investigating murder and robbery was similar to that of the Avogadori, possibly as the result of an earlier delegation of authority by the Avogadori, who continued to investigate crimes with a political or social cast while passing crimes associated with violence in the streets on to those likely to encounter them in their normal routine. Whether or not this occurred, meaningful distinctions were implied by the division of responsibility between Avogadori and Signori.

It is significant that murder cases handled by the Avogadori and the Forty often had political or social overtones, whereas the Signori di Notte usually dealt with those that sprang from the immediate violent impulses of a quarrel or fight. At least part of this distinction arose because the Forty, aided by the Avogadori's intimate access to the political situation, was able to render more politically sensitive verdicts. Because of their number and social stature, the Forty could also share the responsibility for their decisions.[32]

The Signori di Notte prepared a case for murder or robbery in a manner similar to that used by the Avogadori, but certain differences were crucial. The six major stages were the same: accusation, preparation of *intromissio,* pleading of the case before the appropriate judicial body, decision on guilt or innocence, suggestion of penalties, and vote on penalties.

A murder committed by a boatman, Giovanni Marmagna, provides a typical example of the Signori in action. Giovanni and his colleagues were returning to his boat when they became involved in a brawl with a vagabond. They drew their knives; and in the excitement of the moment, mortally wounded the vagabond. The crime occurred in the middle of the campo of San Bartolomeo, and a number of witnesses began a spirited pursuit of the culprit, who dropped his knife and fled towards the Rialto. At this point, the Signori di Notte entered the case. Jacobo Marano, a *custode* of the Signori who was patrolling the Rialto area along with a *custode* of the Capi di Sestiere, reported seeing Giovanni run "fortiter" through the Rialto area chased by people yelling "piya, piya." Cornered, Giovanni jumped into a canal and swam to the bank in front of the Cha Boldù, where he was captured by two young workers. They brought him back to the Rialto and turned him over to Jacobo, who led him off to jail. A patroller of the Cinque alla Pace brought in a bloody knife, presumably the murder weapon, which was found on a bridge near the scene of the crime.[33]

A significant difference in procedure immediately becomes obvious: with their patrollers in the streets, the Signori depended less upon reports of crimes than did the Avogadori. The desire for retribution or vengeance for violent crimes must have encouraged reports to both bodies, but the Signori's presence in the streets overshadowed other factors.

In jail, the Signori examined Giovanni in the presence of the doge. By precedent, the Signore representing the sestiere where the crime occurred was responsible for preparing the case. He handled the interrogation and collected the testimony.[34] Curiously, there is almost no direct reference in the *Processi* to the use of torture before 1390 upon those accused of murder, even though torture was regularly used in robbery cases. Giovanni was merely brought before the doge and the Signori di Notte and questioned about what happened. He denied any part in the murder, claiming that he was walking with friends when they became involved in a brawl. In order to avoid fighting, he ran off and fell into the canal by accident. Asked if he had taken any part in the fight, he answered simply, "No." No torture was used, and the interrogation of Giovanni ended at this point. Conviction was possible without confession in Venice, however, and Giovanni was convicted on the basis of other testimony. This provision may account for the absence of torture in such cases.[35]

Nevertheless, the Signori regularly used torture for the crime of robbery. Perhaps the discriminating factor lay in the fact that robbery is a crime against property whereas the murders investigated by the Signori were crimes of passion; and noble Venetian peacekeepers considered the former more dangerous for society than the latter. After 1390, the torture of murder suspects became fairly regular. The format in which these cases are described shows that procedure had changed: examinations were no longer conducted before the doge and the Signori di Notte but in the Camera del Tormento of the Signori.

Because torture was seldom used, the Signori di Notte had to collect extensive testimony in order to build a case. The surviving *Processi* records of the Signori provide condensations of such testimony, but the scribes tended to use formulas to describe the same basic events—as though the witnesses had all seen the same crime and chosen the same words to describe it. One infers that a scribe, either on his own or with the help of the Signore di Notte in charge, worked from rough notes and chose certain major themes of testimony, repeating them virtually word for word for each witness who mentioned a theme.[36] The impact of such apparent unanimity is difficult to judge, but it certainly could not have helped the defense.

Another problem stemming from heavy reliance on testimony was the question of honesty. The traditional weight of the private oath had lost some of its meaning in the relative anonymity of the city environment. Pietro Bono, for example, testified before the Signori di Notte that he had seen a certain Pascal hit a Venetian *custode* in the *contrata* of San Cassian, wounding him twice. When the *custode* died, a surgeon, Antonio Barberio, testified that he had died as a result of Pascal's attack. Further investigation by the Signori di Notte, however, revealed that Pietro's testimony was false.[37] How often false testimony of this sort distorted the picture of Venetian violence remains a question—especially for serious crimes like murder.

An important part of the brief was the testimony of the victim, which the Signori di Notte made every effort to secure. Giovanni's victim died almost immediately; but in murder cases where the victim lived for a time, his testimony was quickly taken by the Signore on the scene. Doctors were also required to summon the Signori di Notte when seriously wounded persons came into their care. As a result, many cases began with last-breath incriminations of murderers. Victims often provided names of other witnesses as well.[38]

Deathbed incriminations could also cause problems. On one occasion, the Signori di Notte succeeded in overlooking the broader implications of a case. When a sailor named Felle da Chioggia was murdered, all testimony incriminated a small man of about fifty named Tarvixio. While drinking and gambling with Felle in the tavern Martini del Grande, Tarvixio became embroiled in an argument about who would pay for the wine. Words turned to violence, and in the melee Tarvixio picked up a heavy spit and hit Felle a great blow ("magnam botam") that eventually caused his death: prima facie, a common case of senseless murder. On his deathbed, however, Felle furnished a different account of the situation. He maintained that Antonio Vendelino, a noble and a communal official, had insulted him while he was gambling and drinking. The insult contained an implication of homosexuality, and Felle responded by grabbing Vendelino by the neck and shaking him. Tarvixio, an assistant of Antonio, then attacked Felle.

According to Felle's account, the crime involved both a noble and a serious insult. Asked if there was anyone else who could provide information about the crime, Felle responded, "Antonio Vendelino and Thadeo Marino." The latter, Felle's employer, was also present in the tavern. The Signori nevertheless overlooked Vendelino and left the case as a simple murder of passion caused by gambling and drinking. Some trouble may subsequently have occurred: four months later the Signori called two more witnesses, both of whom corroborated the earlier testimony and omitted any reference to Vendelino.[39]

The *Processi* of the Signori di Notte usually recorded the testimony of two or three witnesses other than the accused and the victim, when the latter lived long enough to testify. This practice generally secured the case in the minds of the judges if there were no major contradictions. In contrast to practice in much of the rest of Europe at this time, no specific number of witnesses was required to prove a case.[40] Moreover, it appears that the Signori sought more than proof of guilt. They inquired about motivation and levels of violence in order to provide additional material upon which the Giudici di Proprio could base their penalties. Even after several witnesses had given virtually identical testimony about guilt, they solicited further testimony to give a fuller context to the crime. A regular part of each interrogation involved asking for the names of other witnesses. For example, in an unusually serious case of violence involving several young nobles, testimony was recorded in the *Processi* from no fewer than thirty-eight witnesses, even though there was no doubt about guilt.[41] A similar tendency to outline the broader context of a crime may be discerned in the *Raspe* of the Avogadori. This process allowed the penalties to be sensitive to the level and nature of the crime. It also provides a significant key to Venetian society's perception of violence.

The last regular aspect of the preparation of a case was certification by a doctor of the cause of death. In Giovanni's case, the surgeon Magister Albertino testified that Luysio's death was caused by a single stab wound in the right side of the neck. Surgeons' reports were unusually explicit in giving the cause of death, counting the number of wounds, assessing their seriousness, and occasionally detailing postmortem operations.[42]

These were the primary elements, then, of the case: testimony of witnesses, of the victim when possible, and of the examining surgeon. The parallels with the preparation of an *intromissio* by the Avogadori are clear. The major difference to be found in examining the *Processi* records of the Signori di Notte lay in their ability to apprehend criminals in the street. It is also noteworthy that the doge played a more prominent role in these proceedings than he did in those of the Avogadori. This practice was directly related to the fact that murder and robbery were among the most serious crimes. In these areas, the doge, at least in the formulas of the records, maintained a vigilant interest as protector of Venetian order.

The evidence gathered against Giovanni, along with his denial of guilt, was then taken before the Giudici di Proprio. These officials were primarily concerned with property crime; but in the fourteenth century, excepting cases prepared by the Avogadori and presented to the Forty, they were responsible for the trial of murderers also. The nobles Lorenzo Celsi, Pietro Basilio, and Marino Gradenigo heard Giovanni's case, found him guilty, and sentenced him to lose his left eye.[43]

Concerning trial procedure, the *Processi* of the Signori di Notte give scant detail beyond listing the names of the judges and the final proof that a conviction could be secured by a vote of two of the three judges. The later registers do not even mention these; they contain only summaries of testimony. Some further impression of the theoretical operation of the Signori can nevertheless be inferred by looking at the laws of Venice. Material on gathering testimony centered in three areas: specific procedures, torture, and the recording of testimony. Examination of all "malefactores" and "culpos" was conducted on Fridays between the ninth bell and sunset. This session included both simple examination and torture of robbers. That this *parte* was actually followed is supported by a complaint of the Signori in 1338 that during the summer, because of the longer days, they were finished with their business long before sundown. It was decided that in the months of May, June, July, and August they would stay only so long as all six Signori di Notte felt necessary.[44]

This procedure provided for the examination of suspected criminals already in custody. In the case of those still at large, the Signori di Notte had at least two procedures. They could either follow the *contumacia* procedure described earlier or send letters to Venetian rectors between Grado and Cavarzere asking for the capture of a suspect and his return to

Venice. Both approaches assured the Signori the ability to act on a case; neither the absence of a suspect nor his distance from Venice could stop the process.[45]

The torture procedure outlined in the capitulary of the Signori di Notte closely followed the procedure revealed in the *Processi*. *Latrones* ("thieves"), *raubatores* ("petty thieves"), and *taiabursas* ("purse snatchers") were to be tortured when all six Signori agreed.[46] In 1318, it was ruled that when members were absent, torture could begin with a unanimous vote of a quorum of four Signori.[47] After 1329, six *custodi* of the Signori, one for each sestiere, were specially trained and received extra pay for the job. Some became so successful that a grateful Major Council voted them an occasional bonus.[48] It was ruled in 1290 that no one but his examiners was to be with a suspect while he was being tortured. The fact that such a *parte* was deemed necessary suggests that at least for some, strong defense efforts were being pursued. Following torture, a written report of the results had to be made to the doge within eight days.[49]

The law also set up a regular method for recording testimony. Notaries were required to complete the briefs within two months.[50] The Signori di Notte were then required to finish a case within two months after the brief was written.[51] Of course, there were ways to slow down a case. The doge and his councilors could suspend a case for up to eight days during testimony.[52] Once the trial began, they could hold up proceedings for two months.[53] The rationale for this authority again stemmed from the medieval concept of the doge as the font of all justice. The ability to slow the judicial process assured that hasty action did not mar the judgment, that vengeance should not overwhelm justice. In fact, this prerogative permitted the doge and his councilors to prolong cases with political or social overtones—especially when cases were heard by the three Giudici di Proprio, who tended to lack the political representativeness of the Forty. Although a case could theoretically be continued from the first day of taking testimony for more than six months, most cases were actually handled in a month or two.

Little information survives about trial and sentencing procedures. Jacobo Bertaldo outlined the general way in which a case was heard before the Giudici di Proprio at the beginning of the fourteenth century. In the Ducal Palace, at least two of the three Giudici had to be seated to hear the charges, responses, and various petitions. At the end of the pleading, one judge chosen by the others took all the material in writing, proclaiming, "This is assured." The judges then went through the case together, examining the charges, the testimony, and the defense case. Finally, with at least two judges, two lawyers, and the victim and criminal or their representatives present, they pronounced sentence. A scribe assigned to the case was given all the written material and the sentence, which he briefed and returned to the judges to sign. Bertaldo portrays the trial as highly ritualistic, with an emphasis on periodic repetitions of key phrases and symbolic confrontations of key parties.[54]

The Ten

Of all the bodies studied, the Ten moved furthest from tradition and ritual in its judicial procedure. Concerned principally with treason and crimes of speech that seemed to threaten the stability of the commune, it moved with a fluidity in procedure that gave it the ability to adapt to the needs of the moment, an ability the Avogadori and Signori di Notte had only informally. With its power to act on any case without restraint, the Ten became the institutionalization of expediency.

This fluidity was possible for the Ten not only because of the types of crimes it handled but also because it comprised the most important men of the commune. It lacked the dialectical tension between councils typical of the rest of Venetian judicial procedure. The need for cooperation between the Avogadori and the Forty or the Signori di Notte and the Giudici di Proprio put a check on their ability to act, but the Ten escaped this limitation. The whole case, from investigation to sentencing, was handled secretly within the council. Because there were no external controls, the Ten rapidly grew to be much more than a peacekeeping agency.

Judicial procedure within the Ten consisted of five steps reminiscent of those of the other councils—referral, investigation, formal argument, voting on guilt, and voting on penalties—but there were three significant differences in practice. Because the Ten did not report to another council, all action was internal and secret until the council decided to make it public. Second, the investigative procedures were highly flexible, and the accused had fewer institutional safeguards. Third, there was no *gratia* procedure to allow for the adjustment of penalties by the Major Council or the Senate. The Ten's decisions were final.

The noble Paladin Premarin was involved in the Cretan Rebellion of 1364. On June 26, the Ten decided that for the security of the commune it was necessary to have him brought before them. They ordered him sent to Venice in irons, along with two other suspects.[55] Upon his arrival in September, the Ten set up a *collegio* to investigate Paladin's part in the conspiracy, using torture if necessary. The *collegio* consisted of four members of the Ten: Marco Priuli, a councilor; Giovanni Loredan, a head of the council; Nicolo Contarini, an inquisitor; and Aureo Pasqualigo, an Avogador. No outsiders were involved; and two days later the Ten voted on the penalties for Premarin. They ruled him guilty "because of the evil deeds he committed" in the rebellion of Crete, the vote being thirteen in favor, no votes against, and one abstention.[56]

Guilt established, penalties were immediately proposed and voted upon. This reduced outside political interference, eliminating the opportunity for external pressure to be applied before sentencing. Such an approach was virtually the opposite of the Forty's; but the Ten was a smaller and more important body of men who tended to be more unified on the penalties necessary. The Forty also dealt with cases less threatening to social order. Finally, because the Ten prepared the entire case, the members were probably more prepared to act—having already weighed the social and political implications of their vote before the final meeting. As a result, though the procedures may seem the opposite, the results were much the same: politically and socially sensitive action taken against violent crime.

Marco Priuli proposed that Premarin have his tongue cut out and that he be jailed for the rest of his life. Giovanni Loredan argued that this was too severe, proposing that Premarin merely spend the rest of his life in jail. The Cretan rebellion had threatened the republic in a sensitive place, however—its eastern connection and one of its primary sources of grain. On the first ballot, the doge, supported by most of his councilors, gained a majority vote. Premarin was to be taken to St. Mark's Square where, between the columns of justice, his tongue would be cut out. He was then to be hanged and left for two days as an example.[57]

From a century's accumulation of documents, examples of this sort could easily be multiplied. Because the basic procedure was so flexible, however, it is difficult to generalize a definite pattern beyond the five stages outlined earlier. For specific cases, the procedure can be broken down into more detail. The method by which the Ten received its information was highly important. After the 1320s, it had its own regular patrols, including the Capi di Sestiere, the Capi di Contrata, and in times of trouble, even the civil militia. Matters of concern to the Ten were also referred by other councils or patrolling bodies. A typical case involved Marco Rizo, apprehended by the Signori di Notte for proclaiming in St. Mark's, "Oh good people, help me take these dogs to jail." Rizo lost his tongue and was banned perpetually from Venice when the incident was referred to the Ten. Furthermore, the Ten ordered that if he ever returned he would have his eyes put out and be banished again.[58]

It is unclear whether such cases were unusual, the Ten stepping in only when it felt other councils were not acting correctly, or whether referral was so normal that it was not noted in the records. Two facts support the latter interpretation. First, the Ten consistently ordered special patrols and procedures for bodies it did not control, such as the Cinque alla Pace and the Signori di Notte, to ensure that arrests would be referred to them. Second, the Avogadori were charged to see that each council considered matters legally proper to it. Theoretically, with their entry into all important bodies of state, the Avogadori could see that cases concerning the Ten would be brought before it. If these provisions functioned as they should have, much of the Ten's business would come from this source. The doge and ducal councilors, regular members of the council in their traditional position at the apex of the peacekeeping structure, probably referred cases as well.

The most famous sources were the anonymous informants of the Ten, who dropped their accusations in the lions' mouths strategically located about the city. General histories and guidebooks still keep this romantic notion alive, but in the fourteenth century this form of denunciation was officially frowned upon by the commune. A law passed by the Major Council in 1275 required that anonymous accusations not be used and that anonymous letters be burnt unread.[59] In 1387 the Ten claimed it had been acting under the provisions of this law. The council complained because many unsigned notes then being left at the Doge's Palace, St. Mark's, and elsewhere had to be burned. Asserting that this was not in the best interests of Venice, they ruled that any note left anonymously in these places should be reported to the ducal councilors and handed over to the Heads of the Ten to decide if the council should investigate further.[60]

From 1387, therefore, anonymous accusations were used after screening by the Heads of the Ten. Because the ducal councilors were the first to see the letters, they could presumably exercise prior censorship; but legal authority rested with the Ten. It is significant that this power was not granted to the Ten but taken by it within the context of its original powers, with the justification that the continuation of the old ruling "could endanger the commune." [61] Such a broad construction of its area of responsibility put the Ten beyond legal restraint. Legality, however, was not the only context of Venetian government. Custom, family, and self-interest regularly superseded law; all continued to limit the Ten to a degree.

Anonymous letters may have influenced the Ten clandestinely between 1310 and 1387, but signed letters and reports, especially from the nobility, were accepted legally. The Ten seldom reported how a particular case was brought to its attention, but a great number of the lesser crimes of speaking against the commune or the doge must have been reported either directly or through the Avogadori. In that these crimes were the main criminal business of the Ten, one infers that direct accusation was the primary method of referral.

The nebulous nature of the referral of business to the Ten—now from another council, now from a private individual, now from an anonymous letter—made that council even more powerful and feared; it seemed to be ubiquitous.

In criminal matters, the Ten had several options for investigation. The Inquisitors of the Ten, two of whom were elected monthly from among the council members, could carry out the investigation. As their name indicates, their primary function was this task. A second option might be a *collegio,* an ad hoc group consisting of four members—a head of the Ten, an inquisitor, a councilor, and an avogador. Such groups investigated more important or difficult cases; and even here membership was drawn from within the council.

Often the Ten merely appointed a few of its leading members to investigate a case. If a matter was not too important, this approach avoided an elaborate *collegio* but did not overburden the inquisitors. A smaller, more unified group could also be appointed for cases requiring speed and secrecy. For example, during the investigation of the Falier conspiracy, the Heads of the Ten were empowered to examine a servant of Nicoleto Greco. This was a pressing situation, but it did not require the delicacy used in examining an important noble. The Heads of the Ten could act quickly, extracting the information they sought with no interference and a maximum of security. A small investigating group, then, gave the council the flexibility either to pass on responsibility in minor cases or to operate quickly and secretly in important ones.[62]

Occasionally, in cases that seriously threatened the security of the commune or involved many members of the nobility, the Ten was compelled to step outside its narrow circle and appoint a larger body of advisors. It did so during the Falier conspiracy and during a large-scale sodomy investigation in February 1406 m.v. Eight councilors were added to the Ten to assist in the investigation, which implicated at least seventeen nobles from the families of Zancani, Marcello, Loredan, Alberti, Zane, Molin, Moro, Bollani, da Riva, Michiel, Cappello, and Contarini, as well as eighteen non-nobles.[63]

Inasmuch as the penalty for sodomy was burning, the case had the potential to create an explosive situation among the nobility. To contain this danger, the Ten sought to spread responsibility as widely as possible. Some idea of the breadth of support gained can be inferred by looking at the arms licenses granted those examining the case for their personal safety. Families included the Foscari, Corner, Pisani, Zorzi, Grissoni, Morosini, Emo, Badoer, Barbaro, Querini, Caravello, Mudazzo, Vitturi, Dandolo, Correr, Barbarigo, Mocenigo, Nani, Trevisan, and Bragadin. Officers included the doge, ducal councilors, Avogadori di Comun, Ten, Procurators of St. Mark's, the Ten's special addition, and the chancellor of the commune.[64]

As was customary with major cases, the Ten provided instructions about how the investigation was to be carried out. First, the Signori di Notte were to be excluded from the case and restrained from taking any further action. This body had apparently been overreacting; and hasty action could be divisive, alienating those needed for support. The enlarged Ten could proceed with caution and develop the case without stepping beyond the political realities.[65]

The investigators then determined which of the accused were clerics. This was a question of jurisdiction: in theory, the clergy was not subject to secular authority. In this case, the clerical status of Clario Contarini became an important question. The Bishop of Castello, appointed by the pope to review Contarini's status, was too timid (or perhaps too wise) to rule against him.[66] The Ten nevertheless acquired jurisdiction by prevailing upon the pope to appoint a more amenable examiner to the case. The second bishop, Vito Memo of Polensen, forced Clario to admit that he was not a cleric. With this admission in hand, on August 31, 1407 the Ten ordered the destruction of all material dealing with Contarini's clerical status. Because he was convicted of sodomy and no longer under the protection of the church, the Ten ordered him burned between the columns of St. Mark's by the Signori di Notte, who reentered the case as executioners. The other sodomites had suffered the same fate earlier.[67]

The third provision for the investigation stipulated that all evidence and confessions were to be locked into one box—to which the Signori di Notte were denied access. Finally, all material was to be examined and a list of the guilty given to the Signori di Notte, who would act as the police arm of the Ten and arrest the culprits.[68]

Their investigation of this sodomy case highlighted the Ten's ability to cut through traditional ways of dealing with criminal activity. Although homosexuality was not a crime normally heard by the Ten, in this case it presented a serious threat to the stability of the commune because so many men from important families were involved. The Signori di Notte, who were technically responsible for investigating such crimes, did not meet the political and social requirements of the situation. By taking over the investigation, the Ten brought to the proceedings the requisite power and sensitivity essential for the maintenance of the status quo.

Although the Ten used torture in its investigation, it is difficult to gauge to what extent it relied on this expedient. Reports of its use appear to be incomplete. In Register 6, covering the years from 1363 to 1374, only twelve clear instances of torture are recorded, out of seventy-two cases heard. This figure may be low. Torture may have been used by other councils before deciding a matter was serious enough to pass on to the Ten. Once the Ten received a case, however, it had to vote whether to use torture. Of the twelve instances of torture recorded, only four resulted in clear convictions; six led to acquittals, and two to results not reported. These results seem to demonstrate an open-minded approach to the use of torture. One might advance the alternative explanation that where guilt was unclear a good dose of torture was as effective a deterrent to further crime as a conviction. A man who had been under suspicion and tortured, even though he was freed, was well warned about the consequences of further transgression. He was both an advertisement for obedience and an illustration of the fairness of the Ten in freeing those whose guilt could not be established. In the personal world of the fourteenth-century city, such human examples of the commune's power could be effective.

There is no final evidence to explain the significant number of men tortured but acquitted and freed. Instances of this occurring, however, vary inversely with the social status of those involved. If torture was used as a deterrent, the technique was limited to those without political power. Persons of standing were better able to retaliate.

After an investigation was complete, the case was brought before the entire council. It was usually presented with the introduction, "si videtur vobis per ea que dicta et lecta sunt contra" ("if it seems to you because of what was said and read"). This indictment did not give much information about the material actually "dicta et lecta." Following the name of the accused, came, "quod procedatur contra eum" ("whether to proceed against him") and "si" ("yes") the vote for acting against the accused; then "vel non" ("or not"), followed by the votes against acting; and, finally, the "non sinceri," or those who abstained. "Capta" ("carried") was written, along with a plus, in front of the winning vote; for the Ten this entailed a simple majority.

The first example of this format is preserved in Register 3 in the year 1325;[69] but earlier actions show that the formulas had been used from the first recorded cases after the Querini–Tiepolo conspiracy.[70] The procedure was similar in the Major Council, the Forty, and in the Senate. The basic format was modified by the addition of extra details in important cases. When the Ten decided to prosecute the noble Jacobo Querini for his part in the abortive Barozzi conspiracy of 1328, it included the detail "occasione proditionis per eum tractate" ("in the matter of the conspiracy led by him").[71] Even this expansion of the regular formulas was not too informative. A better measure of the magnitude of the crime was the penalty. The seriousness of Querini's traitorous activities was proved by his decapitation between the columns before the Ducal Palace.[72]

One final aspect of the Ten's judicial proceedings remains to be examined—the granting of *gratie*. A *gratia* was not merely the remission of penalties; it was any of a number of actions that modified the original judgment. Unlike other councils, the Ten granted few *gratie*. Furthermore, *gratie* do not appear to have been granted outside the Ten to cases disposed by it. This freedom from review by other judicial bodies was unique to the Ten. The system of having one council check upon another was well established in the ritual of Venetian governance.[73]

An argument against this contention could be based upon the theoretical authority of the Major Council over all other councils. As the creator of the Ten, it could claim a final authority for all convictions. Even this link was weakened when the Ten was independently constituted after the Arengo of 1339. Ultimately, theory must give way to the reality that there are no recorded instances of the Major Council reviewing judgments of the Council of Ten. The Ten's convictions were changed only by the Ten.

Bertaldo would not have appreciated the absence of "il rito" in the machinations of the Ten. Its flexibility precluded the tradition and ritual of the older methods of dealing with violence used by the Avogadori and the Forty and by the Signori di Notte and the Giudici di Proprio. In a society ruled by a closed nobility, however, the refinements of state ritual must at times give way to a more fluid analysis of power. The Ten shared these capabilities with other Venetian councils, but its sui generis style of operation was of matchless utility to the state when a crisis arose. Perhaps the strongest feature of the Venetian system was its ability to choose from among a range of procedures one that best matched the political, social, and perceived needs of the situation.

Chapter III

THE LAW AND PENALTIES

Law and Violence

Because it is codified and relatively easy to find in archives, law is one of the first sources investigated by those interested in social responses to violence.[1] This approach has some disadvantages because law is an extremely conservative institution. It often represents value systems long out of use that remain despite significant changes in current procedure. As a result, the law may often reveal little about actual practice. Moreover, during the Renaissance, custom and law were so intertwined on a day-to-day basis that it was virtually impossible to separate them. Contemporaries made some progress in distinguishing the two, at least on the theoretical level, but they were hampered by the task of keeping track of the legislation passed by the growing number of councils with legislative responsibilities in the complex communal governments of the period.

Trecento Venice presents a good example of this technical difficulty. The core of Venetian criminal law was codified in the *Promissio Maleficorum* of the early thirteenth century. Although this document remained a basic reference, it was modified only slightly in the next two centuries, while judicial procedure in criminal cases underwent significant changes. *Parti* were passed in the Major Council, the Forty, and the Senate; but little attempt was made to integrate these various sets of laws, although they were often contradictory. After its creation in 1310, the Council of Ten also played a key role in certain areas of criminal legislation, especially for treason and speech. The sheer mass of the legislation of these councils made it almost impossible to keep track of what the actual law of Venice was at any given time.[2]

Aware of the confusion caused by this multiplicity of laws, the nobility attempted a number of solutions at the end of the thirteenth century and at the beginning of the fourteenth. During this period, the number and powers of communal councils were being expanded, so a conciliar solution was tried. The Avogadori were made responsible for collating the laws and providing a legal reference service for the commune. One of the results of this action was a series of registers listing the most important laws passed in the Major Council. Capitularies were also set up for many of the councils, especially for patrolling bodies and courts. These capitularies comprised the laws and working procedures that applied to a particular council, patrolling body, or court. Although lacking the force of law, they were the source of much legal practice, as were both the recommendations of the Avogadori and custom.[3] In criminal matters, however, Venetians were content to leave decisions about penalties almost entirely in the hands of judges or judging councils rather than referring to legal precedent. Law was too inflexible and impersonal for the Venetian style of judgment.

The law itself admitted this. The *Promissio Maleficorum* is an appendix to a larger and more prescriptive compilation of civil laws organized by Doge Jacobo Tiepolo in the early duecento. It begins with a short statement of purpose by Tiepolo: "We hold that justice requires our unceasing vigil and concern in order to correct excess and punish crime." He argues that a studied compilation of criminal law should therefore be applauded by all. Although this introduction is short, it gives an interesting perspective on the function of law in preserving order. Tiepolo saw the responsibility of law in its relationship to correction and punishment, but there is a fatalistic acceptance of the inevitability of crime in this preamble: "unceasing vigil" would bring only correction and punishment or at best the control to keep crime within acceptable limits. One finds little belief in the capacity of law to decrease the level of criminal activity, through either severity or rationality.[4]

The *Promissio* begins with a long section on robbery which, unlike other sections dealing with violent crimes, includes a detailed scheme of penalties. Its position at the beginning of the criminal code, in addition to the detailed penalties, indicates that robbery was of greatest concern to the ruling group that wrote and applied the law. Robbery was likewise evaluated without reference to violence, on the basis of the value of property taken. Penalties were carefully graded into several levels of severity, according to the value of the loss. The scale began with a simple whipping for those who stole less than one lira (in cases of first thefts) but rapidly escalated to the loss of an eye for stealing goods valued from five to ten lire. Anyone who stole more than forty lire was to be hanged. For second offenses, however, the law contained no gradations: hanging was the penalty. The law also dealt in detail with penalties to be imposed for breaking and entering with the intention to rob or for carrying weapons during a robbery.[5]

The sections on assault and murder are much briefer. Simple assault carried a fine of 25 lire, or placing the criminal under a ban of the commune. Penalties for assault that drew blood were left to the discretion of the judge.[6] The disparity between robbery and assault is clear. Penalties for robbery were carefully prescribed, but those for assault that drew blood were left to the discretion of the judging body. This distinction pervades the *Promissio.* Judicial discretion is permitted in penalties for violence, but carefully codified penalties are specified for property crimes.

This distinction produced several important results. First, penalties for violence were more likely to include personal factors. Second, since penalties for robbery were prescribed without reference to violence, its consideration entered into the discussion of robberies preserved in the criminal records only in extreme cases. The Signori di Notte, with primary responsibility for robbery cases, were much more concerned with establishing the value of the property taken than with examining levels of violence. Most important, the judicial discretion for violent crimes within the parameters established by law implies that the penalties reflected contemporary perceptions of the seriousness of these crimes rather than a continuing legal tradition. This result was especially true of crimes tried before the Forty, where a sizable group of nobles weighed the crimes, personalities, and punishments of criminals without much reference to formal law or even to customary penalties. Within similar crime categories, there were wide ranges of penalties, based primarily upon perceptions of violence and the personalities involved.

Homicide was treated in the same way as assault, the penalty being left to the discretion of the judge. In fact, even if guilt was not securely established through a confession or testimony, the law allowed judges to sentence according to their "conscience." The importance of law was negated by the laws themselves.[7]

The penalty for rape was clearly spelled out in the *Promissio.* Whether the victim was a virgin, an unmarried woman but no longer a virgin, or a married woman, rape had a fixed penalty. If the defendant was found guilty, he was to be jailed for up to eight days, being freed when he paid the equivalent of the victim's dowry; this sum was determined by the judges, introducing an element of judicial leeway. If the criminal could not pay the fine within eight days, he was to lose both eyes.[8] Trecento records, however, contain not one case where rape was punished by cutting out the eyes of the criminal. The little corporal punishment meted out concentrated on beating and branding. Although the law of 1232 seems more definite about rape than it is about assault or murder, this apparent specificity is compromised by a final clause ruling that if the crime was not clearly rape or the proof of guilt was insufficient, once more the penalty was to be left to the judge's discretion.[9] Given the nature of rape, especially as it is perceived in a male-oriented society, one concludes that judges regularly claimed such authority.

In the correction of the *Promissio* made in 1331, attributed by some manuscripts to Andrea Dandolo, a yet broader latitude was formally granted. The Forty and the ducal councilors were instructed to judge rape cases in such a manner that all concerned were indemnified, including the victim, the commune, and whoever else might have been injured. What those indemnities should be the law left undefined, leaving the penalty to the discretion of the Forty.[10]

Continuing this theme in the last section of the *Promissio,* Tiepolo summed up the whole of the criminal code by stating that it would be impossible to enumerate every possible crime and posit penalties for each; the determination was to remain in the hands of the judge for those crimes not covered. Inasmuch as the code considered only robbery, assault, murder, and rape in any detail and, excepting robbery, tended to leave wide latitude to the judges anyway, it is apparent that the *Promissio* did not place many limitations on judicial decisions.[11]

The precepts of the *Promissio* are typical of the Renaissance style of justice in Venice—individualistic and personal rather than fixed upon an abstract concept of justice embodied in the law. Symbolizing this attitude, one of the sculptures on the capitals of the columns before the Ducal Palace represents Justice holding the traditional scales and sword; but in this case Justice is presented without a blindfold. Venetian law removed the blindfold from justice by asking judges to evaluate each case with their eyes open, mindful of the character and condition of both culprit and victim. To understand the Early Renaissance perceptions of violence, one must examine the cases themselves and the penalties imposed.

Penalties and Violence

Within the process of imposing penalties for crime is a constant tension between retribution and social control. These elements are difficult to disentangle because they are interrelated on both the emotional level and the intellectual and because they constantly change in relationship to individual crimes. In certain societies or for certain crimes, vengeance predominates, while in other societies or for other crimes penalties are intended to preserve order. Carlo Calisse has argued that the Renaissance tended to focus on the utilitarian aspect of penalties: "Punishment [following the Middle Ages] was conceived in a new way. The different purposes assigned to it in the Middle Ages were abandoned and it re-acquired a political or utilitarian object for the State and Society." [12] Venice exemplified this transition; vengeance became secondary to rational punishment while at the same time and in the same context the institutions and procedures concerned with peacekeeping went through a period of growth and rationalization.

Calisse argues further that the utilitarian aspect of this transition placed a new emphasis on cruelty and terror: "The penalty aimed both to punish the criminal and by inspiring terror to prevent repetition and imitation.

Such a system provided very cruel penalties. There was death made terrible in many ways: mutilation, blinding, torture, flogging, exposing in cages, unspeakable prisons all with a view to inspire fear." [13] Although this might be the logical result of a desire to control crime through penalties, it does not correspond to the Venetian situation. There, a heightened rationality led to a tendency to weigh penalties almost as if they were an investment in control rather than an indulgence in a blood bath of fear. Moderation and restraint typified the approach of this merchant-banker nobility to the punishment of most crime.

This rationality is evident even in cases where the commune raised penalties in order to deter a particular offense. In 1359, the Major Council decided that the traditional penalty for bigamy was not strict enough to discourage potential offenders and increased the severity of the sanction.[14] Although bigamy was a serious crime in the eyes of the church, the council's reaction contained none of the cruelty Calisse describes. Realizing that the primary motive for this crime was the profit bigamists sought from dowries, the council attempted to remove that incentive and handle the question as the business matter it appeared to them to be. The fine was increased to a minimum of 100 lire, and the bigamist was specifically required to return the full amount of all dowries taken. This was not a penalty to strike fear into the hearts of bigamists. It was designed to balance the profit potential of bigamy with the danger of financial loss if detected. In fact, the *parte* makes this logic clear: the earlier penalties of the Signori di Notte were inadequate since men were still willing to take the risk of committing bigamy "because of the small penalties." To offset the attraction of this crime, the fine was raised and any doubts about full restitution were removed.[15]

Moderate investment in penalties should not seem strange in this society of bankers and merchants. A good part of their world was controlled through investments, and it was only logical that they carried this technique over into other areas requiring careful control. When the need was felt, however, the courts were still capable of violence. The Forty sometimes ordered public executions replete with bloody mutilations and symbolic pageantry. The Signori di Notte executed and mutilated in a more restrained style. The Ten could execute even a doge; one moment Falier led the commune, the next he was secretly dispatched by the same efficient order-keeping system that dominated all Venice.

Such moments of final justice were measured events. There were no wholesale blood baths. Each penalty was carefully gauged to the crime, to the status of the criminal and of the victim, even to the need for exemplary state violence at a given time. Brutality in discrete quantities, balanced by the certainty of punishment, seems to have been the goal. The courts drew on a wide range of penalties for criminal violence. Mutilation, for which there was a strong medieval tradition, became a secondary judgment, replaced to a great extent by fines and jail sentences. Moreover, during the fourteenth century, jail sentences, for technical reasons, began to replace fines as well. There is strong evidence for arguing that for many crimes the duecento saw mutilation replaced with fines and the trecento saw fines replaced by jail sentences.

The fact that jail sentences played such an important part in Venetian penology during the trecento is at variance with the traditional historical view about the development of jails. Harry Barnes, in his classic *The Story of Punishment,* wrote: "The eighteenth century was the period of transition from corporal punishment to imprisonment, and, though the process of change was most rapid after 1775, there can be no doubt that the general movement was in progress during the entire period."[16] Others have argued that penal incarceration can be traced as far back as the Middle Ages, but only in England, where a unique legal tradition made such penalties a viable alternative to fines and mutilation.[17] Nonetheless, imprisonment was a normal part of Venetian criminal punishment a full four centuries before the Enlightenment.

The reason for the transition from fines to jail sentences was on the surface rather paradoxical: jail sentences reduced the number of prisoners in the Venetian jails. Fines tended to cause excessive crowding because convicts were held in jail until they could pay their fines. The result was a logjam of lower-class prisoners with little hope of raising the sums necessary to pay their fines.[18]

One method of controlling this problem was the use of the *gratia.* Because granting a *gratia* required the cooperation, in theory at least, of most of the important men of Venice,[19] one might conclude that *gratie* were inaccessible to all but the powerful. The problem of crowded jails, however, forced the use of this clumsy procedure to empty them. A *gratia* allowed the partial remission of fines on the basis of time served, need, or good reputation; but most *gratie* set up time payment schedules complete with interest. Despite its awkwardness, the use of *gratie* churned out more then eighteen thousand adjustments to penalties in the period, almost all designed to clear the jails of men owing fines.[20]

In light of this problem, it became simpler to put a criminal directly into jail for a few months as a penalty for his crime and thus avoid the problem of leaving him there indefinitely until a *gratia* could be worked out. To an extent, the choice between jail or fine became a social or economic decision, the upper classes being fined and the lower classes sent to jail. There were exceptions, of course: jail could be used to make a small penalty more severe for a noble, or a small fine could be levied against a worker. The mixture of fines and jail sentences suggests that consideration was given to the ability of the criminal to pay. As a form of hidden taxation, a fine was economically preferable to a jail sentence, if the crime was not too serious and if the court expected that the fine would be paid.

Table 3.1 shows the relative proportions of types of penalties for rape (including attempted rape) and assault. Rape and attempted rape were both relatively minor crimes, and jail sentences were the most prevalent penalty, followed closely by fines. Banishment and corporal punishment were relatively rare. For assault, a similar emphasis was placed on fines and jail sentences, although fines predominated. This was probably related to the fact that assault cases heard by the Forty involved a larger proportion of substantial people.

Table 3.1. **Penalties for Rape and Assault, 1324–1406**

	Rape		Assault	
	Number	Percentage	Number	Percentage
Jail	305	51	301	40
Fine	242	41	373	49
Banishment	24	4	51	7
Corporal	25	4	31	4
Total[a]	416	100	569	100

Source: A.S.V., Adv., Raspe, Reg. 3641–3645 (1324–1406).

[a] The total is smaller than the number of penalties because penalties were often combined.

There were few penalties involving corporal or capital punishment. These types of punishment can be divided into four categories of severity: discipline (whipping or minor torture), mutilation, execution, and mutilation plus execution. Corporal punishment for rape and assault was restrained. For assault, of 569 cases heard by the Forty, 15 involved mutilation of the criminal and 16 some form of corporal discipline. For rape, there were 20 cases of discipline and 4 of mutilation. The brutal penalties that Calisse maintains were designed to intimidate the people were imposed neither for minor crimes like rape nor for more serious crimes like assault.

The differences between penalties imposed upon nobles and those imposed upon workers reveal the economic and social distinctions involved in social control. In rape cases, among 84 nobles successfully prosecuted, 37 received fines (44 percent); 14 received jail sentences (17 percent); and 33 received a combination of jail sentences and fines (39 percent). Among 173 workers, 24 received fines (14 percent); 89 received jail sentences (51 percent); and 60 received a combination of jail sentence and fine (35 percent). The proportion of fines and jail sentences was reversed for the two groups, jail sentences predominating for workers, who were less able to pay fines. Both groups had a high level of mixed penalties, but for rather different reasons: for a worker, the mixed penalty was a means of taxing whatever wealth the criminal had while simultaneously reducing the amount of time he would take up space in jail; for nobles, the mixed penalty was designed to add severity to the usual fine. In a mixed penalty, the law was imposed more sternly, because time in jail weighed heavily upon all. Jail sentences for nobles were relatively short and were reserved for the most serious crimes. Only 8 nobles were jailed for more than a year for rape, and a majority were jailed for less than half a year. (This total includes both cases where jail was the sole penalty and those where jail was used in conjunction with fines, a total of 46 cases.)

An analysis of assault cases heard by the Forty reveals a similar breakdown. The contrast is less striking because these cases involved a wider range of penalties than did rape cases and because the workers tried tended, for technical reasons discussed later, to be more established. Yet the distinction remains strong. In 121 cases, eighty-three nobles received fines (69 percent); twenty received jail sentences (17 percent); and eighteen received mixed sentences (15 percent). In 195 cases, fifty-five workers received fines (29 percent); sixty-nine received jail sentences (35 percent); and seventy received mixed sentences (36 percent). In both areas of crime, the pattern was clear: workers received jail sentences and nobles received fines. The government could not use fines efficiently as penalties for the lower classes because their inability to pay created more problems than were warranted by the revenue to be gained. Naturally, there was also a considerable amount of social favoritism involved, but this fact can be balanced against the perennial problem of crowded jails. In this context, the profit from fines, when they could be collected, argued for such penalties, especially for minor crimes like rape.

For major crimes—murder and robbery—Venetian practice came closer to Calisse's generalization. Tables 3.2 and 3.3 show that the great majority of murder cases involved corporal or capital punishment, most often execution.[21] But there were significant variations within these categories, Venetian judges creating distinctions in the manner or nature of penalties to fit their varying perceptions of the circumstances surrounding the crimes.

In capital punishment, there was a significant distinction between simple executions and more elaborate, ritual executions that included public mutilation. The latter were moments rich in the symbolism of state control, as Bertaldo described in his panegyric *Splendor venetorum civitatis consuetudinum*. A typical example resulted from the murder of Richa da Treviso by her husband, Giovanni. Giovanni's crime was not the passionate outcome of a family quarrel, as were so many murders of this sort; by contemporary standards, it was a planned and cold-blooded act. One night after everyone was asleep, he carried his wife from bed, dumped her in a canal, and watched her drown while she cried for mercy.

The Forty chose a penalty for Giovanni that expressed the nobility's antipathy to such heartless deeds. He was taken by boat to the far end of Venice then returned to the place where the crime was committed on the island of Giudecca, his crime being proclaimed all the while by a communal herald. There, his right hand was cut off and hung around his neck by a chain—symbolizing the literal removal of the offending member. Giovanni was finally taken to St. Mark's Square, where he was solemnly hanged between the columns of justice. This public ritual was designed to free society of its shared guilt, to bring public vengeance to the malefactor, and to reaffirm one of the basic meanings of the state: that it would protect its members from criminal violence.[22]

Table 3.2. **Penalties for Murder**

	Number	Percentage	Percentage corrected for unreported[a]
Jail	42	10	13
Fine	18	4	6
Banishment	39	9	12
Corporal and capital	220	52	69
Total	319		100

Source: A.S.V., Adv., *Raspe*, Reg. 3641–3645 (1324–1406); Signori di Notte, *Processi*, Reg. 6–12 (1348–1403).

[a] There were 427 cases, but in 155 the Signori di Notte did not report penalties imposed. The number of penalties listed above remains larger than the number of convictions because some penalties were mixed.

Aspects of this public execution had particular significance. The trip across Venice assured that a maximum audience would participate in the ceremony. Much speculation about the mentality of such crowds has concentrated on their collective bloodlust or the existence of a mob mentality that sanctions normally unacceptable types of brutality. Another aspect of such events, their ritual nature, warrants careful consideration. Successful ritual takes human emotions and redirects them toward some acceptable goal, permitting even the bloodiest ritual to become a transcendent experience. In that the state seeks a broader legitimation than reason alone can provide, ritual execution reinforces the basic myth of that state. Venice is a stable society and will provide order and security.

The abundant details in Bertaldo's account of the ideal Venetian procession also show the ceremonial character of communal justice. The doge was to present himself to the people as the representative of custom and usage in order "to teach the people to shun evil and strive for the good." To this end, he displayed the "majesty" of the ducal office through the "rich and spendid clothing" he wore, demonstrating the rewards of just living. On his right, he displayed the judge as the representative of his full power ("merum imperium") to judge criminals. Seeing the judge at the right hand of the doge also taught the people to avoid evil "because of the fear of being themselves judged." Finally, the doge displayed his sword, which was carried immediately behind him, to remind the people of his "avenging power." [23]

Table 3.3. **Corporal and Capital Punishment for Murder**

	Number	*Percentage corporal penalties*	*Percentage all penalties corrected*
Discipline	3	1	1
Mutilation	72	33	23
Execution	75	34	24
Ritual execution	70	32	22

Source: A.S.V., Adv., *Raspe*, Reg. 3641–3645 (1324–1406); Signori di Notte, *Processi*, Reg. 6–12 (1348–1403).

Ritual execution was used with restraint, however, and reserved for those whose departure would be generally applauded. When there was some doubt about the sympathies of the people, executions were carried out quietly. Doge Falier lost his head in the Ducal Palace, and the conspirators who followed Marin Boccono were dispatched in private, their bodies not being displayed in St. Mark's Square until the next day. In both cases, there was perhaps a lesson—but no ritual. This reticence characterized most treason cases handled by the Ten. Ritual was reserved for moments of public consensus.

In Venice, capital punishment was reserved for the most serious crimes. For robbery, it was used freely, and for sodomy and counterfeiting, which were infrequently prosecuted. Most other crimes were punished with jail sentences or fines. Calisse's view notwithstanding, cruelty does not seem to have been regarded as an effective deterrent.[24]

To evaluate these moderate penalties more fully, one must find a scale that relates jail sentences to fines. Fortunately, contemporary records contain the equivalencies the courts of Venice themselves saw: basically that one year in jail equals 200 lire di piccoli.[25] In order to avoid confusion or an appearance of absolute equivalency between fines and jail sentences, a neutral point scale has been derived. It makes it clear that an artificial scale of comparison is being used, based upon equivalencies established in Venetian documents. If 10 lire di piccoli are equated with 1 point (10 lire di piccoli being about the minimum fine), a year in jail equals 20 points, which reconverts to 200 lire di piccoli, as already noted. Although other monies besides lire di piccoli were in use in Venice, lire di piccoli were by far the most prevalent currency for fines, and those few fines in other currencies can be converted to lire di piccoli by using contemporary exchange rates.[26] The resulting point scale allows a comparison of the penalties for nearly all violent crimes, because virtually all penalties were either fines, jail sentences, or a combination of the two.

For all but the most serious violent crimes, penalties tended to be either very mild or very severe, reflecting what seems to have been a calculated application of governmental power. This is reflected graphically by a typical reverse J-curve (see Figure 3.1). Fines and jail sentences were kept minimal in order to limit crowding in jails but guarantee penalties for all offenders. On occasion, however, the judges reacted strictly to a crime. As a result the vast majority of penalties cluster at the bottom end of the point scale; then comes a wide range of little used penalties followed by a much smaller group of severe penalties. This pattern holds for all crimes studied except murder (where the penalty was usually death or serious mutilation), reflecting a rational, almost technical response to the problem of overcrowded jails. To clear the jails yet consistently penalize criminals, government was forced to tailor fines to culprits' ability to pay, within the context of the seriousness of their crimes and the need to keep jail sentences to a minimum. A fine beyond a convict's ability to pay meant jail time, often protracted by the complexity of the *gratia* procedure discussed earlier, just as surely as a regularly imposed jail sentence. Moderation was the only answer, short of returning to wholesale mutilations or banishments, unlikely in a city with a labor-hungry merchant marine and nascent industrial development.[27]

Figure 3.1 presents an overview of the phenomenon. The penalties for eleven hundred prosecutions fall, in a majority of cases (56 percent), in the minimal ranges of up to 10 points: 100 lire di piccoli or six months in jail. By the time penalties reach 30 points, 84 percent of all fines, jail sentences, or combinations of the two are included. Yet a meaningful proportion of the remainder falls at the far right of the scale, at or beyond 100 points (44 percent of the remainder or 8 percent of the total). Most penalties involved six months or less in jail or an equivalent fine; but in a small yet significant number of cases (eighty-two out of eleven hundred), the penalties were very stiff, demanding five or more years in jail or the equivalent.

This balance between the moderate and the severe is revealed more clearly by checking the variation from the average curve for each crime. Table 3.4 shows surprisingly little variation from the average curve for major assault, attempted rape, rape, and speech crimes. Assault, even when divided into major and minor, tends to follow this same pattern, with a significant deviation only in the 1 to 5 and 100+ point range. Thus the minor assault curve would start at a higher point than that of the other crimes, reflecting a higher percentage of lower penalties, and push the reverse J-curve to the left. Nevertheless, a sizable group of penalties (6 percent, or 16 out of 281) required at least two years in jail or fines of 400 lire di piccoli (40 points or more). Although major assault merely moves this pattern to the right, with a greater emphasis on strict penalties, more than half of the cases are included in the 5 to 20 point range (58 percent), meaning that in most cases jail sentences were not longer than a year. At the severe end of the scale, however, the seriousness of the crime required a somewhat greater concentration of penalties: approximately 15 percent of those convicted received penalties of 100 points or more.[28]

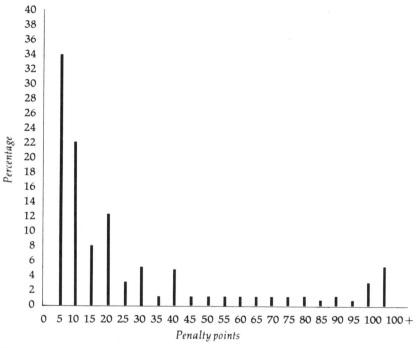

Figure 3.1. Average penalties. *Source:* A.S.V., Adv., *Raspe,* Reg. 3641–3645 (1324– 1406); Dieci, *Miste,* Reg. 1–6, 8 (1310–1374, 1392–1406).

Despite the similarities, this division between major and minor assault reveals that Venetians distinguished between the two crimes, even though the data contain examples of matching penalties. The need for statistical analysis of the premodern period is obvious; even when statistics are imperfect, they prescribe important limits for the historical imagination. These data also reveal the danger of using the mean as a normative indicator for crimes that follow a reverse J-curve. Table 3.4 reveals how atypical a figure the mean can be: only 4 percent of all penalties imposed for major assault fall on the mean point. Almost three-fourths (74 percent) fall below the mean. Penalties were nevertheless remarkably restrained for both major and minor assaults.

Penalties for rape follow a similar curve, showing little difference between attempted rape and completed rape—the means and the curves being relatively similar. For both, a majority of cases (55 percent for attempted rape, 52 percent for rape) are within the first 10 points of the
scale; and the bulk of all penalties (87 percent for attempted rape, 80 percent for rape) within the first 30 points. It is evident that both crimes were
considered minor to an equal degree. The hook of the reverse J-curve
would be found here as well, with 9 percent and 5 percent of the penalties
falling on or beyond 100 points. Once more, the courts punished culprits
either mildly or, on occasion, strictly but made little distinction between
the attempted crime and the successful. This equality may be a partial
illusion, but it nonetheless reveals a significantly different perception of
rape, which is discussed in Chapter 10.

Table 3.4. **Penalty Variations from Average Reverse J-Curve**

Penalty points	Average percentage	Variation				
		Minor assault	Major assault	Attempted rape	Rape	Speech
5	34	+12	−22	−2	0	+6
10	22	− 2	0	0	−3	+3
15	8	+ 2	0	+4	0	−3
20	12	0	0	0	0	−4
25	3	0	0	0	0	0
30	5	0	+ 4	0	0	−4
35	1	0	+ 2	0	0	0
40	4	0	0	−2	+2	−2
45	1	0	0	0	0	0
50	1	0	+ 2	0	0	0
55	1	0	0	0	0	0
60	1	0	0	0	+2	0
65	1	0	0	0	0	0
70	1	0	0	0	0	0
75	1	0	0	0	0	0
80	1	0	0	0	0	0
85	0	0	0	0	0	0
90	1	0	0	0	0	0
95	0	0	0	0	0	0
100	3	− 2	0	−2	0	+4
100+	5	− 5	+ 7	+3	−3	0
Mean penalty		11.9	40.0	22.8	22.6	22.5

Source: A.S.V., Adv., *Raspe*, Reg. 3641–3645 (1324–1406); Signori di Notte, *Processi*, Reg. 6–12 (1348–1403); Dieci, *Miste*, Reg. 1–6, 8 (1310–1374, 1392–1406).
Note: Only variations of more than 1 point are reported.

Each of the crimes discussed thus far fell under the jurisdiction of the Forty, but the pattern also holds for crimes of speech, which were the responsibility of the Council of Ten, thus strengthening the interpretation of a general pattern for crimes other than murder and robbery. As Table 3.4 shows, the majority of speech penalties (65 percent) are included in the 1 to 10 point range; and a full 82 percent fall within the first 30 points. The right hook of the reverse J-curve would be sharply present, placing 12 percent of the total on or beyond the 100 point mark. For crimes of speech, time in jail was also minimized—even the Ten used severe penalties only in unusual cases.

Although Carlo Calisse has argued that the "rationalized" approach to crime control in the Renaissance resulted in stiff and often bloody penalties, this generalization is not supported by Venetian data about typical violent crimes. The state reorganized its peacekeeping apparatus into a bureaucracy and maintained an extensive police force in the streets, but it opted for generally mild penalties. In a broad perspective, Venetians had more to consider than striking fear into the hearts of potential criminals. For serious crimes like robbery and murder, punishment could be both bloody and symbolic; but for other violent crimes, technical considerations kept the response to a milder level than Calisse's theory implies. The continued need for labor, plus a desire to keep the incarcerated population from becoming unmanageably large and costly, meant that payable fines (not requiring a wait until *gratie* could provide time payment schedules) and short jail sentences were the normal penalties for violence. These penalties, sure but not destructive, were the most rational of all. Furthermore, with little interference from criminal law, they were tailored to fit the perceived seriousness of the crimes, assuring that Venetian justice would not be blind.

PART TWO

The Social World of Violence

Within a generation of the Serrata, Venice had become a two-class society, with a noble elite at the top and the rest of the population lumped as a mass below. Among contemporary chroniclers the distinction between *nobilitas* and *populares* was the limit of social analysis.

Nor were the chroniclers naive: it was obvious to them that the gap between the nobility and the rest of society was so vast that further distinctions would have been otiose. Florence, by contrast, a city with no clearly defined elite, developed a highly sophisticated social analysis to describe the shifting patterns of the social groups that vied for power through status. Venetians, living in a setting where status was neatly delineated by the Serrata, saw their world in clearly defined terms. The social world of violence faithfully mirrored this dichotomy.

There is not enough sophistication in the two-class distinction to permit meaningful social analysis. Without an ideological context, class analysis may be merely a way of aggregating data to make them more meaningful or to uncover a reality of which contemporary society was only imperfectly aware. As such, it is a tool of the historian who wishes to consider an intermediate range of facts between the life of an individual and the life of a society as a whole. From time to time, however, this purely analytical social breakdown may reveal certain areas of real identity within artificial classes that can contribute to the understanding of society without requiring an acceptance of the whole complex of Marxist class analysis. Class is used in this context as an artificial tool of measurement; at times that tool may cut to the heart of society, but more frequently it merely aids in slicing extensive data into more manageable units for analysis. This analysis uses a straightforward division of Venetian society into five groups in order of descending rank: nobility, clergy, people of importance, laborers, and marginal people.

Chapter IV

THE SERRATA AND SOCIETY

The Nobility

Because of its legal definition, the nobility was the clearest social grouping; and it transcended the limits of arbitrary class definition. Although it was a more uneven group than some have maintained, the old truism that the nobility's wealth was based on trade and investment in trade has not been seriously questioned. Some were *rentiers* or large landholders, but even these men were extensively involved in trade. Differences within the nobility were linked with age of wealth. Ancient families like the Morosini, Michiel, or Falier could trace their lineage of wealth and leadership back to the first civic memories of the commune. Others, like the Zane, Malipiero, and Dandolo families reached prominence only in the twelfth century. Following the spectacular Venetian gains of the Fourth Crusade, yet another generation rose to richness on the shoulders of Venetian imperial expansion, led most visibly by the Tiepolo family. Throughout this pre-Serrata period, the term *nobility* was applied to an elite not yet legally defined. Noble status did not necessarily guarantee political status, nor did it imply a feudal style of life; it merely singled out the best.[1]

In the years immediately following the Serrata (1298–1320), this fluidity was eliminated and noble status was determined by membership in the Major Council. An article by Stanley Chojnacki, however, argues that considerable changes in the composition of the nobility continued until 1379. These changes grew out of the legal enfranchisement of new families and the attrition of the old. But this thesis is based upon an attempt to extract data from unlikely sources. As Chojnacki has admitted, his figure of a 32 percent change in the composition of the ruling class between 1293 and 1379 "is a sort of best guess." [2] The figure is weakened because membership lists of the Major Council between 1261 and 1297 were used as the starting point for comparison. These lists give a rough approximation of the make-up of the elite just before the Serrata, but Chojnacki's analysis depends upon the make-up of the Major Council just after the Serrata. What was needed was a comparison of the first group of families sitting in the Major Council after 1297–1298 and subsequent groups. This would have measured the rate of movement into and out of the elite after the Serrata. The openness of the post-Serrata elite can only be judged in terms of its starting point. All Chojnacki had to work with were incomplete lists of thirty-eight years of pre-Serrata members, which may have been indicative of post-Serrata membership, but were not substantial enough to warrant his claim of a "systematic exploitation of systematic sources." [3]

Chojnacki also neglected to examine the differential growth rates within the period from 1298 to 1379. Most scholars agree there was a rapid addition of families to the Major Council, and hence to elite status, in the years immediately following the Serrata. Chojnacki has published the relevant texts. They show that the original lenient standards for admission to the council were reduced further in 1300, to require only the approval of four of six ducal councilors and a simple majority of the Forty, with a quorum set at twenty members. Under these conditions, one would expect the routine addition of important men who had not originally fitted into the elite under the legalistic provisions of the Serrata. But after 1307, and especially following the Querini–Tiepolo conspiracy of 1310, there was a progressive tightening of requirements for admission until, in 1319, they included a favorable vote of thirty members of the Forty and two-thirds of the Major Council, plus an investigation of one's petition by the Avogadori. Failure to pass this scrutiny was penalized by a fine of 300 lire to discourage unworthy claimants.[4]

The period from 1298 to 1379 cannot be viewed as uniformly fluid in admission to the elite, when such basic changes were being made in the procedure for admission. Chojnacki has identified forty-two new families among the elite after the 1290s, but according to records in the Venetian archives, only eight of these families were added after 1310.[5] Additions to the nobility between 1320 and 1381 were largely restricted to members of cadet branches of older noble families who returned from the colonies or to mainland tyrants who were granted honorary status.[6] Taking the broad period from the 1290s to 1379 distorts the real picture of stability after 1320, when change was limited either to families dying out or to the admission of one large group of families following significant service to the state—the thirty-one families added in 1381 after the war of Chioggia.[7]

At first, the Serrata referred only to legal membership on the Major Council. With time, it came to define a broad political elite, because by the 1320s virtually all important offices of the state were elected from the members of the Major Council. However, social status implied more than political power, even with the robber-baron mentality of the Renaissance city-states. Florence's Magnate class, representing at least in theory a hereditary elite, was excluded by the Ordinances of Justice from political authority. Yet, through Guelph party ties and social maneuvering, they retained considerable prestige and power. In Venice, the Serrata defined who the political elite would be, rather than who it would *not* be, and the merging of the political and social elites in that city was more rapid and complete.[8]

Trecento Venice came to regard nobility and the political elite as synonymous. Before that time, Venetians and other northern Italians associated nobility with ancient lineage, ownership of land, marriage ties, political power, military prowess, and other relatively subjective criteria.[9] Lane argues that the association of nobility with membership in the Major Council began in 1323, when a hereditary principle legally linked the two together: "Thereafter, the old line between nobles and commoners disappeared. Membership in the Great Council became the basis for that distinction. All members of the Great Council were considered nobles and nobility was viewed not as a matter of personal life style, but as hereditary."[10] Law and political power, not the humanist's *virtù*, provided the basis for status. However, this date could be pushed back at least a decade. Following the Querini–Tiepolo conspiracy of 1310, a *parte* of the Major Council, in the course of making a distinction between noble conspirators and commoners, stated that nobles were "those who are or may be on the Major Council."[11]

The early 1320s seem to be a conservative point from which to date the Venetian nobility of the Serrata. The work of the Serrata was completed, and whatever the original meaning of that term, it had come to mean a closing of the elite. New members did not enter again, except in unusual circumstances like the war of Chioggia. Because of this stability, the nobility of Venice provides a good opportunity to examine a legally defined group's attitude toward, and participation in, violence.

The Clergy

The clergy of Venice were a far less unified group. The primary distinction within the category followed that of Venetian society itself, between noble and commoner. Parish clergy tended to be drawn from the latter class; the higher offices in the church were filled by members of the important noble families.[12] There was a further distinction between regular and monastic clergy.

Because of this diversity, the clergy as a class is a weak group for social analysis. It has the problem of being easily identified but poorly defined, tempting the historian to juggle meaningless data. Perhaps the best course would be to regard the clergy as a separate society. Most clerical violence was handled by the church, however, and was tied to a different administrative structure. This class category therefore will be used primarily to segregate a group of people who do not really fit into any social category successfully. Only occasionally, as in the discussion of sexual crime and petty violence—where Boccaccio's reports of worldly monks and promiscuous nuns are given some support—can a few conclusions be drawn for this grouping.

Important People

The category comprising important people, including those having status in the form of wealth or minor offices but not noble standing, is also weakened because of its diversity. This small group fell between the nobility and the mass of workers. Because of the closed nature of Venetian society, this group might have had revolutionary potential; but most members were in co-opted positions: their economic well-being and status depended directly upon the state and the established order. This dependency created important ties that actually strengthened the stability of Venetian society.

The category includes petty communal officials; non-noble merchants and boat owners operating within the controlled economy of Venice; professional people like doctors, lawyers, or professors; and important foreigners. The least apt members of this category are the petty communal officials who may be grouped at the bottom. They were usually drawn from the laboring class to hold such jobs as patrollers of the streets, inspectors, and heralds. There was a double advantage to the nobility in using the lower classes in the "contact" positions of government (where government came into daily contact with its subjects), especially in a social world where bureaucratic control was relatively new. First, it gave some of those who had been excluded from major offices a feeling of superior status, along with occasionally impressive monetary rewards. More important, in jobs like policing, or fine and tax collecting, it tended to focus popular discontent with governmental authority on this group rather than the nobility. The records of violence provide a litany to the efficacy of this policy, whether it was conscious or not. Although these officials were low in status in comparison with others in the group, their position as representatives of the authority of the commune set them above the rest of society, marking them as important men, at least in terms of violence.

Merchants and boat-owners were a more substantial element of the class, but they were equally dependent upon the government. The number of non-noble merchants is difficult to estimate. Lane pointed out that important naval posts continued to be given to non-nobles after the Serrata. Occasionally a merchant ship command was given to a non-noble, either directly or under the nominal control of a young noble. The whole rich and protected merchant-galley fleet was nevertheless closely regulated by the Venetian Senate, which was dominated by the senior members of the nobility. Non-noble merchants were therefore not likely to oppose their benefactors; they, too, were effectively co-opted.[13]

Foreigners of status are a special group within the category, because they were not members of Venetian society. As a trading city, Venice was host to a large number of transient and semipermanent foreign merchants and sailors. Those who were labeled in the criminal records as merchants or nobles are included in the category of important people, and they seem to have been treated as such by the Venetian courts. These foreigners were as dependent upon the established order as their native counterparts. Their economic privileges, and even their continued residence in Venice, were ultimately in the hands of the nobility.

The activities of doctors and lawyers were also carefully regulated by the commune. Lauro Martines argues in *Lawyers and Statecraft in Renaissance Florence* that legal training in that city was an important vehicle for upward mobility. It would be interesting to compare these findings with the social situation of lawyers in Venice, where upward mobility was limited by the closed nature of the ruling class. Perhaps it is a consequence of this limitation that a large proportion of doctors and lawyers in the criminal records were foreign born. There may have been something about the static nature of the social situation in Venice that made such professions less attractive than they were in Florence.[14] The predominance of commerce as a basis for wealth, however, must have played a role as well. A Florentine, working within a more diversified economy, could find numerous possibilities—banking, trade, industry, law, and politics—for amassing wealth. The Venetian had a more limited economic vision, although not so limited in the fourteenth century as some have assumed.

As in Florence, lawyers, scribes, and notaries played an important role in providing continuity in governmental office. Rotation of office was less rapid in Venice than in most other cities, but noble officeholders in many positions remained mere gentlemen-profiteers, forced by their amateur status to rely upon their better trained inferiors. Scribes and notaries, as keepers of the communal written memory, had significant additional power. Misuse of this power is easy to document. For example, Mapheo Natale, a notary for the Giudici al Forestier, had been "convinced" by the noble Sclavo Dolfin to forge documents in a case then before the court in order to help a friend. The forgery was caught and investigated by the Avogadori di Comun. As a result, Mapheo was deprived of all offices and benefices. Mapheo's penalty demonstrates how lawyers and notaries, even with their practical influence in running the government, subsisted at the mercy of the nobility.[15]

This need may have fostered client–patron relationships. Dolfin seems to have had some claim to Mapheo's loyalty, although it may have been simply a matter of money. There were a number of signs in the trecento that this group of important men without noble status was being converted into a client class. The symbiotic relationship between Andrea Dandolo and his chancellor, Benintendi Ravegnani, was a prominent and an apparently honorable example of such a relationship. The extent of clientage is difficult to ascertain, but it is evident that lawyers and notaries were closely tied to the Venetian nobility.

These professionals, closest to the nobility but legally excluded from it, rather than being a threat to their superiors actually became a support and a buffer for them. Moreover, a small measure of upward mobility into this buffer group allowed some fluidity in society, while maintaining status required a concomitant identification with the nobility. It is not surprising therefore that there was little open social unrest among members of this group.

The Workers

Laborers fill the largest category in the records. Within this class, one distinguishes three main groups: ship and marine-related workers; industrial workers (mainly cloth and glass); and service workers, such as butchers, bakers, shoemakers. The organization of Venetian workers was unusual because, unlike that of Florence, the guild structure was an arm of the state.[16] In Florence, the guilds competed with communal government for political control; and during the trecento they were largely successful in influencing policy. In Venice, the defined nobility and the domination of the economy by merchants obviated the need for noble membership in guilds. In a way, the commune of Venice was itself the guild of merchants.

Consequently, Venetian worker guilds lacked political power. Their main similarity with Florentine guilds lay in their control of the labor force. In both communes, guild legislation sought primarily to ensure the quality of workmanship and to organize laboring masses in a way that assured profits for guild masters and wealthy investors. The guilds helped keep a certain order in both cities, but in Venice they were administered in a centralized fashion by the government; there was no question of competition for power.[17]

Sailors were not organized into a guild. Lane attributes this to the fact that they, like merchants, "were too numerous and the functions performed by the commune left no sphere in which such a guild might have operated."[18] This was true, but there was an additional factor: many seamen were among the most marginal of Venetian laborers. Guild membership implied a stability foreign to their lifestyle. In criminal records, one often finds them identified not only as sailors but as vagabonds or wanderers (*pelligrini*) as well. Frequently they were also foreigners or men with names that indicated recent foreign origin. In addition, they were regularly recruited from the prisons; the *gratia* records reveal that many prisoners were pardoned from jail terms for unpaid fines to allow them to join communal fleets. Finally, instruction to policing bodies suggests that marginal people were even swept up off the streets into seamen duties. All this indicates a very low status for sailors, which may have seemed the optimum condition to Venice's merchant capitalists. It cut their labor costs to a minimum.[19]

Industrial workers became progressively more important in the fourteenth century, with the growth of the wool and silk industries. Early in the century, the cloth industry was concerned primarily with local production for local use; but by mid-century it began to expand into foreign markets and draw on the skills of imported workers, especially those from Lucca. Skilled labor from industrial mainland cities posed a problem for the commune. These laborers and their masters were not accustomed to the closed Venetian political and social organization. Their violence against it is instructive in coming to an understanding of the role of tradition and habit in the maintenance of a closed society. Cloth workers were, in fact, among the most violent groups in Venetian society.[20]

Service industries in Venice were quite diverse. Unfortunately, little is known about their place in the work force or in society. There are indications that their guilds were organized early and that they were among the most successfully controlled workers in the commune. They worked for a predominantly Venetian market, and their subservient position is easily understood. Like the notaries and lawyers, they existed in the service of the nobility, who utilized their skills and controlled their guilds. From this broad division of the Venetian working class, one might assume that social unrest would be concentrated among the lower levels of the marine workers and in the cloth industry.

It is unfortunate that the surviving records of the guilds from the fourteenth century reveal only their theoretical organization and rules. Records of their actual operation are lost. Given the control of the communal government over the guilds, however, it is likely that beyond their role in production and peacekeeping they were primarily fraternal and charitable organizations on the model of the Venetian confraternities. Workers therefore, though the largest group in the society, lacked organization and a formal power base; thus their violence tended to be isolated and individual.

Marginal People

The final group to be considered contains those marginal people at the bottom of city life who are almost invisible to history. Some members of this group can be identified: petty servants, slaves, street whores (in distinction to courtesans), beggars, and wanderers; all were occasionally noted in the records of violence. It is impossible to determine how many others, referred to by first names and perhaps places of origin, also fit into this group. The number of socially unidentifiable people in the records of violence is quite large, and it would be significant if they could be assigned to the marginal category. It would give evidence of a sizable and violent class at the bottom of society. More likely, however, the unidentified included low-level workers as well as the marginal: people with so little importance that their occupations were not significant to the record keepers.

The data are not conclusive, but they indicate that this group was quite large, providing the human capital reserves usually associated with urban economies based upon inexpensive, relatively unskilled labor. This interpretation is supported by Venetian legislative efforts to attract labor to the city at times when its human capital reserves were low. Whatever the numbers, the living conditions of these marginal people, combined with their lack of knowledge about and commitment to the order of Venetian society, made them potentially an extremely violent group. The criminal statistics, for all their imperfections, provide a glimpse into this world of violence that supports this generalization.[21]

Estimates of Size

A major analytical problem with this five-class division of Venetian society is a lack of firm data on the size of each of these groups. For Early Renaissance Venice, demographic data of any type are limited. Lane probably came closest to a general figure when he numbered population at about 120,000 persons in the 1330s.[22] The plagues of 1347–1348, 1382, 1397, and 1400 seriously reduced the population, but recovery was remarkably rapid after these demographic catastrophies. The people of Venice and other major cities not only increased their rates of reproduction but also replaced population loss by drawing laborers from the countryside and, in Venice, from overseas colonies.[23]

More important for social analysis than total population is the division into the social categories outlined earlier. This division can be based only upon rough estimates, but even these have some value in giving a perspective on the social data from the records on violence. For the nobility, the figures have the most validity. A good estimate would place the nobility at between 3 percent and 4 percent of the population. This figure is based on chronicle references to the number of males capable of doing military duty in the city in 1338.[24] Below the nobility, one can only make intelligent guesses or extrapolate from sixteenth-century figures. This latter approach seems, within wide ranges of error, to be the most valid; such broad categories probably did not vary too much in relation to one another in the context of premodern merchant-capitalist society. Doubtless there were major shifts, especially within occupational categories; but for the sake of comparison, a sixteenth-century breakdown remains the best available.

This provides a picture of a Venetian society with a noble elite making up 4 percent of the population; a clergy making up 3 percent; important people below the nobility accounting for 11 percent; laborers accounting for 77 percent; and marginal people for 5 percent.[25] In the fourteenth century, the percentage of clergy may have been slightly higher, and the group of important people below the elite may have been considerably smaller. Marginal people were certainly more numerous, because in most census material they fail to appear in anywhere near their actual numbers. Still, figures in the range of nobility 3–4 percent, clergy 3–4 percent, important people 8–11 percent, workers 75–80 percent, and marginal men 5–10 percent, are reasonable estimates for the fourteenth century. Despite the possible range of error, if these figures are used with caution, they will be useful for putting into perspective the abundant social data on violence from the records of trecento Venice.

How many violent crimes were committed by each social group? The data reveal only how many crimes were prosecuted, and this introduces a bias common to all studies of criminal violence, that of the social selection that occurs before prosecution. If Venice was an exceedingly just society, as has been argued, this would be a minor problem: it could be assumed that prosecutions represented a faithful sample of crime itself.[26] But the operation of the judicial process, along with the data in this and subsequent chapters, indicates that this was not the case. Thus, along with the presentation of statistical data that follows, it is necessary to examine the factors most likely to influence prosecution in order to form some tentative conclusions about the social nature of criminal violence.

By itself, a statistical approach to the social world of crime is not sufficient. Statistics provide a structure, but history requires more. The limits prescribed by the data must also be interpreted. In what follows, this is the primary goal: to provide not only structure but also feeling and place.

Chapter V

THE NOBILITY AND VIOLENCE

The Myths of Order

In an age when nobility was universally reviled for its lawless ways, Venetian nobles were reputed to be particularly peaceable. The myth of Venice contributed and continues to contribute to this view, with its stress on noble unity and self-sacrifice for the common good. According to that myth, nobles were willing to put aside individual goals and emotions for the greater good of society. Following the Serrata, there was certainly some merit to such behavior. An equally potent modern myth—that of bourgeois commitment to law and order—implies another reason for such peacefulness. The bourgeois revolutions of the late eighteenth and nineteenth centuries or the bourgeois counterrevolutions of the twentieth, however, belie this stereotype. In fact, the nobility remained the most violent people in society. They were not a peaceloving bourgeois nobility more interested in money then honor. The paradoxical phrase *bourgeois nobility* expresses the heart of the matter: as a group they were committed to order; as individuals they perceived themselves as members of a superior class and were often violently disruptive. The myths about peaceful bourgeois elites err because they overlook the broader social world in which elite mentalities were formed. For Venice, that world was still partly courtly and feudal. Nobles included in their world-view many of the perceptions and values of the courtly world, even though these were being modified by their own economic mode of life. It was still possible for a portly member of the *popolo grasso* to fantasize about himself in terms of courtly romance.

The name the Venetian elite adopted for themselves after the Serrata implied this perceptual context: they styled themselves, arbitrarily, *nobles.* It was a style, a view of their place in the world, that informed their lives in many ways. They read or listened to courtly literature and the *chansons de geste,* some even in the language of southern France rather than Latin or the evolving Venetian dialect. They also staged and participated in jousts in St. Mark's Square. In 1364, a tournament was held in honor of the king of Cyprus, who was returning from France by way of Venice. Local nobles participated in this joust along with visiting nobles like the lord of

Ferrara. A Venetian chronicler, Caroldo, stressed that first place went to a Venetian, who for his valorous comportment, was rewarded with a gold crown worth 300 ducats. The equal attention to honor and money symbolizes the unseen contradiction between bourgeois and feudal values.[1]

So complete was the confusion of old and new ways that the commune periodically had to pass legislation to discourage nobles from riding horses through the narrow streets of the city islands. Although early versions of the gondola were more suitable and walking probably more efficient, the nobility preferred the trappings of an older style of life.[2]

It is not surprising then that Venetian nobles were somewhat schizophrenic in their relationship to violence. As a group, they were rationally committed to a controlled environment, but as individuals they often practiced a highhanded and violent way of living that aped the unruliness of nobles on the mainland. This high level of personal violence is suggested in Table 5.1. For the four major violent crimes, the nobility was prosecuted for 18.3 percent of all cases although their proportion of the total population was only 3 to 4 percent. This share indicates that in comparison with other groups nobles were highly violent. To infer some reason for this overrepresentation one must look in more detail at noble involvement in each type of crime. There are reasons to expect some overreporting in the areas of speech and assault and significant underreporting in murder and rape. Despite these qualifications, the high level of prosecution of nobles, in a system controlled by the nobility, suggests a prevailing awareness of the dangers inherent in violence among nobles and the prevalence of that violence.[3]

Speech and Assault

Table 5.1 shows especially strong deviations in speech and assault, the nobility being involved in 30 percent more speech crimes and 17 percent more assault crimes than their proportion of the population. In both areas, however, the statistics are inflated, albeit in a meaningful way. First, insults, threats, and words took on greater significance in the upper echelons of society, where words could be transformed into action that might damage society itself. The speech of the nobility was therefore closely monitored. Idle threats and bickering among the lower classes, except in their more ominous manifestations, were of little interest to the controllers of society, or were too hard to detect to be prosecuted.

What these figures reveal, however, is the careful watch over the speech of nobles. The legendary unity of the Venetian elite must be questioned in light of such surveillance. An intrinsic element in that unity was a careful monitoring of words against other nobles and against the state. By this means, the state turned the evolving myth of Venice into more than a unifying theme of urban imperial pride: it also became the law of the land. Myth and control are difficult to untangle, but there is no doubt that in the Early Renaissance active control of dissent within the elite helped to make the myth a social reality. Thus the state had not only its own myth and its own mythology, it had an orthodoxy of speech to uphold as well.

Table 5.1. **Violent Crimes Committed by Nobles**

	Number	Percentage[a]	Deviation[b]	Mean penalty	General mean	Modal penalty	Median penalty
Speech	78	33.9	+29.9	13.4	22.5	10.0	9.7
Assault	122	21.4	+17.4	16.0	24.8	10.0	9.9
Rape	83	20.0	+16.0	24.7	22.7	5.0	11.0
Murder	18	4.2	+0.2				
Total	301	18.3	+14.3				

Source: A.S.V., Adv., *Raspe,* Reg. 3641–3645 (1324–1406); Signori di Notte, *Processi,* Reg. 6–12 (1348–1403); Dieci, *Miste,* Reg. 1–6, 8 (1310–1374, 1392–1406).

[a] Percentage of total criminal population for crime.

[b] Based upon the assumption that the nobility accounts for 4 percent of the population.

The figures on assault cases involving nobles are also inflated because records exist only for those cases heard by the Forty, who primarily tried crimes committed in the course of communal business, either in the form of interaction with communal officials in the streets, in litigation, or in the normal course of noble office holding. To a degree, then, this deviation reflects both the active contact between nobles and government and their higher status. A comparison with the assault statistics for important people, however, whose contact with the government was as regular as that of the nobility, reveals that this cannot be the only factor. Assault by important people falls closer to the range of their proportion in society—they were much less involved in such crimes.

A major distinguishing factor between the two groups was the elite mentality of the nobility who felt that the state was at their service. When that service became interference, the noble's loyalty often ended. Rhetoric placed the noble within society and the Serrata placed him on top of it, but older values like noble honor occasionally placed him beyond it, with violence as the result.

That sense of being at once in charge of the law and beyond it is exemplified by a case of private torture involving a noble, Triadano Gritti, in 1384. He believed a servant had damaged his home, but he lacked the proof to proceed against her legally. In a feudal fashion, he practiced private justice by hiring a certain Paolo to torture the woman and gain a confession. Paolo worked diligently—the torture involved her toes and head—but without clear results. Although the commune objected to this private torture and sentenced Paolo to jail, Gritti was absolved. Private torture was not permitted, but the nobility was wary of offending one of its own. Gritti called to justice served as a warning against such violations, but only his functionary was punished.[4]

A more typical assault case involved the noble Jacomelo Emo. In the summer of 1359, he was submitted to the indignity of being searched by a humble *custode* of the Signori di Notte, Pietro, who found and confiscated a concealed weapon. The laws against carrying concealed weapons were continually being renewed by the Major Council, to which Emo belonged; but the interference was annoying and degrading to his sense of honor. His response was not unusual: he waited for Pietro near the latter's home in the campo of San Tomà and wounded him seriously with a sword, causing "much blood to flow." The penalty for this assault on communal authority was a restrained fine of 200 lire di piccoli. Emo may have thought this a modest price for assuaging his offended honor.[5]

Table 5.2. **Penalties Imposed on Nobles for Crimes of Speech**

	Number	Percentage of total
1–10 points	55	70.5
11–20 points	10	12.8
21–30 points	4	5.1
31–99 points	1	1.3
100–149 points	2	2.6
150+ points	0	0.0
Unclear	6	7.7
Total	78	100.0

Source: A.S.V., Dieci, *Miste,* Reg. 1–6, 8 (1310–1374, 1392–1406); Adv., *Raspe,* Reg. 3641–3645 (1324–1406).

These cases reveal a paradox about the behavior of Venetian nobles: the commune defined and defended the prerogatives of the nobility; yet nobles were among those most disruptive of this defense. It is significant that this basic contradiction, rather than violently destroying Venetian society, became an integral part of the way it functioned. The very fact that the Forty took the time to hear such cases, when councils like the Cinque alla Pace or the Signori di Notte might normally have heard them, may be viewed as an adjustment to the threat of the nobles' destruction of their own social order through violence. Nobles were too important to be dealt with harshly for most of these crimes. The commune sought to warn without antagonizing by striking a balance between the assurance of penalty and the danger of inciting the proud to vengeance.

This balance prevailed for crimes of speech and of assault. Penalties for speech crimes were generally moderate, as Table 5.2 demonstrates. If graphed, the data would reflect a typical reverse J-curve, though the right hook would be small, indicating that few strict penalties were imposed. This phenomenon is paradoxical in that the state carefully monitored the speaking activity of nobles and viewed dissent as a dangerous threat. Two factors tended to moderate the penalties: first, the commune was wary of creating rifts within the ruling class through harsh penalties; second, because it watched the nobility more carefully, a greater percentage of lesser crimes was prosecuted. This is reflected in the low average penalty for noble speech crimes (13.4 points), in comparison to the general average (22.5 points).

In some cases, nobles could be penalized severely for minor crimes. Aluysio Venier, son of Doge Antonio Venier, along with a friend from an important family, Marco Loredan, left some objects on the bridge that led into campo San Ternita—a set of horns and a sign designed to insult (as the records relate) the virtue of Giovanni dalle Boccole, also a noble, and his wife, sister, and mother-in-law. Although it was no more than a youthful joke in bad taste, the commune responded without humor. Both pranksters were given two-month jail sentences, fined 100 ducats, and forbidden to enter the campo of San Ternita for ten years. An incident like this at any other level of society would not have warranted communal attention, but insults among the ruling class could not be overlooked.[6]

Table 5.3. **Assault Penalties for Nobles**

	Number	*Percentage of total*
1–10 points	74	60.7
11–20 points	23	18.9
21–30 points	13	10.7
31–99 points	6	4.9
100–149 points	4	3.3
150+ points	0	0.0
Unclear	2	1.6
Total	122	100.1

Source: A.S.V., Adv., *Raspe*, Reg. 3641–3645 (1324–1406).

Penalties for assault follow a similar pattern (see Table 5.3), clustered at the lowest levels with a small group of more severe penalties. In this instance, however, it would be difficult to assert that nobles were tried for a wider range of crimes. As noted earlier, most of these cases involved serious crimes; and more severe penalties might be expected. In fact, the average penalty for the nobility (16.0) falls considerably below that for all classes (24.8).

One could claim that these figures indicate that nobles received special treatment from their courts. Yet Venetian law and practice required a careful consideration of the social status of criminal and victim, and all the courts were aware of the dangers in imposing strict penalties on powerful men. From this view, the treatment accorded nobles was not special at all; it was consistent with the Venetian perception of justice. Statistics, however, reveal that nobles received lesser penalties. One of the most persistent aspects of penalties for violent crimes was their social awareness. Although penalties for all classes describe a reverse J-curve, which means that there were considerable overlaps, the mean penalty becomes progressively higher as the social scale becomes lower.

Rape

Table 5.1 shows that nobles committed a higher proportion of rapes than their numbers would suggest. It might be supposed that nobles were more often accused of rapes by purported victims seeking monetary awards from the courts. This almost never happened, however; the likelihood of profit from false accusation was small. Moreover, it is hard to imagine a crime handled by the politically sensitive Avogadori and Forty, composed completely of nobles, being exploited to the detriment of the noble class. One would therefore expect the prosecution of rapes by nobles to be low rather than high.[7]

On the other hand, one might argue that because these crimes were more important they were more likely to be reported and tried. However, rapes by important men—those just below noble status—fall neatly within their class; and moreover it will become clear later that rape by nobles was regarded as a particularly minor crime.

If there is a skewing of the data, it more likely occurs in the other direction: crimes were underreported. Nobles bought off or intimidated their victims or carried out their crimes in such an organized fashion that they escaped detection. A good measure of this power is revealed by the recurrent pattern of a noble buying the support of his victim's relatives or servants. In 1357, a minor noble, Francescino dalle Boccole, was actually helped by the mother of his victim. She brought her daughter, who had not yet reached puberty, to the noble and helped as he raped her twice. Both received severe penalties; Francescino was jailed for two years and fined 200 ducats; the mother spent one day in a berlina, the Venetian equivalent of a pillory, was whipped from San Marco to Santa Croce while her guilt was proclaimed by a herald, and spent one year in jail.[8]

A similar pattern can be seen in the rape of an eight-year-old girl by a more important noble, Nicoleto Zorzi. Nicoleto paid a certain Bianca, who had access to his intended victim (the daughter of Francesco Grassi), to do the dangerous work of stealing the girl and hiding her away for his crime. As the documents delicately related, Bianca brought this girl to her own room and there "prepared her" for Nicoleto. Nicoleto then arrived and with Bianca's help succeeded in his assault.[9] Because of the money and power of the nobility, such crimes must have been rarely reported. In many cases, the victim or her relatives were undoubtedly bought off with bribes or dowries or scared off by the power of the culprit's family. The statistics probably reveal only a small proportion of rapes by nobles. This analysis is reinforced by the fact that rape by nobles was primarily a crime committed upon social inferiors, 84 percent of all attacks victimizing women of lower social status. Despite these factors, a high level of rapes by nobles survives in the records. If nobles had the power to escape prosecution in some instances, why did they not do so in virtually all? There are two likely reasons. Some crimes were too public to be covered up, or the families were too upset to accept a cover-up. More important, rape was such a minor crime, especially for nobles attacking their social inferiors, that covering it up was often not worth the effort or expense. It was simpler to face a day in court.

The noble Moreto Tomado's career as a would-be rapist illustrates this attitude. In September 1352, he came before the Forty for breaking into the house of a boatman named Andrea in an attempt to rape his wife. The social distance between a boatman's wife and a noble was immense, and the Forty fined Tomado a paltry 20 soldi di grossi. It was unlikely that he could have bribed Andrea to forget the matter for less. Three months later, Tomado was back before the Forty for breaking into the house of a miller named Victor in an attempt to rape his wife, Colette. Though a bumbler, Tomado was still a noble and his victim again of low social standing. The Forty voted him another insignificant fine, 50 lire di piccoli, exactly what he would have paid if apprehended for carrying a knife longer than the legal length in the streets. Tomado paid the fine immediately, as was noted in the margin of the text. For Tomado and most nobles, rape of inferiors was so minor that it was often not worth the effort of attempting to cover it up.[10]

The data on noble penalties for rape shown in Table 5.4 support this interpretation. More than 70 percent of the penalties fall in the 1–20 point range, and the predominant point category is the lowest (48 percent of all rape penalties are in the 1–10 point range and 25 percent in the 11–20 point range). The average penalty (24.7) is also low, despite the admixture of cases where the victim was of high social standing. Only nobles raped noble women, but this was considered a serious crime. The difference is impressive; the average penalty for thirteen rapes of noblewomen is 52.7 points, but the average penalty for rape of lower-class women is 19.3 points. Class awareness and bias are clearly delineated by this disparity. The *Promissio Maleficorum* called for consideration of the quality of criminal and victim; statistically it is evident that the Forty was carrying out that mandate.

These figures are given more substance by a case involving a young noble, Paolo da Canal. In May 1351, he was accused of breaking into the home of a carpenter named Marco and raping his wife. The incident caused an uproar, and there were a number of witnesses available to testify against him when the Avogadori prepared the case. But Paolo's peers in the Forty overlooked the Avogadori's case and acquitted him. Six months later, he was back before the Forty with a similar crime they were less willing to overlook. Although once again his crime was illegal entry and rape, his victim was the wife of Marco Corner, a noble of major social and political stature. Youthful excess had become excessive. Paolo had crossed a line no less real for being perceptual rather than physical, which transformed his offense from minor into major violence. He and his accomplices, Moreto Vitturi and Moreto de Buora, were fined 20 ducats each, jailed for three years, and banished from Venice and all its territories for another three years.[11]

Table 5.4. **Rape Penalties for Nobles**

	Number	Percentage of total
1–10 points	40	48.2
11–20 points	21	25.3
21–30 points	5	6.0
31–99 points	11	13.3
100–149 points	3	3.6
150+ points	1	1.2
Unclear	2	2.4
Total	83	100.0

Source: A.S.V., Adv., *Raspe*, Reg. 3641–3645 (1324–1406).

Murder

Although in other violent crimes the nobility behaved more like a feudal nobility than a merchant elite, in murder cases they did not deviate significantly from the norm (see Table 5.1). It is possible that murder committed by nobles was underreported. Because the crime was so serious and the penalties so devastating, the judicial system may have been unwilling to hear any but the most socially dangerous cases. When a noble murdered someone from the lower classes, it may have been less strain on the fabric of the system to overlook the crime. The power and wealth of the nobility must also have frequently provided the means to escape detection. Paid assassins or minions could shield the wealthy from direct involvement and leave no record of their culpability.

A typical instance of a noble using a hired murderer involved the noble banker, Zanino Soranzo. A business dispute with fellow banker and noble, Semelino da Mosto, led Zanino to hire a certain Blasio, a carpenter, to assassinate Semelino. For the deed, Blasio was to receive 100 ducats plus living expenses in Treviso for two years, presumably so he could hide out until it was safe to return to Venice. When Blasio was caught, found guilty by the Forty, and executed, Zanino fled.[12] That Zanino would hire an assassin for settling a dispute with a noble peer weakens the myth of Venice that members of the nobility worked out their controversies peacefully and equitably, this being one of the underpinnings of their continued success. Zanino certainly did not subscribe to this code, and the nobility's response was severe. Because he fled, the commune offered a reward of 400 ducats for his capture; if he were caught, his penalty would be the same as Blasio's. The law was harshly enforced in these cases, to keep the nobility from dissolving into antagonistic factions rife with feuding. Like most nobles, however, Zanino had the wealth and power to protect himself when he decided to violate one of society's strictest taboos. How many cases like this were successful but undetected is impossible to estimate; but it is clear that hiring a murderer was an available option for the nobility.[13]

Table 5.5. **Murder by Nobles, Motivation**

	Number	Percentage of total	Percentage of category
Self-interest			
Against commune	2	11.1	25.0
Business gain	3	16.7	37.5
Criminal gain	2	11.1	25.0
Influence litigation	1	5.6	12.5
Total	8	44.4	100.0
Passion			
Casual	1	5.6	10.0
Family quarrel	3	16.7	30.0
General quarrel	4	22.2	40.0
Sexual quarrel	0	0.0	0.0
Vendetta	2	11.1	20.0
Total	10	55.6	100.0

Source: A.S.V., Adv., *Raspe,* Reg. 3641–3645 (1324–1406); Signori di Notte, *Processi,* Reg. 6–12 (1348–1403).

Most nobles prosecuted for homicide killed in the heat of passion, when their power to disguise their crimes was lost (see Table 5.5). The sample (18 cases) is too small to be conclusive, but a majority (56 percent) were crimes of passion occurring during moments of emotional contact. Violence leading to death was too serious a crime to become a style of life or a form of self-interest.

The case of Tomaso Moro exemplifies this type of motivation. Tomaso

and a friend were walking across campo San Giacomo del Lupo one evening when Bartolomeo Garzone and a companion began flipping stones at
them. This insult called at least for hostile words. The young men
stopped and argued, and eventually weapons were drawn. So far, things
were normal. Such incidents usually ended with minor bloodshed and the
Signori di Notte, Cinque alla Pace, or Capi di Sestiere fining the culprits if
they were unlucky enough to be caught. In this case, Tomaso struck too
well; and although the fight was broken up by some passing nobles,
Bartolomeo eventually died. Public, passionate, and unpremeditated,
Tomaso's crime was typical of the murders for which nobles were prosecuted.[14]

Even murders committed out of self-interest tended to have a strong
element of the passion of honor. Crimes involving communal officials, in
particular, seem frequently to have been spontaneous overreactions to
minor aggravation. In 1400, Tomaso Dandolo and his illegitimate son
were tried for killing a *custode* of the Capi di Sestiere who had attempted
to arrest them for being involved in a street brawl. Although the crime
had an element of self-interest, in that it might have allowed Dandolo to
escape prosecution for fighting, the real motivation was the heat of the
moment and annoyance at the interference of a communal official. Tomaso and his son ultimately managed to flee the city and thereby escape
the penalty imposed.[15]

Another bit of evidence tends to support the contention that murders
more carefully planned and executed by nobles escaped detection: most
victims of murders committed by nobles were also nobles. Most victims
of other violent crimes committed by nobles were members of the lower
classes. This suggests that such murderers often escaped prosecution either because there was less interest in the unexplained death of members
of the lower classes or because nobles were too important to prosecute for
these crimes. There was also less informal contact between the lower
classes and the nobility that would lead to the unpremeditated homicides
for which nobles were most often arrested. These data, however, support
another interpretation: the nobility may have considered themselves so
superior to the lower classes that murder was inappropriate. A slap expressed disdain, a murder suggested equality. Both factors were probably
at work, lack of reporting and lack of the motivation to kill members of
the lower classes.

Though not fully reported, penalties for murder by nobles were evenly
distributed.[16] Seven of the fourteen penalties involved execution, four of
these being of a public, ritual nature; three called for mutilation, so that
ten can be categorized as severe. Four fines were levied, in cases where
guilt was unclear or self-defense provided some justification for the accused. Even for nobles, then, prosecution for murder was a deadly busi-

ness. Nevertheless, through either self-control or subterfuge, the nobility managed to keep its level of prosecution down. For homicide, their style of violence was replaced by prudence.

Violence generally permeated the style of life of the nobility. They may have been bourgeois by economic criteria, but they remained to a significant extent noble in self-perception and self-definition. Their style included a high level of violence toward the lower classes and a sense of superiority that extended even to their own governmental and social system. When such things interfered with their wishes, be it a petty official trying to search a noble or a boatman's wife rejecting a noble's advances, the result was the assertive violence characteristic of established elites.

Nobles as Victims

The victim of violence reveals as much about his social world as the perpetrator. In a world of random violence, one would expect the distribution of both victims and perpetrators to be proportionate to the social distribution of the population. This was not the case for perpetrators, and it is not the case for victims. The deviations are significant for developing a further understanding of Venetian violence. Table 5.6 presents the general data on nobles as victims, revealing a significantly different picture from that of nobles as perpetrators. As one might expect, these crimes were consistently reported, creating a total positive deviation of approximately 5 percent, considerably lower than the 14 percent deviation of nobles as perpetrators.

Table 5.6. **Nobles as Victims of Violent Crime**

	Number	*Percentage of all victims*	*Deviation*[a]
Assault	75	13.2	+9.2
Rape	14	3.4	−0.6
Murder	31	7.3	+3.3
Total	120	8.5	+4.5

Source: A.S.V., Adv., *Raspe,* Reg. 3641–3645 (1324–1406); Signori di Notte, *Processi,* Reg. 6–12 (1348–1403).

Note: Speech crimes are not included because the commune did not deal in any significant numbers with speech crimes victimizing workers or those below.

[a] Based upon the assumption that the nobility accounted for 4 percent of the population.

Nobles as Victims of Rape

While nobles deviated by more than 16 percent in their commission of rapes, as victims they hardly deviated at all. Although noble males had the greatest proclivity to commit rape, noble females, according to these figures, were raped at a rate close to that prevailing throughout Venetian society. This statistic is misleading, however: in rapes of noblewomen where both victims and the perpetrators could be identified, all perpetrators were male nobles, a small (but active) group. This situation resulted partly from the practice of isolating young noblewomen once they reached puberty; moralists recommended such a practice, and the literature reflects it.[17] Equally important was the fact, already noted, that rape of a noblewoman was a serious crime, no longer a casual expression of male aggressiveness but the violation of a carefully guarded possession. Considering the average penalty of 52.7 points, it is not surprising that lower-class rapists found other victims. Thus, by reason of her isolation and social rank, a noblewoman was not sexually within reach of a lower-class man. Social taboos, more than sexual ones, separated them. Rape of a noblewoman by a non-noble would have been a crime committed more against the state than against the woman herself.[18]

Adultery between noblewomen and non-nobles, though rare, did occur. In 1391, Lucia, the wife of Marco Barberigo, was convicted in absentia for adultery with Francesco Karelo, a priest at the church of San Samuele. She had apparently received him in secret at her home when her husband was away. Despite the fact that a priest was not necessarily far below the nobility in social position, Lucia was sentenced to two years in jail and the loss of her dowry. If she did not present herself in Venice within two months to begin serving her term, the jail term was to be doubled. Her crime was considered much more serious than mere adultery, because the line between a noblewoman and non-noble man was, in sexual terms, virtually impassable.[19]

The fact that noblewomen were raped no more often than others, then, does not reflect the fact that they were raped only by a small proportion of the total male population. In terms of the limited group of men who could attack them, their rate of victimization was quite high. All the careful protections of family, though effective, could not protect noblewomen from sexual assault by noble males.

Nobles as Victims of Murder

As victims of murder, nobles also fall close to the norm; but here the statistic is more straightforward because other classes did murder nobles. This observation might seem to contradict the preceding analysis about rape; but in Early Renaissance Venice, murder, unlike rape, was a very serious crime and those who committed it violated a severe taboo, no matter what social categories were involved. Also, noble males—as communal officials or merchants—were more generally exposed to the violent tenor of lower-class life than were homebound women.

Nobles were nevertheless killed by other nobles more often than by any other identifiable class. Of thirty-one murders, twelve nobles killed other nobles, one important man killed a noble, nine workers killed nobles, and eight marginal people killed nobles. Given their relatively small numbers, nobles were responsible per capita for the most murders of nobles. The only group that came close to the nobility in per capita rate was the marginal men. Being transient, they were the least likely to accommodate themselves to the society in which they were living for the moment; and they may have been less aware of the significance of their crimes. They could also be hired as assassins more easily.

Nobles as Victims of Speech Crimes

Data on nobles as victims of speech crimes are not very telling, given the commune's selective concern with speech crime; but there is significance in the evidence that prosecution was necessary to enforce the vaunted unity of the nobility. Dissension within the group at the verbal level was prosecuted regularly, although most of it centered upon communal business. In part, it was triggered by conflicts of interest; but by far the largest part developed out of conflict between the pride of individuals and the legal power of the state: in essence, the conflict between the nobility's sense of prepotency and its own collective attempts at social control.

Zanino Pisani epitomized this conflict in a case brought before the Forty by the Avogadori in 1367. While being tried by the Cinque alla Pace for beating a prostitute, he exploded in a fit of temper at the noble judges, singling out as his target Pietro Paolo Querini, whom he went so far as to threaten. As a result, he was fined an additional 100 lire di piccoli by the Forty and having learned his lesson, managed to keep quiet before this body. Zanino was irate about his treatment at the hands of the Five, yet he singled out only Pietro. Apparently there was some previous tension between the two that led him to believe that Pietro was pushing the case against him. The Forty thus stepped in to enforce noble unity.[20]

These cases, which occur regularly, are reminiscent of one of the well-known antecedents to the Querini–Tiepolo conspiracy: Pietro Querini was arrested and convicted for refusing to be searched by a Signore di Notte, Marco Morosini. The resulting words between the two culminated in Querini publicly kicking Morosini in the streets of the city. Such petty public violence symbolized, at least for later chroniclers, a moment of open conflict between two major factions that prefigured the final confrontation of the conspiracy. As a partisan of Doge Pietro Gradenigo's faction, Morosini represented their use of the law to harass their opponents. Querini's refusal to be searched and his attacks on Morosini represented the opposition to the Gradenigo power, centering in the Querini family and their supporters. As the chronicler Marco Barbaro rightly pointed out, this was no simple moment of gratuitous violence; it stemmed from "the devil who was seeking to destroy this government." How often the devil interfered in this way it is difficult to judge, but the careful monitoring of such activity by the commune shows that the state was conscious of the danger of public divisiveness within the nobility.[21]

Quarrels over state policy were another area of dispute. Although one might assume that the law would not interfere in these disagreements, Venice was more concerned with the appearance of unanimity than scholars have understood. Even in the area of debate about public policy, unseemly dissension was proscribed. In July 1367, at a meeting of the Senate, Nicolo Polani disagreed in an overly violent manner with Giovanni Grimani about state policy on silver. There was no physical contact, but Nicolo was fined 100 lire di piccoli by the Forty.[22] A similar case in 1336 involved a ducal councilor, Pietro Bellegno. Bellegno's comments during a meeting were considered inappropriate by the Forty. It is not clear from the laconic records what he said, but the wording of the indictment is suggestive: he was accused of using "verbis iniuriates" against his fellow councilors. In the social life of the nobility, where strong family and personal pride were molded by the commune to fit collective goals, words could indeed be injurious. Bellegno's verbal injury to his associates also cost him 100 lire di piccoli.[23]

A final example of insults among nobles illustrates the difficult area of nobles intimidating other nobles in their capacity as communal officials. In 1385 m.v., the Signori di Notte were examining the mysterious death of one of the slaves of Francesco Venier. When the wounds on the corpse made them suspicious of Francesco himself, both Francesco and his brother Lorenzo insulted and threatened Pietro Michiel, the Signore di Notte in charge. Rather than backing down, Pietro brought the Veniers' words to the attention of the Avogadori. The brothers were eventually fined 100 lire di piccoli each by the Forty.[24] The final outcome of the murder investigation is unknown because the records of the Signori di Notte from that period are lost. Still it is clear that nobles were sometimes insulted and threatened, not only in anger and frustration but in order to corrupt the operation of the system. Important nobles had stronger weapons than threats: money and influence were better lubricants for the wheels of justice or the government bureaucracy. Still, the case of Francesco and Lorenzo Venier showed that some threatened violence as an alternative.

Although nobles speaking against nobles was by far the largest group in this category, nobles were also popular as victims of verbal abuse from other classes. The only two prosecutions brought against marginal people for speech crimes involved nobles. Laborers insulted nobles more often than any other lower-class group, important men placing a close second. The numbers are too small to permit conclusions about these divisions, but it is clear that nobles were per capita the greatest sufferers of the injurious words the commune elected to prosecute. Those who abused them were usually their peers.

Nobles as Victims of Assault

Although nobles committed 21 percent of the assaults, they were victims of only 13 percent (see Table 5.6). They were nevertheless attacked about 9 percent more frequently than a random distribution of assaults would predict. As in speech cases, they were most often assaulted by other nobles. A total of 47 of the 75 attackers of nobles were also nobles (63 percent of the cases). More social contact, in conjunction with an elite attitude that encouraged violent interference with communal policy, led to a higher level of violence, whether verbal or physical.

Motives for these assaults are difficult to assess because in a large proportion of the cases the records give no reason beyond a simple dispute. Where motives are given, disputes over communal business and problems about litigation in which victim and aggressor were both involved account for the vast majority of crimes. A typical case before the Giudici di Petizion involved two noble neighbors, Marco Vidal and Zanino Caotorta, residents in San Ermacor. They were disputing the ownership of some property, but the courtroom failed to contain their disagreement. As they were leaving the church of San Salvador, the issue was raised again; Marco lost his temper and wounded Zanino with a large knife. There was no indication that Zanino's life was in danger, but the Forty took the unusually severe action of sentencing Marco to two years in jail.[25]

What distinguished this type of assault from the normal violence of city life was that it attacked the orderly economic and social life of the commune. Courts and the whole litigation procedure had evolved to allow the peaceful transfer of goods and settling of disputes. To an extent, in the highly articulated government of the trecento, that was still what government meant. Because of their power, nobles who thwarted that objective were more threatening than any other group. They could divide the Venetian ruling class into warring factions. That this did not happen, given the level of interpersonal violence between nobles, can in part be explained by the careful legal attention given to these disputes by the commune.

Other social groups were wary of assaulting members of the nobility because of the seriousness of the crime. According to the records of the

Avogadori, nobles assaulted by non-nobles were usually communal officials. The crimes were more attacks on communal authority than on the
nobility, although the two were so closely intertwined that in the end the
distinction may not be meaningful. A sailor named Zanino illustrates this
type of assailant. He apparently was not one of those satisfied sailors
who, according to Lane, manned the Venetian merchant marine. He was
angered by the communally appointed *patronus* of his ship, the noble
Marco Venier. In a disagreement between the two, Zanino became so
enraged that he called Marco "a bastard and many other things," finish-
ing his tirade with an openhanded slap. In the violent world of the Venetian sailor, a slap hardly warranted attention; but slapping a noble official
was another matter. Zanino realized this and disappeared immediately.
Considering the style of a sailor's life, moving on to new horizons was
probably not a difficult choice. But the Venetian machinery of social control lumbered into action; a simple slap finally being heard in court before
the Forty, its damage argued by the Avogadori. Zanino may never have
known it, but the point was made; he was sentenced to one year in jail
with three months in which to surrender himself or face having his sentence doubled. The contrast with crimes involving only nobles is telling.
They may have been called the same thing, handled by the same criminal
procedure, and judged by the same court; but even Zanino knew they
were not the same.[26]

An aspect of lower-class violence against the nobility that creates problems in the data is the possibility that some of these assaults were paid for
by nobles. Even when the document names a lower-class assailant and a
noble victim, the crime may have originated within the nobility. A factor
that makes this unlikely in cases before the Avogadori and Forty was the
number of noble officials victimized, where the problem clearly lay between the assailant and the official. Cases like the wounding of the noble
cleric, Bertucio Querini, in 1345, may nevertheless represent an area of
violence between nobles concealed by the nature of the documents. Two
sailors and a cloth worker banded together to wound Bertucio, at the in-
stigation of Morosino Morosini. Morosino's motive was unclear, and he
was never brought before the Forty; but his helpers did not fare so well.
The Forty sentenced one sailor to four years in jail; the other, if caught,
was to spend six years in jail and be perpetually banned from Venice and
its territories. The cloth worker, when finally caught by the Cinque alla
Pace, suffered the loss of his right hand and perpetual banishment.[27]

Even without the data to determine how much lower-class violence
against nobles was directed by other nobles, it is clear that nobles were
primarily responsible for crimes against their own class. A higher level of
contact contributed to this, especially for crimes of assault and speech,
which were often motivated by litigation or communal business in which

nobles were regularly involved with nobles. As a class of victims, however, the nobility did not deviate as strongly as they did as a class of criminals. The statistical reason for this is straightforward: as victims, they drew their criminals from the relatively limited pool of other nobles; while as criminals, they drew their victims from the whole range of the population. As victims, although they drew their aggressors from a limited number, the nobility still tended to deviate on the plus side. In cases of rape, 3 to 4 percent of the total population raped noblewomen at a rate so high that without breaking down the statistics further it appeared that these women were being raped at a rate normal for the whole population. To put it crudely, fifteen hundred men were doing the work of forty thousand. In other areas of violence, the comparison was worse. Within the nobility, violence went far beyond the levels normal for society as a whole. Paradoxical as it may seem, the nobility *as individuals* were the biggest problem for the nobility *as the commune.*

Chapter VI

IMPORTANT PEOPLE

A Subordinated Class

Below the nobility came a small group of important people, whose criminal behavior was in sharp contrast. They matched more closely the stereotype of the Renaissance burger—peaceful men eager to act within the legal restrictions of society because their business and status depended on communal stability. Merchants, professionals, and civil officials who wanted to succeed in Venice had to be accepted by the nobility. As a consequence, the group of important people was subordinated by the ruling class, not in competition with it.

Table 6.1. **Violent Crimes Committed by Important People**

	Number	Percentage[a]	Deviation[b]	Mean penalty	General mean	Modal penalty	Median penalty
Speech	17	7.4	−2.6	18.3	22.5	20.0	8.5
Assault	65	11.4	+1.4	21.8	24.8	10.0	10.5
Rape	32	7.7	−2.3	25.4	22.7	30.0	19.8
Murder	40	9.4	−0.6				
Total	154	9.4	−0.6				

Source: A.S.V., Adv., *Raspe*, Reg. 3641–3645 (1324–1406); Signori di Notte, *Processi*, Reg. 6–12 (1348–1403); Dieci, *Miste*, Reg. 1–6, 8 (1310–1374, 1392–1406).

[a] Percentage of total criminal population for crime.

[b] Based upon the assumption that important people account for 10 percent of the population.

They came closer to embodying the myth of Venice, to fulfilling the ideal, than did the nobles. Rather than becoming a revolutionary class fighting for a place at the top, they remained an orderly buffer group contributing toward the preservation of the commune. The remarkable stability of the Venetian state depended not only on the organs of social control but also on the co-opting relationship between important men and nobles, a relationship that isolated and protected the nobility. In that relationship, important men became lap dogs or guard dogs but seldom revolutionaries.

Table 6.1 shows the peaceful nature of the group in general. Their total level of violent crime is proportionate to that of society as a whole even though the figures are likely to be high. Because both speech and assault were closely monitored for the upper classes, there were more prosecutions. These figures are also inflated by the inclusion of foreign nobles and low-level communal officials, who in many ways do not fit into the group. It is therefore safe to argue that important people were considerably less violent than their numbers would indicate.

Assault

Important people were prosecuted for a significant number of assault crimes. Because of their superior status, however, they were less likely than the lower classes to be given summary justice in the streets by the Signori di Notte or the Cinque alla Pace. The commune could afford a hearing by the Forty for these more important people. The Forty was especially interested in cases growing out of litigation or communal business, and the wealth and social standing of important people made them more likely to be involved in such activities. As a result, criminal prosecution in this area probably focused on them as much as on the nobility. But although they were a considerably larger group, important people were prosecuted about half as often for assaults as were nobles (11 percent for important people, 21 percent for nobles). Per capita, nobles were prosecuted four times as often.

Moreover, a large number of the assaults attributed to important people occurred among a group that made up the lower stratum of this group at best—the police patrols of the commune. Although these individuals were economically inferior to other important people, their position and relative authority raised them above the lower classes. These protectors of communal order were among the most violent people in the city. A total of 29 percent of all assaults by important people were committed by police patrollers (19 out of 65 cases). Although the numbers are small, it is interesting to note that this group, approximately 0.4 percent of the population (based on a police to population ratio of 1 to 250), accounted for 3.3 percent of all the assaults tried by the Forty, resulting in a significant inflation of the criminal records for their group. If foreign nobles, military officers, and police patrollers are excluded, the assault figures for important people can be cut by 40 percent. Despite these inflating factors, the original figure of 11 percent is low, implying that the vast majority of this group was peaceful indeed.

In a manner typical of a middle class, this group tended to commit assault out of self-interest. The explosions of passion of the lower classes and the stylish violence of the nobility were alien to the important people. A typical example of assault involving self-interest involves Nicoleto da Cola, a shipowner, and Dragano Buticularo, a communal tax official.

Nicoleto was shipping wine and Dragano was responsible for searching ships to estimate the value of the wine carried. Nicoleto complained about Dragano's method of search, then stabbed him as he was leaving a boat. Passion and self-interest were mixed, but the primary issue was economic gain.[1]

Table 6.2. **Assault Penalties for Important People**

	Number	Percentage of total
1–10 points	30	46.2
11–20 points	18	27.7
21–30 points	3	4.6
31–99 points	5	7.7
100–149 points	3	4.6
150+ points	1	1.5
Unclear	5	7.7
Total	65	100.0

Source: A.S.V., Adv., *Raspe,* Reg. 3641–3645 (1324–1406).

Important people normally avoided open violence, however, because it was detrimental to their interests. More than any other group, they understood and feared the losses resulting from the penalties that could be imposed. In addition, they stood to lose the offices they held from the state or the official support the ruling class had given them as ship captains, guild leaders, or professionals. Table 6.2 reflects the typical pattern for penalties: almost three-quarters of assault penalties for this group are concentrated in the 1-to-20-point range. Within this range, however, important people were treated more severely than nobles. The average penalty for assault for nobles (16) falls almost 6 points below that for important people (21.8). Nonetheless, the latter group was still penalized less than society as a whole, their point average falling 3 points below the general average (24.8). This is consistent with the general pattern for penalties noted earlier: the lower the social position, the higher the penalties.

The victims of these assaults, although the sample once again is small, fell predominantly within the class and below. Nobles, however, were victims at a rate about twice their per capita level of the population (9 percent). This fact, plus the high level of assaults within the group (49 percent), can be attributed partly to the nature of the cases selected to be heard by the Forty. It also reflects a higher level of contact. This is certainly true within the group. How true it is in relation to the nobility is harder to judge, because in the other categories of violent crime, nobles were rarely victimized by important people. For example, there was only one reported murder and there were no reported rapes. Perhaps assault was the only form of violence both minor and immediate enough to grow out of the higher levels of contact. No assault cases were reported in which important people attacked marginal people. Apparently these cases were either rare or too unimportant to warrant the attention of the Forty. A similar explanation can be advanced for the number of attacks upon workers, which was smaller than might be statistically expected (29 percent).

Assault data are difficult to work with because so many interlocking factors are involved. Still, it is safe to conclude that although the reported levels of assault match the proportion of the class, when the total picture is considered, important people were less violent than other classes. Because this was the area of their highest criminality, they were obviously not a violent group. When they did become involved in assault, their crimes were motivated by self-interest; they selected their victims from within the class or below; and they were penalized below the average for society as a whole.

Important people committed so few speech crimes (17) that almost no conclusions can be drawn (see Table 6.1). They were probably as closely monitored as the nobility, but they did not match their estimated proportion of the population, being responsible for only 7 percent of these cases. The normal pattern of penalties is repeated, punishment being either very light or occasionally very severe, with little in between. The average number of penalty points is as expected—18.3, falling neatly between the average for the nobility (13.4), and the general average (22.5). Given the sample, however, little can be inferred about the speech crimes of important people except that they apparently followed the same pattern as assault.

Rape

As shown in Table 6.1, rape cases also provide a limited sample for evaluating the violence of important people. Although they are within the expected parameters, being responsible for 8 percent of the total criminal population, the sample includes only 32 cases. Their penalties, shown in Table 6.3, reveal only a progressively smaller number of cases as the penalties become more severe. A reverse J-curve might emerge if there were more cases, a prediction based on the general continuity of this curve throughout all classes, but the data are inconclusive. Even the average penalty, although higher than that for the nobility, does not fit the usual pattern of increasing as social status decreases. The mean penalty for important people (25.4) is higher than the mean for nobles (24.7) but not significantly so; and rather than being lower than the general average, it is almost 3 points higher. In the context of the other data, this is unusual, but the size of the sample and some peculiarities in reporting help to explain the anomaly.

As rapists, important men almost exclusively attacked victims below their own class (97 percent), or at least they were prosecuted only for those crimes. From a social perspective, their crimes did not warrant such stiff penalties; but there was another important factor—the age of the victims. The high average penalty resulted from the fact that 8 out of 32 rape victims of this group were *puellae*, girls who had not reached puberty. The average penalty of 42.2 points for this crime seriously inflates the general penalty average of the group. Important men raped *puellae* about twice as often as did any other class and received almost twice the average penalty for doing so. It is thus not surprising that their general average for all rapes should fall just above the mean.

Table 6.3. **Rape Penalties for Important People**

	Number	Percentage of total
1–10 points	11	34.4
11–20 points	4	12.5
21–30 points	4	12.5
31–99 points	6	18.8
100–149 points	1	3.1
150+ points	0	0.0
Unclear	6	18.8
Total	32	100.1

Source: A.S.V., Adv., *Raspe,* Reg. 3641–3645 (1324–1406).

Another factor in the high penalties for rape might have been a lack of empathy among the nobles for the criminal behavior of this group. What was considered a youthful lark for a noble became more serious when the perpetrator was not a noble, especially if he came from a group singled out for special privileges by the nobility. In the end, the sample remains too small and too many variables intervene for definite conclusions to be made; but it is clear that for unaggravated rape the penalty fell below the mean for all rapes.

When the victims are considered, it becomes obvious that rape was an exploitative crime against social inferiors. Especially when one considers the inclination of important men to attack girls not yet sexually mature (a particularly exploitative aspect of these crimes), this propensity suggests an assertive attitude toward rape. Lower-class women were more accessible as victims. Important women, in imitation of upper-class mores, were probably more isolated and carefully watched. Adding to this tendency was the fact that a lower-class victim might be silenced with money if necessary, whereas important women were less likely to accept such payments. Social status also gave important men a superiority and power over the working classes that made their rape easier. Alessandro da Parma, a *rector scolarum,* was wealthy enough to hire a wetnurse for his wife. The wetnurse's eleven-year-old daughter became Alessandro's victim. The commune punished Alessandro severely for the crime, giving him a six-month jail sentence and a fine of 150 ducats, two-thirds of which went for the young girl's dowry.[2]

Another example of ease of access to the lower classes involved a lesser important person, a police patroller of the Signori di Notte. This man adopted a daughter named Pasqualina, an option probably open to him because his post gave him a small financial advantage. The girl became his victim: he raped her in his own house although she was not yet ten. Once again the Forty responded with strictness and added some exemplary punishment as well. He was sentenced to a year in jail and a fine of 50 ducats. As a warning to others, he was beaten and branded between the columns in the Piazzetta. In both cases, access to the victim was eased by position and wealth.[3]

Important men raped at a rate in proportion to the size of their class. This is unusual: when skewing factors are considered, they seem to be as criminally active in this area as the rest of society, excepting of course the nobility.

Murder

Murder also falls within the expected parameters for the group, as Table 6.1 demonstrates. As with assault, the figures are inflated by the unusual violence of police patrollers. Of forty murders, eleven were committed by police. Though the sample is small, this also suggests that as a group Important people were less violent than might be inferred from the actions of police patrollers. For substantial important people, murder was as much to be avoided as it was for the nobility.

Murders of passion and murders of self-interest divide in exactly the same way for important people as they do for nobles, with a slight predominance for crimes of passion (56 percent to 44 percent). Murders of self-interest attributed to important people were more often committed by hired assassins. Nobles were equally able to hire assassins, but perhaps their hirelings were caught less often or discovered less often to be in noble pay; or perhaps the high-handed style of the nobility led them to commit more murders on the spur of the moment, especially when communal officials or others got in their way. Important people, achieving their positions through subservience to the commune, learned to resist the temptation of immediate violence. For them, rationally planned crimes were more attractive, especially when the penalty for murder was too unpleasant to chance direct involvement.

Foreign nobles, classed here as important people, also inflated these figures, though they also frequently tried to avoid personal involvement by hiring assassins. Magister Nicolo, a surgeon in Padua, hired Antonolo and three others to kill Guilelmo Aliprando, called Bezio. No motive is recorded, but Bezio was successfully cut down in Venice, although Antonolo and his associates were caught. Antonolo and Dionisio of Milan lost their eyes and were banned perpetually from the city. The other assassins got off more easily, one serving two years and being banned, the other being fully absolved. Magister Nicolo, who paid for the assassination but stayed in Padua, escaped punishment. All the commune could do was ban him perpetually from Venetian territory (which may have been a hardship, but certainly not on the order of losing one's eyes) and offer a reward of 500 lire to anyone who apprehended him in Venetian territory. If he were ever foolish enough to be captured, he would receive the same penalty as Antonolo and Dionisio.[4]

Victims followed the expected pattern, falling within the class or in lower classes. Per capita, the highest level of victimization was within the group, a full 30 percent of homicide victims being important people. High levels of contact, both economic and social, were primary factors in this tendency. Remembering their rational approach to murder, one may note that important people were shrewd enough to avoid murdering nobles, or at least to avoid being detected.

The penalties for murder underline the danger of the crime. Of twenty-four cases where penalties are reported, fifteen involved execution. Thus the majority of important people convicted of murder died for their crimes. In seven cases, the death was bloody, ritual execution, the kind of retribution designed to reinforce fear of the law in the minds of the people.

In murder, as in the other violent crimes considered, important people came close to the stereotype of the bourgeoisie: a peaceful class particularly averse to major violence. When the violence of patrollers and foreigners is excluded, the data suggest that the rest of the group, perhaps closer to a class in an economic sense, was proportionately less violent than the norm for its percentage of the population. On the average, the penalties for important people were higher than those for the nobility but lower than the general average. This is consistent with the admonition in the penal code that judges take social standing into account in deciding punishment. Victims also followed the normal pattern, falling primarily within the group or below. The only distinctive area was sexual violence, with the predilection toward rape of *puellae*. Apart from this, important people appear to have been an ideally subordinated, stable buffer group. Perhaps sexuality was the one criminal area where they could express their superiority over weaker victims without jeopardizing their status.

Important People as Victims of Murder

As victims, important people, although they were among the less violent, suffered a high rate of violent crime directed against them. This phenomenon is not surprising: their government positions were the main contact areas between the people and the power of the state.

This point has not been sufficiently stressed in analyses of the stability of Venetian government. A buffer group of low- and middle-level office-holders helped to deflect animosity from the nobility. Police patrols, guild discipline, delivery of summonses, collection of fines, and a host of other bureaucratic duties requiring contact with the lower classes were handled by non-nobles. When a Venetian came into contact with government, it was usually in the person of a member of this buffer group. Unless he was inclined to see beyond the annoyance of the situation, he would direct potential antinoble hostility toward the official before him.[5]

Police patrollers were among the most frequently attacked members of this buffer group. A typical case involved Pietro Purus, a *custode* of the Signori di Notte who was searching for a certain Francescino, a boatman and vagabond who had missed the sailing of his ship. At the Rialto, with the aid of one of the special patrols of that high-crime area, he located Francescino and arrested him. They walked their prisoner across Venice without incident, but at the entrance to the Ducal Palace, beneath which lay the jail, Francescino drew a concealed bread knife, stabbed his captor, and fled. Pietro died from the wound. There was apparently no personal animosity in Francescino's attack; on the contrary, Pietro was the victim of violence because of his position.[6]

Another example of the animosity patrollers could generate in the line of duty is demonstrated by the murder of Marino da Verona, another *custode* of the Signori di Notte, by Anechino, a German cloth worker. Marino and a fellow *custode* were headed toward San Simeone Profeta in the middle of the night on an errand when they came upon three Germans in the streets. To be out after hours was theoretically illegal, and they could have arrested the Germans; but they were on other business and the crime was minor. Marino's associate politely reminded them "that this was not the time to be outdoors." A short while later, however, they encountered two of the Germans still wandering the streets and this time spoke to them more forcefully; but the men were drunk and rowdy and began to shout in German. Marino's associate warned that "if they did not go home, they could go to jail"; and to make his point he raised his sword, still in its sheath. One of the Germans threw a stone at

Marino's partner, hitting him in the head and knocking him down. Marino immediately chased the man who had thrown the rock, only to be cut down from behind by the other, who had been carrying a concealed weapon. Minor resentment suddenly escalated to violent murder.[7] Many of the murders of important men fall into this pattern.

Where money was involved, the animosity against communal authority became most severe and the use of a buffer group most effective. Nicoleto Felone, a communal herald, confronted this situation when he attempted to collect a fine from Nicoleto Damiani, a carpenter. Felone tracked Damiani to a monastery and demanded payment. Damiani murdered Felone and fled the city. The Forty sentenced him to perpetual banishment, a realistic penalty for a man who had escaped; but if he were caught in Venice or its territory, they sentenced him to a ritual execution, complete with chanting herald, mutilation at the scene of the crime, and hanging between the columns in San Marco. Damiani was probably careful to avoid this fate by staying outside the limits of the authority he had defied.[8]

Other malefactors were not so lucky. Pietro Famizi, who killed his torturer after being sent to the Camera del Tormento by the Ten, was beheaded in a restrained ceremony between the columns of justice.[9] Jacobo da Vigonovo and Marco Chodeschino received the whole symbolic treatment, dying the day they were sentenced for the murder of a police official.[10] This type of penalty—with public display of the criminal, proclamation of guilt, and mutilation before execution—made it clear that the murder of communal officials would not be tolerated.

Another reason for the high levels of violence against important people was the absence of the protection provided by noble status. A crime against a noble was on the face of it more serious than a crime against an important person, even though the commune sought to minimize violence against its officials. As a consequence, important people were murdered by a more socially balanced group than were nobles. Nobles murdered important people 4 percent of the time and fellow nobles 30 percent of the time. Important people killed one another at a rate of 17 percent but murdered nobles at a rate of 3 percent. Laborers were responsible for 63 percent of the murders of important people but only 29 percent of the murders of nobles. In contrast, marginal men murdered nobles at a rate of 26 percent and important people at a rate of 16 percent. Given their proportions of the population, nobles and important people were murdered at about the same rate. Noble status provided protection from violence by the rest of society but the nobles' proclivity to murder one another kept the statistics in balance. In contrast, the social balance in the murders of important people shows that they were less protected by status.

This group suffered the anomaly of being relatively nonviolent themselves but the victims of a high proportion of their society's violence. Such an unhappy situation may have increased their natural tendency to support tight governmental controls. In consequence, although they were the most potent group excluded from political status by the Serrata, rather than being revolutionary, they became ardent supporters of the status quo and of restrictive measures to preserve it. Individual examples of this support outside the general data on violence are rare, because the only visible people of important stature below the nobility were men like the grand chancellors whose position made them unlikely to exemplify anything but extreme support for the state. It is interesting to note that the cooperation between Andrea Dandolo and his grand chancellor, Benintendi Ravegnani, led to the writing of Dandolo's chronicle, one of the first major literary examples of the myth of Venice. This chronicle stresses the cooperation between nobles and important *popolani* toward the goal of building the greatness of Venice. In the mythic consciousness, there was clearly no conflict between important people and nobles either.

Important People as Victims of Speech Crimes and Assault

Similar patterns emerge in crimes of speech and assault. Higher levels of contact and less hesitation because of the status differential led to significantly more violence against important people by the lower classes. Assaults against patrollers of the commune played a major part in this pattern, with crimes ranging from simple slaps or punches to serious wounds. Also occurring at this level were outbursts against minor officials acting as agents of the commune rather than as keepers of the peace. While on official business, Pietro Rizo, a minor official at the Fontico Tedesco, became involved in an argument with Marco Muxe. Marco was content to argue, but a friend, Francesco d'Armano, took minor violent action. The Avogadori recorded this assault in an interesting colloquialism that can be rendered in English as giving him "a shot to the jaw (levavit pugnum et dedit dicto Petro . . . ut est dictum subtus barbam)." [11]

A considerable amount of this violence was directed at guild officials or minions of the Giustizia Vecchia, which was also concerned with overseeing guild activity. A case involving a wax worker named Zanino reveals a typical form of violence-provoking tension. Francescino Turri, the *gastaldo* of the guild, was at the shop where Zanino worked, examining candles to see if any were poorly made. When he started going over Zanino's work, the latter asked, "What are you trying to do?" The *gastaldo* answered, "I'm looking to see if these candles are well made." Looking through a group, he picked out a few and announced, "These are poorly made." Zanino hit him once with his open hand and threatened to do more.[12] This was a minor matter, but the response to guild or governmental interference could be more violent, as the case of Luca Paolo demonstrates. Luca was a silk worker and a judge in the guild court. In that court, he ruled that a certain Marco and his brother were not qualified to practice their occupation. Outside the meeting hall of the guild, Marco accosted Luca; and after insulting him by calling him "really crazy" and denigrating him for being neither a Lucchese nor a Florentine (implying that only people from these cities were competent to judge silk workers) he struck him with a sword and injured him seriously.[13]

The hostility to guild control revealed in these crimes supports the general view of the Venetian guild system described earlier. Guilds were carefully controlled by government for the benefit of the nobility. This control could occasionally protect workers, but it also kept them from amassing wealth. Quality controls designed to protect a merchant's market were an annoyance, as in the case of Zanino; and limitations on entry into a craft, though to the advantage of master craftsmen, created little satisfaction among those qualified to be more than mere workers. Perhaps this was the case in Marco's attack on Luca. Examples could be multiplied, but the point remains clear: guild regulations and the close governmental supervision of guild labor created high tension between workers and their superiors. From the perspective of the workers, the men enforcing these restrictions often were not nobles but low-level officeholders—little more than successful laborers themselves.

There was senseless violence as well: Colleta, wife of a minor official, was stabbed by a silk worker for singing a new song from Padua; but such cases were extremely rare.[14] Communal business, guild business, and occasional litigation were the main reasons for violent attacks upon important men. There were also attacks upon the distributors of grain for the communal grain dole. Although grain was important for survival, especially in times of famine, it was sold, not given. In 1392, Benasuto, a dealer in spices by trade, was appointed by the Capi di Sestiere to collect money due the commune for grain distributed in Dorso Duro. It was a thankless task, as Benasuto found out, being stabbed four times by a certain Cristofo Trentavasi when attempting to collect at his house. This type of case was quite common, implying that the grain dole, which probably did much to preserve the peace of the commune, had its negative side as well.[15]

In the area of speech, the level of crime drops off. Perhaps this indicates not a lower level of such crimes but a lesser inclination by the commune to prosecute those accused of speech crimes against important people. Indeed, as one proceeds from noble victims down the social scale there is a significant and steady drop in the number of cases. Noble victims account for ninety-two cases; important victims for forty; labor victims for seven; and marginal people, as one would expect, for none. For the reasons already discussed, the forty cases involving important victims involve a more socially balanced group of offenders than do speech crimes against nobles.

Important People as Victims of Rape

Rape is the one area where there was no positive deviation for important victims. The probability of an important woman being raped was close to the norm, perhaps even below average. In this area, a higher level of contact through officeholding and business encounters was not meaningful. Women held no offices, nor were they regularly involved in business, except as laborers in certain stages of the cloth industry or as servants or slaves. Important women were not found in these positions, which probably explains the difference between the figures for rape and those for other violent crimes against important people.

Nobles were, per capita, the most active group raping important women (18 percent of all rapes), although in raw figures the laboring class had a considerable edge. In terms of their proportion of the population, however, they fell short of the level expected from random distribution by class (71 percent of all rapes). The primary reason for this is the high level of involvement in sex crime among nobles, which combines with normal levels of criminality among important and marginal men to make rape by laborers statistically less likely.

In the world behind the numbers (and the sample is too small for strong conclusions), it is a safe assumption that rapes of important women, like those of noblewomen, were evenly if not fully reported. There was no financial incentive to report the crime and little reason based on status to suppress it.[16] It is possible that the fear of animosity or reprisals from nobles—the result of social bias—may have resulted in some failure to report rapes of important women by nobles. If this is the case, the level of noble criminality was even higher than the records reveal.

It was noted earlier that no cases were reported of a worker raping a noblewoman, and it was argued that this resulted in part from the gulf between the two, which made the act much more than a minor crime of passion. The line between important women and laboring men was not so clearly defined, but there was still a sense of social place. Important women were also more secluded and protected, especially from the lower classes. Nobles, who might carefully plan and carry out their crimes, were not so restricted as lower-class men. The latter were more likely to select neighbors or women in the streets as victims, passing up the less accessible important women.

Important people, though a rather disparate social group, had several attributes in common that make them useful for aggregating and analyzing the data on violence. Most essential, they served as a buffer group between the nobility and the rest of society. As a result, though they were not particularly active as perpetrators of violence, they played a significant role as victims. They occupied positions of government involving social contact where the power of the state to coerce met the power of individuals to resist. Although their own style tended to be peaceful, violence often impinged on their existence. It would not be apt to leave the impression that they were a class of martyrs, however; their rewards, though not at the level of those of the nobility, were sufficient in terms of power and status to make the risk acceptable.

Chapter VII

WORKERS AND MARGINAL PEOPLE

Violence as a Way of Life

For the nobility, violence was to a degree part of their style of living; but for workers and those below them, it was a way of life—a means of survival or an expression of deep frustration. Problems within the statistics, however, obscure this picture. Table 7.1 indicates that workers were less violent than any other group in society, falling at least 12 percent below their proportion of the total population. For several reasons, one would expect quite a different set of statistics. According to current theory, high violence levels should have been linked with the marginal existence of many workers, which created circumstances of considerable alienation and frustration, especially in the marine and cloth trades. Many workers were also recent immigrants, less adapted to the self-discipline required by urban life and less aware that they had anything to gain from nonviolence. Even artisans from other cities had to make a significant adjustment to the lower status of guilds in Venice. In this they differed from their superiors among the important people and from the nobles who had created the system of Venetian order.

Table 7.1. **Violent Crimes Committed by Workers**

	Number	Percentage[a]	Deviation[b]	Mean penalty	General mean	Modal penalty	Median penalty
Speech	117	50.9	−24.1	18.8	22.5	10.0	6.0
Assault	348	61.2	−13.8	20.5	24.8	5.0	10.1
Rape	272	65.4	− 9.1	24.3	22.7	10.0	10.0
Murder	297	69.6	− 5.4				
Total	1034	63.0	−12.0				

Source: A.S.V., Adv., Raspe, Reg. 3641–3645 (1324–1406); Signori di Notte, Processi, Reg. 6–12 (1348–1403); Dieci, Miste, Reg. 1–6, 8 (1310–1374, 1392–1406).

[a] Percentage of total criminal population for crime.

[b] Based upon the assumption that workers account for 75 percent of the population.

In fact, several factors imply that the reporting of violent crime for laborers was low. It appears clear that crime reports vary inversely with social status, at least for the less serious or less visible crimes committed against workers within or below the group. Minor assault cases were often handled with summary justice in the streets by the Signori di Notte, Cinque alla Pace, or Capi di Sestiere. The only reflection of this type of justice to survive is the record of the *gratie* given to some of those convicted; and from this slim evidence there is no way to reconstruct the social breakdown for these cases. It is safe to assume, however, that assaults involving workers were deemed less important than those involving nobles or important people. In a similar manner, minor speech crimes were probably not even monitored. Certain rape cases involving workers were also occasionally considered too insignificant to report or prosecute, especially those that ended in marriage. Even a few murders of highly mobile and unestablished people by others in the same circumstances may have gone unnoticed. All these factors suggest a significant skewing of the data. It should be stressed, however, that although there were strong reasons for expecting low levels of prosecution among nobles, their reported levels of violence were amazingly high; thus assumptions of bias in the data must be treated with caution.

A better perspective can be gained by looking at the behavior of workers in each of the four areas of violent crime under study. It will become apparent that the factors that would lead one to expect high levels of violence were in fact present in trecento Venice.

Speech

Low levels of prosecution for speech crimes reflect an inability or an unwillingness to prosecute offenders among the lower classes. Table 7.1 shows a low level of prosecution in this area, approximately 24 percentage points below the estimated proportion of workers to the population. There may be another factor at work here typical of attempts to control crimes of thought. For physical crimes that are openly disruptive, the assurance of a penalty may be the best deterrent; but for verbal sedition, arbitrary enforcement is often an effective form of control. If all instances of questionable speech are monitored and controlled, an air of oppression is created; but an occasional almost whimsical action creates a public example and reinforces the fear of authority without consolidating that fear into resistance.[1]

The low level of prosecution for speech crimes definitely does not indicate that the working classes were without complaint against the nobles and their government. Recorded speech crimes show strong class overtones when the opacity of the formulaic style of the scribes is broken. It seems strange that verbal crimes were reported in the least detail, almost as if the act of repeating the words repeated the crime itself. Occasionally, however, the silence is broken, as exemplified by the wife of a Florentine worker named Francesco da Firenze. In 1350, while Venice was preparing for war against Genoa, this woman called for the destruction of the Venetian nobility, whom she termed "magnates." Her ire was apparently roused by the commune's attempt to register all able-bodied men (including her husband) in the civil militia. Her actual words as recorded by the Ten suggest an unusual understanding of Venetian society and tradition, even though she was the wife of a worker and a recent immigrant. She began her complaint: "Those who register and are responsible for the registering of the militia should finish like those of the Barozzi house." [2]

Her words refer to the execution twenty-two years earlier of the Barozzi traitors, leaders of an enigmatic conspiracy which in its failure caused the destruction of the family.[3] By implication, she was calling for the execution of the people compiling the lists of militia and of the people who had ordered that compilation, as traitors—the Capi di Sestiere and their men, who were doing the registering; the Council of Ten (including the doge and his councilors), who had ordered the registration; and the entire Major Council, which stood behind the measure and had made it necessary by their war policy. This may be exaggerating the vision of a worker's wife, but the rest of her speech makes it clear that she hated the whole ruling class. She concluded by hoping that the ships of the fleet "would sink and that their owners would burn up along with the other magnates of Venice." [4]

Although this woman shows a Florentine point of view—equating Venetian nobles with Florentine magnates—she apparently had a good basic knowledge of Venetian society from a lower-class perspective. Her reference to the Barozzi conspiracy recalled an event finished two decades earlier and barely mentioned in the chronicles, which must have been still alive in the public mind. Her attack on the ruling class and its war is typical of those dispossessed of power and alienated from a society: let those who rule be destroyed.

A second example highlights the deep antipathy toward the nobility among some workers. During a quarrel about work standards imposed by nobles, Antonio, who worked in the cloth industry, said, "Bah, forget about weakly threatening these nobles, instead give them a knife in the throat; the penalty for killing a noble after all is the same as that for killing a man of base condition." [5] The penalty for murder was usually death, so Antonio was roughly correct, although a worker was more certain to die for killing a noble. More important than his perceptions of penology is his basic antagonism toward the ruling class. Nobles were beyond the range of arguments advanced by workers, even beyond their threats. There was equality only at the level of head-to-head violence. The records of prosecution for crimes of speech reveal that such class antagonism existed throughout the period. Even though the lower classes probably lacked a clear perception of their position and certainly lacked a modern conception of class conflict, the existence of class antagonism is clear. When a ruling class defines itself legally, setting itself apart from the rest of society in an attempt to protect its rule, antagonism against that clearly defined class is a natural result. Lane's interpretation that there were minimal class tensions in Venice cannot be maintained on the basis of the evidence of speech crime; nor does it fit logical expectations about social conflict within a closed society.

Table 7.2. **Penalties Imposed on Workers for Crimes of Speech**

	Number	*Percentage of total*
1–10 points	38	73.1
11–20 points	4	7.7
21–30 points	1	1.9
31–99 points	1	1.9
100–149 points	4	7.7
150 + points	1	1.9
Unclear	3	5.8
Total	52	100.0

Source: A.S.V., Dieci, *Miste,* Reg. 1–6, 8 (1310–1374, 1392–1406); Adv., *Raspe,* Reg. 3641–3645 (1324–1406).

The penalties workers received for crimes of speech reveal this distinction from another perspective. Table 7.2 indicates that penalties follow the pattern typical for this offense but with a more pronounced concentration on both heavy penalties and on very light. The mean penalty for workers (18.8) is higher than that for nobles (13.4), even though speech crimes of nobles were a greater threat. This indicates that the speech of at least some workers was taken seriously.[6] But the greatest difference in penalties for speech crimes can only be inferred, not documented. The striking contrast between high and low penalties suggests an arbitrary approach to the crime. This observation is supported by earlier evidence that the speech of the upper classes was more carefully monitored. All prosecution for speech crimes may have been somewhat arbitrary; but it was especially so among the lower classes. This arbitrariness, so atypical of Venetian justice, may have been designed to quiet worker complaints more through fear than through the normal administration of justice.

Assault

Punishment for assault, as shown in Table 7.1, also occurred at a lower rate for workers than their numbers would suggest. Two important factors qualify this discrepancy. As noted earlier, minor assault was usually handled by summary justice in the streets. Second, the cases heard by the Forty concentrated upon assaults involving government officials or litigation. Because worker contacts with these situations were fairly limited, reported incidents should be low. Given these considerations, it is likely that workers were involved in assault at a level at least as high as their proportion of the population. In the area of serious assaults requiring the attention of the Forty, however, they were no match for the nobility.

The kinds of victims of assault by workers suggest the special nature of the cases heard by the Forty. Important people, primarily government officeholders, by far predominate (46 percent). This fact supports the hypothesis that important people served as a buffer group for the nobility; here, in one of the few instances of criminality against the upper classes, the victims were those who represented governmental authority to the workers—not the nobility but important men. In eighty-eight of ninety-two cases of assault by laborers on important people, the victims were government officials, although only eighty-one of these cases (88 percent) were clearly related to government business. A concentration of cases of this type would naturally appear in records of the Forty, but cases involving other classes were much less skewed: only 28 percent of noble assault victims were important people; and 49 percent of the victims of important men came from their own class. Of the eighty-one cases, forty-seven involved police patrollers, 58 percent of all worker assaults against important people. Speech patterns reveal animosity against the nobility, but assault patterns show that on a day-to-day basis hostility was expressed at the point where government made its power manifest.

A few instances of this violence tell the story better than the statistics. The case of Matheo Solsa is typical. Stopped by a *custode* of the Signori di Notte for a routine search, he was carrying a concealed weapon. The penalty for this being a fine of at least 100 lire di piccoli, instead of surrendering his weapon, the worker used it to wound the *custode* in an attempt to escape.[7] This was the simplest form of contact violence. It is impossible to know whether Matheo struck in frustration or anger or for self-protection; perhaps all three played a part. The crucial component in this violence is Matheo's position as a worker. For a noble, the fine would be negligible. If he decided to assault a patroller, it would be as a matter of style or honor; for a worker, however, such a large fine almost invariably meant time in jail until some form of *gratia* could be worked out. His violent act was a form of survival, not a style of living.

Guild authority created similar tensions. Although the Venetian guilds were an extension of the power of the nobility, contact with workers was made not by nobles but by important men. Conflicts with this authority sparked similar reactive types of violence. Pietro Angelo was a carpenter who worked in the Arsenale. In March 1358, he was ordered to work overtime by a certain Nicoleto, an official of his guild. When Pietro did not show up, Nicoleto fined him 5 lire di piccoli. Pietro retaliated soon afterward by tossing a stone at Nicoleto that hit him in the head and caused "blood to flow." The Forty heard this case rather than a guild court and sentenced Pietro to six months in jail and a fine of 25 lire di piccoli. The commune responded to this attack on guild authority as if it were an attack on government authority, suggesting once again that a unified vision of the state prevailed in Early Renaissance Venice.[8]

Table 7.3. **Penalties Imposed on Workers for Assault**

	Number	Percentage of total
1–10 points	99	49.3
11–20 points	39	19.4
21–30 points	20	10.0
31–99 points	14	7.0
100–149 points	6	3.0
150+ points	3	1.5
Unclear	20	10.0
Total	201	100.2

Source: A.S.V., Adv., Raspe, Reg. 3641–3645 (1324–1406).

The next highest incidence of victimization falls within the worker class; but the records concentrate on important assaults and are most biased. Both worker assaults on workers (38 percent) and worker assaults on marginal persons (1 percent) must have been much higher; but these cases did not merit the attention of the Forty. The gratia registers, which report many lower-class crimes, show that by far the largest portion of assaults by workers involved victims from within or below the class. The fact that the surviving material from the Avogadori does not agree with the gratia registers supports the conclusion that assumptions of underreporting are correct.

The motive for the assaults tried by the Forty have already been discussed. Attacks against communal authority were the dominant category (52 percent). Another motive was litigation (24 percent), although it is surprising to find workers involved in a significant amount of litigation. Even family matters were occasionally brought into communal court, revealing how deeply government penetrated into traditional social relationships.[9]

Penalties for assaults by workers resemble the penalties given for speech crimes, as Table 7.3 demonstrates. The large sample fits the pattern already identified, with almost a majority of the cases in the range of 1 to 10 points and 4.5 percent in the range of 100 or more. The mean (20.5) for workers again falls below the general average (24.8), but this reflects the absence from the sample of the marginal workers not identified by the sources, implying an average somewhat higher if all penalties could be socially categorized. The average for workers, although low, is significantly higher than the average for the nobility, repeating the consistent pattern of these statistics.[10] Considering that assaults by nobles were almost by definition more serious crimes, the special treatment they received at the hands of the Forty becomes especially apparent.

The assault statistics for workers, even at this underreported level, indicate that Venetian workers expressed considerable physical dissatisfaction with society. Their physical anger, however, was aimed not so much at the men responsible for communal policy as at those who enforced it.

Rape

In rape, workers also fall considerably below the expected levels of criminality (see Table 7.1). At all social levels except the highest rape was not a serious crime, and it was surely underreported among workers. Equally important, a rapist sometimes could marry his victim, reducing the prosecution levels as a result. Such cases sometimes reached the courts where the judges permitted the rapist to pay his debt to society either by marrying his victim or by serving a jail sentence or paying a fine. For instance, in 1390 Guido of Padua, a cloth worker living in Venice in San Simeone Profeta, was convicted of raping Micola, daughter of Antonio da Barleto. Micola may have been no great catch—the Forty made the choice easy by imposing a stiff penalty if Guido did not accept her as his bride. Facing two years in jail and a fine of 200 lire di piccoli, a penalty more severe than the average for raping a noblewoman, Guido agreed to marry Micola and credit her with a dowry of 200 lire di piccoli. Other examples of such marriages can be found, but it seems likely that most cases did not reach the courts.[11] Low levels of reporting, plus an acceptance of marriage before prosecution may account for the negative deviation of worker rapes. In reality, with the exception of nobles, workers were probably as active in this crime as other classes.

Most rapes occurred within the class (71 percent); those that did not were primarily directed toward lower classes (22 percent). That the nobility was untouched shows that workers understood that rape of noblewomen was far too serious to contemplate—a serious form of social assault. These problems did not arise with marginal women, who per capita were the favorite targets of working-class rapists. In the end, however, contact rather than social position probably played the largest part in this selection process. Lacking the resources of the nobility, workers committed rapes at the neighborhood level, often knowing their victims.

For the Forty, this created the problem of distinguishing between rape and fornication or adultery. Low penalties reflect this uncertainty (see Table 7.4). About one-half of all penalties fall between 1 and 10 points. Penalties of 100 or more points constitute fewer than 6 percent of the total, and these cases primarily involve *puellae* or important women. It might appear that workers and nobles received about the same penalties for rape, but this is an illusion of the statistics: the rape of noblewomen was more than twice as serious as the average rape, greatly inflating the statistics for nobles. Without these cases to pull up the average, the average penalty imposed on nobles would fall to 5 points below that of the workers (19.3).

Table 7.4. **Rape Penalties for Workers**

	Number	Percentage of total
1–10 points	85	49.7
11–20 points	27	15.8
21–30 points	8	4.7
31–99 points	21	12.3
100–149 points	9	5.2
150+ points	1	0.6
Unclear	20	11.7
Total	171	100.0

Source: A.S.V., Adv., *Raspe*, Reg. 3641–3645 (1324–1406).

In rape, then, workers were perhaps active at their per capita level, but the crime was of little significance, often hardly worth the bother of reporting. Workers tended to victimize their equals or those below, reflecting the fact that the crime was not planned and arose from opportunity. Penalties were mild, but more strict than those for nobles. The consideration of potential penalties may have deterred some workers; but rape was mostly a crime of passion in which few stopped to consider the legal consequences.

Murder

The murder statistics given in Table 7.1 show that workers participated in this crime at their smallest negative deviation. Given the nature of the statistics and the number of workers involved, the variation is not significant; and one may assume that workers committed murder at about the same rate as the rest of the population. Hidden in these statistics is the fact, noted earlier, that nobles occasionally hired members of the lower classes as assassins. Nevertheless most murders occurred within the limits of one class: workers killed workers, nobles killed nobles or had them killed. Instances of workers killing nobles, even including cases where it is not clear whether they were acting on their own, are so few as to have little impact on the data. It is therefore reasonable to view these data as an indication that in the area of murder laborers were independently quite active.

The breakdown by victims is normal, given the relative size of each class: noble victims accounted for 2 percent of the total, important people for 15 percent, workers for 72 percent, marginal people for 9 percent, and clergy for 2 percent. The one anomalous area is murder of important people, which is linked to the contact between workers and communal authority through patrollers, heralds, and other officials. The records of murder prosecutions, however, are not biased like the assault records; virtually all prosecuted murders are reported in the registers of the Signori di Notte and the Avogadori. Thus the disproportionate murder of important people reflects their rate of victimization more accurately than the assault statistics.

These murders occurred under circumstances similar to those for assault. Angelo Antonio was patron of a ship and Rolandino was one of his sailors. Rolandino encountered his master near the Rialto and accused him of cheating the sailors on their ship. Angelo responded by threatening to have Rolandino whipped and his wife enslaved. Enraged, the sailor replied, "God damn it, not even you have the right to make slaves here." "With these injurious words they walked along arguing in this manner," the records report, until Angelo drew a knife. Rolandino threw a stone and knocked his patron down; then in panic and anger he drew a bread knife and stabbed him once in the right side, "causing heavy bleeding." The bread knife was an effective weapon: as the scribe of the Signori di Notte laconically noted, "the said Angelo died immediately." [12] A violent act with many social overtones, Rolandino's crime was typical in its spontaneous release of violent emotions, hinging upon feelings of powerlessness in the face of superiors. His response to the threat of enslavement was especially telling: "not even you" expressed the limits of the virtually unquestioned power of the upper classes. Angelo went too far in his assumption of authority and died because of it. For other officials, simply "doing their job" was often enough to put them in jeopardy of assault or murder.

The motivations for murders by workers, given in Table 7.5, represent one of the more balanced breakdowns, although crimes of passion are somewhat more numerous among workers than among nobles or important people. This factor suggests that as in Rolandino's case murder and violence were a part of a worker's life rather than a chosen style. The only unusual aspect of these figures concerns business gain, which is inflated because many such cases involved small sums of money but were more like crimes of passion or survival than the business disputes of the upper classes. A quarrel between Nicolo Utino and his employer reveals the underlying aggravations that could lead to sudden explosions of violence. Nicolo worked for Magister Benvenuto da Venzone, and his pay was 50 soldi di piccoli in arrears, a relatively small sum. He approached Benvenuto at work, asking for payment of at least 30 soldi di piccoli, "and thus began an argument between them." Tensions built when Benvenuto picked up a heavy bucket and threatened: "Get out of here before I hit you with this." Rather than backing down, Nicolo touched his bread knife threateningly but did not draw it. Seeing the movement, Benvenuto drew a weapon and cried: "Scoundrel, how dare you reach for your knife in my house!" Nicolo, having asked only for a small amount of pay, found himself in a serious situation. Perhaps Benvenuto was merely trying to weaken his resolve to collect his back pay, but if this was the case, he had underestimated Nicolo's violent resolve. Nicolo drew his knife and stabbed Benvenuto quickly in the neck. Shortly thereafter, Benvenuto died.[13]

Table 7.5. **Murder by Workers, Motivation**

	Number	Percentage of total	Percentage of category
Self-interest			
Against commune	8	4.3	12.9
Business gain	27	14.7	43.5
Criminal gain	23	12.5	37.1
Influence litigation	4	2.2	6.5
Total	62	33.7	100.0
Passion			
Casual	13	7.1	11.6
Family quarrel	10	5.4	8.9
General quarrel	61	33.2	54.5
Sexual quarrel	21	11.4	18.8
Vendetta	7	3.8	6.3
Total	112	60.9	100.1[a]
Unclear	11	6.0	100.0

Source: A.S.V., Adv., Raspe, Reg. 3641–3645 (1324–1406); Signori di Notte, Processi, Reg. 6–12 (1348–1403).

[a] Total is greater than 100 percent because of rounding off.

Workers were more likely to take their frustrations out on those closer to them than their employers. Murders by workers were usually motivated by immediate problems, but these problems touched deeper levels of frustration. Homicide could result from a simple quarrel about the price of a boat ride; an argument about the quality of workmanship; a dispute about the division of labor between workers; or frequent grumblings about the repayment of small debts.[14]

The penalties for workers who committed homicide tended to be extreme, even when self-defense might have warranted some adjustment of penalty. In 60 out of 102 cases, execution was the sentence, and another 32 required major mutilation. The commune was restrained in its response to other forms of worker violence, but drew the line at murder.

For workers, murder was much like assault, a matter not of style but of life. Because of its gravity, it was also the most completely reported type of violence. It is thus significant that as murderers workers came closest to matching their proportion of the population in their criminality. Higher levels of victimization of important men reinforce the pattern noted for assault. At contact points between state authority and the people considerable anticommunal sentiment was expressed. Thus although worker murders may often seem to have been "senseless," violence at the working-class level exploded not so much at the source of the tensions as at the moment when accumulated frustrations became unbearable. This continuing characteristic of lower-class violence is considered further in the chapter on the perception of murder.

Violence among Worker Subgroups

Within the worker group, three broad categories may be distinguished. First, there were protoindustrial workers, laborers in areas like the cloth industry that required considerable capital investment in raw materials and organization and served a market larger than Venice. A second category consisted of service workers, those who served the daily needs of the city, men like butchers, bakers, and shoemakers. Third were the marine workers—boat hands, rowers, sailors, and so forth. The lack of adequate estimates of the size of each group in the Early Renaissance creates an insurmountable problem in trying to analyze violence in terms of these subgroups. Nonetheless, they can be ranked by relative size, which permits some generalizations to be made. The service group was probably the largest. If there were more marine workers this consideration is balanced by the fact that they were often out of the city. Protoindustrial workers would constitute a distant third, as Venice was not nearly so developed in the industrial areas as the major mainland cities.

The relative incidence of violent crime, however, does not follow this breakdown at all. For 535 cases that can be grouped into these categories, 226 (42 percent) involved industrial workers; 198 (37 percent) service workers; and 111 (21 percent) marine workers. Some suggestive hypotheses develop out of these figures. Industrial workers were especially violent, given their smaller numbers, perhaps because they were relatively new to Venice. The city actively recruited them throughout the century, especially after 1348. Though they were familiar with urban life, many may have been troubled by government domination of guilds and the lack of opportunity for guildsmen to participate in government. The enticements offered by the city to lure cloth workers, such as reduced requirements for citizenship, may not have seemed quite so attractive once the full extent of government domination became clear.

Marine workers seem surprisingly peaceful, probably because they were at sea much of the time. That their violent tendencies were more respected than the figures reflect is suggested by the periodic strengthening of patrols when the fleets returned to port. Although they could not make up for their lack of statistical violence during these periods, the sailors made a valiant effort. Service workers, the largest subgroup, were on the whole more established and secure. Many of their number, like the important people, may also have been co-opted by the nobility who made up an important part of their market. Thus their relatively lower levels of violence may have resulted from a more peaceful and secure life style.

The violence of workers in general, although underestimated in the data, may have been about equal to their proportion of the population. In itself, this is surprising because one would expect workers—especially with large numbers of new industrial workers and sailors—to have been a disruptive group. They did their share, but they were nowhere near as violent as the nobility. The significance of this violence was further lessened, from the perspective of the ruling class, by its tendency to focus within the class or below. The exceptions to this were outbursts against communal authority where the victims were generally important men. If the nobility continued to exist atop a violent worker stratum, it was separated from it by a buffer stratum of important men who willingly absorbed this potential violence where it became real. Consequently, the nobility tended to view worker violence as an external phenomenon to be contained (i.e., kept outside) but not highly feared, so long as it remained unorganized and diffuse. As a result, penalties for workers, though stricter than those for their social superiors, were still mild: jail sentences and fines that on the whole seldom required more than a year in jail or its equivalent. Violence was a way of life for the workers, and the state tried merely to keep it within acceptable limits through police patrols and regular but modest penalties.

Workers as Assault Victims

An analysis of laborers as victims of crimes reveals the obverse of this isolated context of worker violence. Laborers as victims are much like laborers as criminals because they tended to victimize mainly themselves.

Rape was the primary exception. For that crime, they also provided a pool of victims for the upper classes.

Reports of speech crimes and assault tend to deemphasize worker victimization. A crime of speech against a laborer was too minor to warrant the attention of the Forty or Avogadori, and physical violence between workers was often handled with summary justice. Thus workers were victims of only 32 percent of the assault cases heard by the Forty. But the *gratia* records show that workers were prosecuted by policing bodies for victimizing workers at a much higher level than the records of the Avogadori report. The Avogadori nevertheless heard more than 180 cases involving worker victims.

A few of these cases directly involved government business, even though laborers held no official posts. A gold worker named Andreas, for example, was assaulted by Galaxio Bono, a minor officer who became angry with him in the course of a discussion at the Cha Dolfin and struck him twice with a dagger, wounding him seriously. Galaxio not only lost his job and received a sentence of six months in jail, he was also perpetually deprived of all communal offices and benefices—a normal part of the penalty for serious malfeasance in office. This case and a few others like it suggest two comments. First, the commune was unforgiving to low-level officials who overstepped the bounds of their offices, especially with violence. Andreas may have been an important worker, but six months in jail, even without the loss of the benefits of office, was a major penalty for an important man committing such a crime. Second, communal business could motivate violence in both directions. Violence against the commune had its counterpart in violence by the commune. A wide range of this violence was acceptable to society, but in this instance—one of the few where the line of acceptable violence was crossed—the commune responded forcefully. At this level of the official hierarchy, at least, the commune established and enforced its own boundaries.[15]

Communal business occasionally involved workers as witnesses before government courts. Although Anna da Verona may not qualify as a worker, her case is representative. Anna was a "matronam in Castelleto," or a madam. She was held and examined by the Signori di Notte in connection with a murder case in which Giovanni d'Artusio was the primary suspect. Upon her release, Giovanni's brother Danieli accosted her and asked about her testimony before the Signori. When she refused to talk, perhaps also because he wanted to pressure her into silence, Danieli beat her. In these rather convoluted cases, workers became victims of the violence associated with communal business.[16]

More significant in accounting for the cases involving worker assault heard by the Avogadori and the Forty were those resulting from litigation before communal courts. It would be fascinating to determine how many workers used the Venetian civil court system. According to the criminal data, laborers not only used the civil courts for litigation but also, like other Venetian classes, occasionally tried to obtain justice outside the courts. Francescino Sourosin's mutilation of his mother-in-law, Besina Mare, provides a brutal example. Besina, a widow, took her son-in-law to court in a dispute over her daughter's dowry and was awarded 8 ducats—a considerable amount of money for a carpenter. Encountering Besina one evening at the *traghetto* that ran from Dorso Duro to San Marco, Francescino began a discussion with her that quickly escalated to an argument, led to blows, and ended bloodily when he cut off her nose. This mutilation was significant. Although there is little reason to expect an attack on one's nose in most societies, this was a fairly common form of assault on women in Venice, originating apparently with the commune itself. Mutilation of female criminals traditionally sought to destroy their value by destroying their good looks just as mutilation of males attempted to destroy their value by cutting off their hands. Women were punished by cutting off their noses or lips, and violent criminals often followed the lead of the state in this regard. Francescino may have thought he was dispensing justice and thus used the traditional penalty for minor robberies by women.[17] Although litigation of this type was the most common cause for assault on laborers in the cases handled by the Avogadori, it was not typical of the violence that laborers normally suffered. That violence was usually the product of the tenor of everyday life in an urban environment that made heavy demands on the working classes. If material on all prosecutions for assault were available, it would provide a vivid picture of that part of lower-class life; but the data no longer exist.

Workers as Victims of Murder and Rape

For the crimes of murder and rape, the data are relatively complete. Almost every murder case was heard either by the Signori di Notte or by the Avogadori. Rape was handled exclusively by the Avogadori. In these two crimes, one major and the other minor, one can find the outlines of a picture of lower-class victimization that can be applied to those areas of violence where records do not exist.

By all fourteenth-century measures, murder was a major crime, perhaps not so serious as robbery, but still a crime that called for major mutilation, banning, or execution. As victims, workers were close to the norm, having a negative deviation of only 13 percent. Still, this figure is surprising, considering that their record as murderers deviated negatively by only 5 percent. In fact, in relation to the nobility, on a per capita basis workers did quite well. A note of caution should be introduced, however, concerning the number of victims recorded in the pretrial records. The murder of a noble was exceedingly difficult to overlook, whereas at least in certain areas of the work force, men could disappear with ease. Too much should not be inferred from such hypothetical underreporting because most workers were integrated into Venetian society through guilds, church, and family. The last especially, one would expect to be aware of murder or unaccountable disappearance. Marginal people, more likely than workers to be underreported in this manner, actually show a significant positive deviation as victims. There probably was underreporting, but it would be difficult to argue that it was significant enough to bring the level of victimization above the norms for society.

Dividing murderers of workers into social classes supports this. It produces one of the most conforming patterns for any social group and for any crime. Although nobles murdered laborers at a negative deviation rate of 3 percent and workers murdered workers at a positive deviation rate of 8 percent, neither deviation is significant. Perhaps the negative deviation for nobles suggests that there was underreporting. This could be true, because it is evident that the severe penalties for the crime made murder convictions dangerous even for nobles. Wealth, influence, and power may have been used to keep down the number of prosecutions. But in order to bring the level of worker victims up to the norm, one would have to assume that approximately three-fourths of all murders of workers by nobles went unreported. It is more realistic to assume that although there was some underreporting it would not change the total number of victims enough to bring about a change in the relationship between worker victims and other victims.

There are some reasons for assuming that the lower figure for murders of laborers by nobles, one of the few areas where the nobles were less violent than the norm, is realistic. Most obviously, nobles had less reason to kill workers. They had the power to take revenge in more subtle ways; and if they sought bloody vengeance, they could hire others to do the work. In addition, the nobility had relatively little contact with the working class.[18] Violence inflicted on laborers by nobles tended to remain more casual and less dangerous. The noble mentality was such that in the normal operation of society they considered workers too insignificant to murder.[19] Killing a worker may have been considered an overreaction that would have detracted from the normal noble style of violence.

Important people, generally a peaceable group, murdered workers at a normal per capita rate. Though less violent than the nobility, they had much more regular contact. Here one can find the expected employer–employee tensions that often led to violence. By far the most frequent murderers of laborers were laborers themselves. This is the only area where laborers deviate positively in the relationship to victims. This is significant because it supports the thesis that the records of speech and assault crimes do not adequately reflect the violent tenor of lower-class life as a whole. Those figures reflect with some accuracy the level of violence against the commune and its officials and the level of violence associated with business and business litigation, but they do not reveal the general levels of violence in society. Murder statistics are less biased; they depict a working class close to the norm as victims and as criminals.

Cases of workers murdering workers reveal something of the violence of lower-class life. The motivations for murder provide a glimpse of this world. There are 103 clear cases of workers murdering other workers, a low figure for eighty years of violent activity but a large enough sample to provide a profile. Many murders can be attributed to the acceleration of casual quarrels into physical violence, as was true in 20 cases. These quarrels were usually the product of chance encounters or minor irritations. One day, for example, a tailor named Panelo was walking near a number of moored ships, including the galley of the Greek emperor, at about the hour of vespers. Coming upon some sailors there, he began abusing them until a Venetian sailor, Antonio called Toderino, got angry enough to give Panelo a couple of shoves. Panelo drew a bread knife, a common weapon in worker murders, and quickly dispatched Antonio. Words had exploded, almost incidentally, into murder. The affair might easily have stopped with shouts, shoves, or wounds, but murder was the virtually accidental result.[20]

Drinking quarrels, gambling quarrels, and murders that can be classified as spontaneous (i.e., where the records indicate that no reason for the murder could be found) generally fit this pattern of rapid acceleration from irritation to murder. Together with minor quarrels, they account for 35 percent of the cases in which workers murdered workers.

The ultimate source of the alienation and frustration expressed in such violence is difficult to gauge, even from the records of violence. One is tempted at first to point to the static nature of the Venetian social system following the Serrata, but it can be debated whether the closed nobility was important to the worker portion of il popolo. For Lane, it was a matter beyond the ken of workers, despite the fact that in Florence at this time workers were attempting to secure the political trappings of status through the right to hold important communal offices. In Venice, crimes of speech against the commune indicate a certain amount of dissatisfaction with the political and social status quo. Murder, however, is not a good indicator of this kind of political bitterness.

It was perhaps more important for the average worker that living was held at the subsistence level through the planning of the controlled Venetian economy and the ready supply of new labor from the mainland. Housing could be poor and diet marginal. On these aspects of lower-class life, the murder records speak indirectly. Fully 37 percent of all worker murders of workers involved minor money matters, mostly simple quarrels. Nicolo da Brabante, a worker for Rigi da Munego, murdered a German cloth worker over a small debt his victim was putting off paying. Nicolo went at around midday to collect his money, but his debtor tried to delay, claiming, "I don't have to repay you until Sunday." That Nicolo was only a common laborer and not a lower-class loan shark is indicated by his response. In the ensuing quarrel, Nicolo suddenly drew a small knife and stabbed his delinquent debtor. The wound must have been superficial: when Nicolo fled, his victim pursued him. Nicolo finally turned and stabbed his victim again, this time killing him. It was a spontaneous act, almost accidental, with little evidence of premeditation.[21]

A similar case involved two sailors, Nicolo da Raguso and Giorgio da Negroponte. Giorgio owed Nicolo a small sum of money, which he apparently could not pay. As a result, they quarreled while on board their galley, moored at San Zaccaria. In the heat of the argument, Nicolo bashed Giorgio over the head with an oar, killing him and ending his chances of regaining his money. Nicolo, however, behaved more rationally after the crime. With the help of a friend, Gurian da Segna, he tied a bag full of rocks to his victim and dumped him overboard. Nonetheless, the crime came to the attention of the Avogadori, an indication of how effectively the Venetian commune could monitor capital crimes. And after admitting his guilt under torture, Nicolo was condemned to death. The Venetian nobility's sense of justice and showmanship is revealed in an extra fillip added to the execution. Nicolo was paraded through the streets while his guilt was proclaimed, as was typical of ritual executions; but in addition, he was forced to drag a bag of stones chained around his neck, a reminder of his disposal of his victim's body, on his last march to the columns of justice in San Marco.[22]

Most telling, perhaps, were the murders that grew out of quarrels about the amount to be paid for a product or service. These tended to be startlingly simple crimes much like Martino Sorto's murder of a German named Leonardo over the cost of riding a *traghetto*.[23] Such disputes were vastly different from the high finance of the merchant-banker elites, but they were not unrelated. Cities drew people from the countryside with a promise of wealth that could sometimes materialize. Much has been written about the potential for non-nobles to gain wealth in Venetian service: sailors investing their wages in goods and slowly gaining their own trading capital; families gaining position by educating their sons to be notaries and thus gaining power in the political structure of the commune. But these cases were the exceptions. Nevertheless, along with heavy exploitation of rural labor and (at least before the plague) rural overpopulation, they drew people to the cities. Murder was also an exception in the Renaissance city, but it reveals more accurately the harsh realities of everyday worker life. The sailor making his fortune or the meteoric rise of Raffiano Caresini from a notary to an important and powerful member of the nobility—these were the myths of the city. A murder over a small loan or over the price of a ferry ride across a canal—these open up the harsher reality of the daily life of the workers.

Most of the remaining homicides where workers murdered workers were the result of sexual quarrels (12 percent), family quarrels (7 percent), and vendettas (6 percent). All except the last seem to fit well in a picture of a lower-class society caught up in the basic struggle for survival, with a reserve of alienation ready to flare into violence at the slightest provocation. Most of the sexual and family quarrels that led to murder were spontaneous or petty. They, too, could have ended with hard words or slaps as readily as with murder. In fact, there is little difference between the motives for murder and those for petty assault.

The pattern of victimization of workers in rape cases differs from the pattern for murder. In 416 cases (correcting for the unidentified victims) nobles were responsible for 12 percent of worker rapes, important men for 3 percent, workers for 81 percent, and marginal men for 4 percent. Whereas nobles were much more active, workers victimized their class at a normal rate. In part, these figures can be explained by the unusual social sense Venetians reveal in their violent sex crimes. As has been noted, rape of social superiors was rare for all classes and rape within classes or of lower classes was prevalent. As a result, workers and those below suffered the most from violent sexual activity.

Workers raped workers at a normal rate of 81 percent. Unlike rapes by the upper classes, these crimes were generally spontaneous acts of a local nature. The victims were usually neighbors, wives or daughters of workers with similar occupations. Typical was the rape of Benevenuta, daughter of Jacobo Dalioto, by Nicoleto. He was a leather worker, as was her father, and they both lived on the island of Giudecca. Nicoleto broke into her home and carried her off, a straightforward rape without much careful preparation with both victim and criminal linked through occupation and habitation.[24]

In some cases, there was a modicum of planning. The attempted rape of Maria, wife of sailor Antonio Francesco, by a rag dealer named Almerico, provides a typical example. Almerico broke into the house where Maria lived, apparently while her husband was away. Hiding himself under her bed, he waited for her return. He was discovered before he could execute his plan and fled. His penalty was a fine of 50 lire di piccoli. Some planning was clearly involved in Almerico's crime, but it was a far cry from the resourceful enterprises mounted by noble rapists. The plan was rudimentary, the chance of failure high, and some familiarity with the victim implied.[25]

The records of worker victimization probably contain only a small fraction of the violent sexual activity directed against them by their social superiors. Perhaps the development of a more relaxed set of sexual values, which is discussed later, helped to make this high level of victimization less traumatic, but the picture of violence practiced upon women with the quasi-acceptance of society provides a rather dismal addition to the levels of violence in lower-class life already surveyed. Young women had to be always wary of their peers. Being alone with a man was often enough to invite attack, and the unpremeditated nature of lower-class violence added to the danger. There was also little protection from noble attack when even mothers and fathers helped deliver their daughters into the hands of the rich and powerful.

The records of rape depict the sexual world of the workers as a wasteland, but this sort of image can be found in the criminal records of any society. The records of sexual crimes, however, reveal a happier (if still illegal) side of Renaissance sexuality. The story of adultery is yet to be told, but in a society where marriages at all levels were matters of family convenience centered on the production of children and where women were often the victims of sexual violence, it is heartening that the warmblooded and affectionate adultery Boccaccio chronicled in the *Decameron* was actually practiced. In an attempt to enforce morality, the Venetian courts penalized these affairs halfheartedly but with little impact on the practice. The Avogadori alone handled 564 adultury cases in the records extant from the period, and there are no signs that the offenses were lessening.

From the documents, however, a harsh picture of lower-class Venice emerges—a society tense with the potential of explosive violence. Life was governed by the difficult struggle for existence among workers who depended upon marginal and often irregular wages. With the paternalistic support of the nobility, a few achieved some upward mobility; but the daily problems of living, eating, and surviving were the basic concerns of most workers. Still, some were not unaware of the broader context of their situation; they could even charge the nobility with responsibility for their plight, as the records of speech crime demonstrate. Occasionally, they also victimized the important men who represented the interference of outside power with their lives.

Marginal People

The lives of marginal people are difficult to analyze because they are the least visible people in history. Statistics tend to be most uncertain at the lowest levels of society; and discussion must be largely speculative, even when numbers are used. A priori, one can assert that the alienation and frustration typical of worker violence should be even more prevalent in the violence of marginal people. As their name implies, they had little place in society except as a source of casual labor. Attracted to the city by the promise of jobs, they struggled to stay alive from day to day at a level that often would have constituted illegal violence from the perspective of the established. The murder of a German vagabond, Federico, gives a taste of this street life. About one o'clock in the morning, Federico was searching for a place to sleep under the Rialto bridge, among the "many Germans and Slavs" who were already sleeping there. When he tried to lie down next to Zanino from Zara, also a vagabond, Zanino roughly threw him into the Grand Canal for disturbing his sleep. Because it was July, the water was probably warm enough for the short swim to the *riva;* but according to witnesses Federico "was not seen to come to the surface again." This is a typical instance of the spontaneous violence endemic in lower-class life, for by any standards, Zanino's motives for violence against Federico were minimal and his premeditation nonexistent.[26]

Table 7.6. **Violent Crimes Committed by Marginal People**

	Number	Percentage[a]	Deviation[b]
Speech	11	4.8	−3.2
Assault	31	5.4	−2.6
Rape	29	7.0	−1.0
Murder	69	16.2	+8.2
Total	140	8.5	+0.5

Source: A.S.V., Adv., *Raspe,* Reg. 3641–3645 (1324–1406); Signori di Notte, *Processi,* Reg. 6–12 (1348–1403); Dieci, *Miste,* Reg. 1–6, 8 (1310–1374, 1392–1406).

[a] Percentage of total criminal population for crime.

[b] Based upon the assumption that marginal people account for 8 percent of the population.

The general statistics shown in Table 7.6 indicate that marginal people were violent at approximately normal rates; but when the figures are broken down, it becomes obvious that they are minimal at best. Speech and assault crimes are clearly underreported. The few speech crimes for which marginal people were prosecuted grew out of direct threats and required no active monitoring of their speech by police patrols.

An interesting example is the case of Cristiano, a slave who was caught fighting with another slave in the street. Marco Loredan, a noble, stepped in and broke up the fight, ordering Cristiano to come with him to be fined by the Cinque alla Pace. Marco was not a police patroller but a tax official; by right of his office, he was empowered to carry arms and break up fights in the streets. Cristiano was unimpressed; in the heat of the moment, he threatened to kill Marco. For this threat, the Forty ruled that he be given twenty-five lashes as he walked between San Marco and the Rialto bridge and twenty-five more before his master's house in San Angelo.[27] This is such a special instance of a crime of speech that little can be generalized from it. Although it is dangerous to argue from a lack of evidence, the best conclusion seems to be that the verbal activity of marginal people was usually unimportant to the ruling class.

The assault cases heard by the Forty present a similar picture. Because the Forty heard important cases or cases involving communal business, marginal people were almost by definition excluded from such matters. The fact they they managed to account for even 5 percent of the total stems from their contact with police patrols or minor communal officials. This contact was not statistically significant enough to put them into competition with the nobility, but it did pull them up to a normal rate for assault, implying that they were quite active. One assumes that if the records of the Cinque alla Pace and other street patrollers had survived they would reveal a greater level of violent activity.

Rape is also probably underreported in Table 7.6. Given the pattern of the rest of society, rape and adultery may have constituted the normal sexual life of this group. Lasting relationships would be difficult, if not impossible, to maintain. If illicit sex was the norm, few cases would have come to the attention of communal authority. The majority of the victims (67 percent) came from within the group, but the reporting is so low that all but the most serious or public cases were probably overlooked. When the crime was reported, the victim was often the slave of a noble, which suggests that slaves enjoyed a more established and protected style of life than did marginal people. Thus, one must assume that the reported crimes are atypical and that they do not accurately reflect the violent tenor of life for marginal people.

In murder cases one might expect to find reports on marginal people more nearly complete. As Table 7.6 demonstrates, it is the only crime where their reported violence significantly exceeds their proportion of the population. In fact, they are the most deviant group for this crime. It is a dubious honor, but nonetheless this is the only area studied where noble predominance in violent crime is broken. Even at these levels, there are grounds for suspecting underreporting. Murders within the class should have been the most numerous, but the deaths of marginal people would also have been the least noticed. Their mobile, rootless lives made unexplained disappearances a normal state of affairs. At this social level, murderers who disposed of their victims successfully were likely to escape suspicion. Marginal people were also occasionally hired as assassins; and when their crimes were well planned, escape was probable. Marginal people were freer than members of any other class to move on after their crimes, leaving Venetian authorities with little but the corpse of another vagabond or beggar. All these factors probably contributed to underreporting.

Certain aspects of marginal life, however, contributed to higher rates of prosecution. Marginal people lived primarily in the streets, even to the extent of sleeping there (as the case of Federico exemplifies), and a higher proportion of their murders took place in public. Because the streets were heavily patrolled at all times and full of activity during the day, the chances of escaping unnoticed were considerably reduced. In addition, most of these crimes were unpremeditated explosions of violence with no thought given beforehand to escape or alibi. For this very reason, however (along with the factors noted earlier), unless the culprit was captured immediately there probably was little chance of apprehension or even identification, making reporting generally low.

Even murder does not provide much of a model for the violence of marginal people. The data base is not large enough, and the data preserved are not secure. Only the individual crimes give some impression of life at the edge of Renaissance society.

Marginal People as Victims

Studying the victimization of marginal people presents similar problems. Most levels of violence against this group were seriously underreported. The reasons are not hard to understand: the very marginality of these people made it likely that they were indifferent or did not understand how to use the system; nor was the system designed to respond to their need for protection from violence. In fact, the most surprising aspect of the data is the extent of prosecution for violent crimes within and against this class: in the areas of both rape and murder, there is actually a small positive deviation in reported violence against this group.

Given the nature of the documentation, there is little recorded victimization of marginal people through assault or speech. Speech crimes against marginal people, although they may have led to more serious violence, were clearly beyond the ability of the commune to control or even to monitor. The commune also had little interest in protecting this group from verbal assaults and threats. It is not surprising that there is no record in the period of a prosecution for speech crimes or threats against a marginal person. For assault, even though the records are mostly restricted to cases arising from litigation or communal business, a small number of charges were brought against attackers of marginal people. Only twenty-four cases in eighty years clearly do not represent the level of violence against this group, but they provide a good perspective on the extent to which these people were marginal.

The commune was much less willing to overlook murder, even at this level. Of 427 murders prosecuted, 55 victims were marginal people, almost 13 percent of the total. Although one reason for this surprisingly high level of prosecution may have been the visibility of crimes against people who lived, struggled, and died in the streets, the visibility of marginal life must be balanced against its anonymity. Marginal people had few of the points of reference that helped even the worker: church, confraternity, even family and neighbors were often unaware of their existence.

Because the sample is small, one cannot say much about the social groups that murdered marginal people. There is only one reported murder by a noble. When nobles committed crimes, even when they did so from passion, they were so much better at executing and concealing them that their victims, especially at this low social level, probably vanished without trace. There was little cause for a noble to murder a marginal person: considering the elite style of the nobility, marginal people were beneath their attention. There were no questions of honor or other issues that prompted violence between the top and the bottom of Venetian society. There may also have been a reluctance to prosecute nobles for a crime carrying very serious penalties when the victims were so unimportant.

The only case prosecuted illustrates some of these problems. Zilio Boldù murdered a vagabond known as Bini, stabbing him before a number of witnesses in a public place. Bini did not die immediately; and as was the normal procedure, the Signori di Notte attempted to obtain his testimony about the person who struck him down. As long as Bini lived, he refused to testify against Boldù. Perhaps he felt that if he lived it would be difficult to cope with so powerful an enemy. A friend who was with Bini at the time of the attack likewise refused to testify against the noble. The case proceeded only because other witnesses with less fear stepped forward to name Zilio. Nonetheless, Zilio only lost his left eye, a painful but minor penalty for a crime that usually ended in execution.[28]

Important people statistically killed marginal people at about a normal rate for their class size (9 percent), while workers were responsible for significantly fewer than their share of these murders (59 percent); but the numbers are too small to be meaningful. One can conclude only that their position at the bottom of the social scale made marginal people easy victims for the rest of society. Marginal people were responsible for the largest percentage of murders of other marginal people, about one-third of the homicides. Their peers were most accessible for the spontaneous violence that characterized the lower classes; the downward pattern of violence stops at the bottom and naturally produces a clustering of cases there.

Rapes of marginal women exhibit a different pattern. A similar change of pattern between murder and rape has already been noted in the case of workers. First, rapes of marginal women were reported at a surprisingly high rate, about one-fourth of all rapes prosecuted. By now, the reasons for this are clear. In a society that sought to protect women from contacts with men except in controlled situations, marginal women were the most available victims. Their style of life did not allow them the luxury of isolation. Like marginal men, they were creatures of the street, and a lone woman was an acceptable sexual target. Like the working-class woman, the marginal woman was further exposed because her status made her a more acceptable target for violence. The penalties for the rape of a marginal woman were themselves so marginal that they did not deter even those who bothered to consider the consequences. More significant, the low penalties for the rape of marginal women indicate a low valuation of the crime by society, so low, indeed, that one might argue that society hardly viewed it as a crime at all.

Accompanying this is the downward pattern of violence, which has become a theme of this section. Although marginal men by far lead in the rape of marginal women (26 percent), both nobles (7 percent) and important men (7 percent)—normally distant from the marginal class—had few qualms about exploiting marginal women. The availability of female slaves and servants, who were unlikely to report their victimization, made this exploitation even easier. A *parte* passed by the Major Council in 1364 sought to show that the commune was concerned about masters imposing upon their slaves and servants. It stated that women so treated became "vile," "less efficient," and often "pregnant," all of which was to the detriment of the commune. The Signori di Notte were instructed actively to seek out such criminals, but the legislation itself admitted that detection would be difficult because the crime occurred in the privacy of the master's house.[29]

Predictably, although required to search harder for these cases, the Signori di Notte did not find any. Rapes of servants or slaves by nobles were prosecuted only when the victims belonged to others. Nor were many of these cases successfully prosecuted, as the rape of Anna, slave of the noble Michaleto Dolfin, exemplifies. The evidence against Checo Duodo, also a noble, was strong. He had taken Anna from her master's home and raped her in an empty house of his in San Giovanni Bragole with the help of a relative, Francesco Duodo. Although it was clear that Anna had at least been carried off, both nobles were absolved of the crime. Apparently the Duodo family had enough power to escape prosecution.[30] A similar case involved a servant of Agneta Sanuto named Catarina. She claimed that Zanino Sanuto, a son of Agneta, raped her in her own room in the Sanuto house. Her claim, much more difficult to prove because of its private nature, was overwhelmingly rejected by the Forty, with 26 votes for acquittal, 9 for conviction, and 4 abstentions. One wonders to what extent the case was decided on its merits and to what extent it turned on the dangerous precedent that would have been set by a conviction.[31]

Statistically, marginal women fared better at the hands of workers; but because of the number of workers most of the prosecuted rapists were drawn from their ranks. Although there is a negative deviation of 14 percent in rapes of marginal women by workers, this figure still accounts for 61 percent of the rapes of marginal women. They were excellent victims for workers both because they were members of an even lower class and thus acceptable targets and because their less protected life style left them open to the spontaneous violence endemic among the lower classes.

Rapes of slaves and servants on boats seem to have been common. Women from upper classes apparently were careful not to enter boats alone, especially the *traghetti*—boats that carried people back and forth across the wider canals where bridges were not available. Marginal women out on errands or merely moving about the city could not always choose to wait for safe company, and they were regularly victimized by boatmen and fellow passengers. Exposed by their style of life, they provided the primary sexual outlet for marginal men and acceptable sexual victims for the rest of society.

Marginal people thus seem to have been frequent victims of rape and murder. Their social position and life style left them dangerously open to attack. They were, at least sexually, a favored prey of the upper classes, who tended to view their victimization with a large measure of leniency. This analysis can be reduced to a simple but significant tautology: the closer one gets to the bottom of the lower classes of Venetian society, the more openly violent was the tenor of life. In turn, this implies a more ready reliance on violence for physical survival. In subtler terms, an addiction to gratuitous violence may have contributed to psychological survival; a moment of senseless violence by a marginal man may have been a way of forcefully creating a place for himself in a society that had no place for him. Throwing a fellow vagabond into the Grand Canal for intruding on one's sleeping spot under the Rialto may seem an overreaction; but it was a direct assertion of one's place in a physical sense. In terms of its psychological overtones, that one act symbolizes the essence of lower-class violence in Renaissance Venice.

Conclusion to Part Two

At the beginning of this section, it was argued that Venetian violence appears to fit into the two-class analysis favored by trecento chroniclers. The violence of nobles was often a product of their elite style, filled with exploitative attitudes toward the lower classes. It was frequently premeditated, but it could also be a spontaneous reaction in defense of noble values like honor or status. This arrogant violence does not belong in the myth of a city of sober countinghouse merchants. But men are more versatile than their myths, and the Venetian noble was often a schizophrenic combination of bourgeois commitment to order and neofeudal commitment to prestige and power. Conventional histories have drawn attention to the more normal and attractive sides of this noble psyche; but if Venetian society is to be understood, this darker side of the elite mentality must also be examined.

Lower-class violence was essentially different from upper-class violence. Similar themes can be found in both, but from the statistics it is evident that lower-class violence was more spontaneous and reactive, tied to the harsh realities of living in a city that required a large supply of subsistence-level labor to man its fleets and developing industries. Lower-class violence tended to victimize other members of the lower classes, usually reflecting petty conflicts where alienation and frustration exploded into violence. In sex crimes especially, a social awareness that some have denied also played a significant role. Spontaneous violence is by its very nature almost impossible to explain, but current theories of alienation provide a model that accounts for some of the data.

From the general figures, workers seem to have been proportionately less violent than nobles. There are many uncertainties with the data, but none accounts for the consistent negative deviations except the interpretation that the nobility was by far the most violent sector of Venetian society. Between the nobles and the lower classes one important addition must be made to the chronicler's social perspective: the group of important people who enjoyed enough wealth, prestige, or political power to be a step above the rank-and-file workers. The importance of this group to Venetian stability has already been broadly outlined. Acting as a buffer between the nobility and the lower classes, important people were often the victims of lower-class hostility toward communal policies. As guild officials, patrolling officers, and executives of various communal organs of power, they represented communal authority to the lower classes. When the response to that authority was violent, they generally felt the brunt of that violence. In contrast to the nobility, this group was the least violent sector of society; they successfully internalized the norms society had adopted for its own maintenance. Here one finds those famous sober, rational burghers. The existence of this buffer group was vital for the continuity of the state with its legally defined nobility. Rather than threatening the stability of the state and the position of the nobility with revolutionary machinations, important people were so subordinated that they shouldered the day-to-day business of the government and accepted more fully than their superiors the laws and ordering principles of society. Doubtless there were some thoroughly corrupt notaries, some thoroughly violent police patrollers, and some substantial men capable of spontaneous violence; but as a group, their stolid avoidance of violence and acceptance of the status quo, including their own exclusion from the nobility, did much to stabilize Venetian society.

PART THREE

The Perception of Violence

Perceptions of violence change over time. The amount of violent activity acceptable in feudal society became unacceptable and criminal in the more complex economic and social atmosphere of the Early Renaissance. In part, the Florentine Ordinances of Justice reflect such a perceptual change. Such shifts create a basic problem for comparative studies of violence, but this problem can become an asset if violence is taken in a more suggestive sense as a key for understanding the perceptual world of a particular society. Because violence is perceived so immediately, patterns of violence and responses to them within a specific context can provide unusual insight into the perceptual codes of a ruling class.

In dealing with perceptions, the historian normally turns to the literature and intellectual heritage of a society; but these sources primarily reveal the consciously articulated and traditional literary views of an intellectual elite removed from the everyday world of perception. *Ricordi,* diaries, and sermons overcome this problem to some extent, but each is contaminated in its own way by the conscious attempt to convey perceptions to posterity. Criminal records also strive to convey an impression; but they transmit living perceptions of violence in a more innocent fashion. They are intended less to convey a view of reality to some future or contemporary intellectual elite than to depict a specific lawless event in the most criminal light possible. They describe those things that are most unsettling about an act of violence to a contemporary audience. If anything, they seek to reinforce contemporary perceptions in the men responsible for judging a crime by stressing the commonly perceived taboos broken by the violence of a specific crime. Moreover, when both judges and prosecutors were members of the same class, and usually of the same narrow senior group within that class, these records provide an excellent opening to their general perceptions of their society as well as its violence.

In a Venetian rape case, for example, a modern observer might be surprised to find more weight placed on a subsidiary aspect of the crime, such as breaking into the victim's house, than on the rape itself. What seems to matter, after all, is the sexual crime. In trecento Venice, however, rape and most other sexual crimes were considered so minor that the records emphasized almost any other violent aspect of the crime in order to build a stronger case against the defendant. In contrast, a modern prosecutor would emphasize the sexual violence to the victim because the jurors' perception of the seriousness of the crime depends upon this aspect of it. For each society, the criminal record tends to convey in a straightforward fashion the violence members of that society could be expected to perceive.

Venetian judicial procedure is particularly relevant for this type of analysis. Although there were no juries, the law left wide leeway to the judges to fit penalty to crime as they deemed appropriate. The records of the crimes, because they were used as prosecution briefs, contain elaborate evaluations of the amount and nature of the violence involved to aid the judges in making their decisions. In addition, the judges, especially those on the Forty, were prominent members of the nobility chosen more for their political sensitivity than for their legal expertise. As astute amateurs, they reflected their peers' perceptions of violence more accurately than a professionally trained body of judges bound to legal precedent. The Venetian judicial system was accordingly a sensitive barometer of the perceptions of the nobility, and the surviving records were geared to those perceptions. Consequently, they convey a unique picture of Venetian social organization and complex attitudes toward violence.

This final section studies the way the Venetian elite perceived the four types of violent crime already discussed: speech, assault, murder, and rape. From this range of criminal violence, a preliminary assessment of the Venetian nobility's perceptual world will be abstracted, especially in its relationship to the violence they found in that world.

Chapter VIII

CRIMES OF SPEECH

Speech as a Form of Violence

In trecento Venice, speech was perceived as a significant form of violent activity. A society that prided itself on its unity, that felt such a need for unity—witness the myth of Venice and its stress on cooperation at all levels—expressed that need in its criminal procedure by protecting communal unity from the violence of verbal disruption. This was not the result of some strange collective paranoia on the part of the nobles; it was a crucial requirement for the preservation of their rule and their state.

Individual nobles could be quite violent and highhanded in their pursuit of honor, place, and power. One danger inherent in this competition, even on the verbal level, was that of the ruling class dissolving into quarreling factions. The orderly function of the commune would be gravely threatened if cliques fought for power in the halls of the government or the streets of Venice. Adding to this perceived danger was the awareness that the nobility was a closed class; open dissension could provide a focal point for alliances with non-nobles that would challenge their monopoly on power. Contemporaries were convinced that this danger was real. The Querini–Tiepolo conspiracy was regarded as such an event, a moment when factioning got out of hand, threatening Venetian order and the nobility's position on top of that order. The memory of that civic lesion was kept alive each year by the commune's celebration of its successful defense against the Querini–Tiepolo faction.

The connection between the conspiracy and the move to monitor speech is evident from the very existence of the Council of Ten, which was created to destroy the remnants of the Querini–Tiepolo faction and control the factioning tendencies of the nobility. The Ten rapidly became the center of government activities designed to thwart treason and revolution. But aside from a few moments of public notoriety in the fourteenth century—thwarting the Falier conspiracy, prosecuting Carrara agents and noble sympathizers in the two wars with Padua, and destroying the remnants of the Cretan Rebellion—their main criminal responsibility was to prosecute those who spoke against the commune, the nobility, or individual nobles.

The power to prosecute for crimes of speech stemmed directly from the

Ten's mandate to control speech as a form of violence against the unity of the state. The original empowering legislation was developed in response to the escape of the most important leaders of the Querini–Tiepolo conspiracy. Even before the Ten was created, the Major Council responded to this threat by effecting the verbal isolation of these men, forbidding any contact in speech or writing with them. On July 2, 1310, the council ruled that no monasteries or religious persons could shelter or communicate with any of the conspirators. The same prohibition, stiffened by a penalty of 500 lire for shelter and 300 lire for communication, was imposed upon all citizens or residents of Venice.[1] Eight days later, when the Ten was created, its powers were defined to include responsibility for all legislation already passed by the Major Council for control of the conspirators.[2] Out of this responsibility grew the Ten's power over speech. From the first days of the Council of Ten, the control of faction and speech were inseparably mixed, and speech was considered a dangerous part of the violence of factionalism.

In its early days, the Ten followed this mandate closely, using the penalties given earlier as guidelines for its own penalties against speech crimes. As late as 1320, the noble Leonardo Emo, who was involved in liquidating the property of Querini–Tiepolo conspirators, was instructed to deposit 200 lire with the Camera Frumenti to pay a fine imposed by the Ten on Angelo Girardo, who had spoken with an old conspirator, Andrea Doro, in Naples.[3] A more curious example, which reveals how seriously the Ten took its charge, involved the scribe Donato Calderario. In 1320, the Ten instructed him to correspond with a conspirator identified only as a member of the Barbaro family. To clear any doubt on the legality of the contact, the council took the time to rule that Donato could communicate with the traitor without being subject to the fine normally imposed upon those who spoke with or wrote to traitors.[4] The prosecution of these verbal contacts with the dispersed remnants of the Querini–Tiepolo conspiracy, which continued well into the 1320s, reveals respect for the disruptive potential of speech.

The Ten rapidly expanded its original mandate in the area of speech, finally gaining responsibility for everything from speaking against the state to "evil words" in general. These controls were intended to prevent disunity within the commune and make it easier to control animosities before more direct violence resulted. In effect, the Ten eventually created an environment where criticism of the commune and its policies was always potentially illegal. With the support of the nobility, the Ten tried to enforce a standard of noncriticism that contributed to the development of a virtual religion of the state. In effect, government in Renaissance Venice became to a great extent a secular religion. A growing orthodoxy of state is seen most clearly in the intellectual sphere—in the laudatory tradition of the Venetian chronicles which eventually developed into the myth of Venice. There were other factors in the growth of the myth, but the habit of silence enforced by the Ten and to a lesser extent by other councils certainly contributed to its development.

The importance of enforcing this verbal unity is proved by the amount of time the Ten spent in prosecuting these crimes. In registers 5 (1349–1363), 6 (1364–1374), and 8 (1392–1406), the percentage of speech crimes prosecuted by the Ten remains remarkably stable and high: 77, 78, and 77 percent respectively.[5] Thus, from 1349 to 1406, apart from the lacuna caused by the loss of register 7, the Ten was concerned with controlling speech in more than three-quarters of the cases it heard.

Verbal Violence against the Doge and the State

The Ten had more than a consistent policy of limiting speech; it devised a conscious strategy of using its broad mandate to control what it considered a primary source of violence in Venetian society. An early example of this can be found in the case of Tusco da Lucca, a cloth worker, who was reported by one of the Capi di Sestiere to have said "evil and dishonest words . . . against the honor of the doge and the whole land."[6] Although the statistics cited in Chapter 7 suggest that the nobility were not particularly concerned with speech among the working classes, Tusco's case was unusual. He was part of a growing group of skilled foreign laborers being attracted to Venice. Cloth workers, however, were one of the most socially active and disruptive groups in Early Renaissance society. One reason Lucchese cloth workers were available to work in Venice was the sporadic labor violence that forced many to leave Lucca. These laborers, although they were needed to build Venice's industrial strength, also bore close watching for their potential social disruptiveness. Tusco was banned from Venice; and if he ever returned, he faced an indefinite jail sentence at the discretion of the doge and the Council of Ten. The threat of an indefinite jail sentence was rare, and in conjunction with permanent banishment it demonstrates how seriously the Ten meant to control disorder by controlling speech.[7]

An extreme instance of this control involved Oliverio, a petty police official who was jailed while the Ten investigated reports that he had criticized the commune's grain policy in the church of San Giovanni e Paolo. Talking about the communal grain policy hardly qualified as treason, but it was an area of speech that could lead to physical violence. As noted earlier, grain distribution by police patrollers was frequently the occasion for violence against communal officials, usually in the form of petty assault. Whatever Oliverio said, it was considered serious enough to warrant investigation by the Ten. Although he was finally released and no action was taken against him, the message was clear: even questioning the operations of the commune was frowned on by the authorities.[8]

This unanimity was demanded most stringently of the nobility itself. In a case similar to that of Oliverio, Giustiniano Giustinian, "nobilis et sapiens vir . . . Potestas Clugie" ("a noble and wise man . . . Potestà of Chioggia") was fined 200 lire di piccoli for refusing to accept communal grain policy in the territory under his jurisdiction. Although in modern terms this is not a crime of speech, he was prosecuted for words spoken against "the rule of Venice." Words were once more seen as a type of disruptive violence to be controlled.[9]

The extent of these requirements for uniformity casts doubt upon the republican nature and the proverbial justice of the Venetian commune, especially as even debates in the councils of state were occasionally grounds for prosecution. In the tense days of the early 1350s when the war with Genoa was being discussed in a special council of twenty-five appointed for the war, the Avogadori prosecuted three members of the council before the Forty for words "against the honor of the doge and commune." The three, Bernardo Vitturi, previously in charge of part of the protective forces in the Eastern fleet, Luchas Mudazzo, and Giovanni Loredan were fined 100 lire each for their part in the debate over communal policy. Although their censured words are not reported, it is difficult to imagine how important nobles could be prosecuted for their part in a debate during a difficult time of policy making when all possible positions should have been considered. In fact, it is difficult to understand how such prosecution could even be contemplated by the Avogadori. Nonetheless, the case was not only contemplated but successfully argued.[10]

Such actions were not rare although the formal nature of the records makes identification of every case difficult. For example, Pangratio Zorzi was successfully prosecuted for getting into an argument over communal policy with Doge Giovanni Dolfin in a meeting of the Forty and fined 100 lire. The formal reason for the prosecution was the insult to the doge implicit in having a heated argument, but the line between insult and debate here is narrow.[11] In 1362, Nicolo Falier was deprived of all communal offices for two years because he spoke against the doge during a debate in the Major Council.[12] Perhaps the strangest of these cases was an attempt to prosecute Giovanni Bembo for saying something not insulting but merely irrelevant during a debate in the Senate. His crime was described by the Avogadori as "having made a statement that was not pertinent (tangencia) in the Senate." Why such an action was considered a crime is not clear, but it reveals the extreme to which such attempts at control were pushed. In this case, the extreme was too far, and the Forty voted to absolve Bembo.[13]

These examples and many others suggest that through such vague categories as insults to the doge or speech against the commune an orthodoxy was imposed even upon the nobility, even within the councils of state. This wide-ranging attempt at verbal control grew out of a respect for the violence of words, especially when they were translated into factionalism within the ruling class, and the deep desire for unity and maintenance of the status quo. This developing orthodoxy was more than protopatriotism or a form of civic humanism. It was used to protect society from the internal tensions that members of the nobility saw as potential sources of violence that could endanger the continued existence of their commune. Only in this context can one understand the willingness of the Ten and Forty to prosecute such crimes.

It is unfortunate that communal notaries used a formulaic style in recording these crimes. Rather than reporting what was said or written, they merely reported that it was done "contra honorem huius civitatis," or that those words were "inhonesta," "contra honorem dominationis," "contra honorem communis et nobilium venetorum," or "contra honorem nostrum." The formulas vary little throughout the period under consideration, concentrating upon two essential points: first, but to a lesser degree, the "dishonesty" or "injustice" of the speech; second, and more important, the fact that the speech had offended the honor of the commune or the relatively synonymous honor of the nobility or the doge.

The formulas are sometimes abandoned to reveal the nature of these crimes against the orthodoxy of the commune. In a partially destroyed text from the early part of the century, it is noted that Marco Rizo was apprehended by the Signori di Notte and brought before the Ten for speaking against the honor of the nobility. Specifically he was accused of having said in St. Mark's, "O good people allow me to throw these dogs [the nobility] in jail." Although Marco's importance is not clear, his words elicited a particularly violent response from the Ten: his tongue was cut out and he was perpetually banished from Venice with the provision that if he were ever to return he would lose his eyes as well.[14]

Continuing lower-class sentiment against the commune is illustrated by a message scrawled in charcoal on the wall of the church of San Boldo at the beginning of the fifteenth century. In dialect, it read: "Mad Venice you have forgotten your poor." The Ten, believing that the words did violence to the honor of the commune, levied a fine of 1000 lire upon those responsible. Although the perpetrators do not appear to have been caught, that was a secondary concern. The size of the penalty, publicly proclaimed by a communal herald, made it clear that slogans scrawled on church walls could subject their authors to severe penalties.[15]

These examples demonstrate the desire of the nobility to restrict criticism of the commune even by the lower classes of the city. Threats from the nobility were considered more dangerous because the nobility comprised men of power. Their dissatisfactions could place the state in serious jeopardy, as the Querini–Tiepolo conspiracy or the fall of Marin Falier readily demonstrated. But in the memory of the nobility there were obscure threats from the lower classes as well, exemplified in the Barozzi conspiracy and in the attempted attack on the Major Council by Marin Boccono and his followers. That both are evidence of class tension in Venetian society should not be forgotten. This tension is also observed in the case of an arsenal worker, Palmerio Paradiso, who was sent to jail for a little more than a month in 1350 when he expressed the bitter hope that a galley of the war fleet would be sunk.[16] This incident occurred during the early stages of one of several wars with Genoa that severely tested the fabric of Venetian society. Before the war was over, this dissatisfaction was transformed into the support the arsenal workers gave to Marin Falier in his aborted coup.

Within a few days of Palmerio's indiscretion, a similar case was brought against the wife of Francesco da Firenze, named Pencina, whose prosecution is described earlier. She had spoken against the officials who were drawing up new lists of the civil militia and against those who were responsible for having these lists drawn up (the Ten), apparently because she opposed the workers of Venice being called up for war. She also castigated the nobility, whom she referred to with the pejorative term *magnate*, calling for the destruction of the Venetian fleet and the magnates who sailed with it and who had ordered its sailing. The Ten reacted with restraint to this affront to communal honor: they gave Pencina four days to present herself before the council and begin serving a one-month jail sentence. If she missed the deadline, her penalty would be two months in jail. In both these cases, the violence advocated was unlikely to materialize, but the Ten reacted with firmness. Public expressions of dissatisfaction with the commune and its elite, no matter how fanciful, were perceived as a grave matter. It is clear that strong undercurrents of class tension surfaced in such crimes of speech. The ruling class may not have feared such tension as greatly as factioning within its own ranks; but the time and effort expended and the penalties meted out by councils like the Ten and the Forty demonstrate a perception of and reaction to class tensions.

Some speech crimes were much more analogous to the modern crime of conspiracy; and the Council of Ten, in particular, used them to prosecute anyone perceived as a threat. Judging words to be violent was a useful pretext for condemning actions not otherwise clearly criminal. For example, Francesco Enzignerio, Deacon of the Scuola of Santa Maria della Misericordia, was prosecuted by the Ten "for words and actions of his used against the honor and order of the state" when he expelled Francesco da Monte from an office in their confraternity. This was hardly a crime, yet speech was a good pretext for acting in an area where the Ten was just beginning to exert its authority. Later it moved to control the confraternities—potentially dangerous bases of wealth, prestige, and power for non-nobles—by overseeing their meetings, elections, and even their size; but at this earlier time, a nebulous interpretation of the speech laws allowed the Ten to act.[17]

A more conclusive example can be found in the way this catch-all crime was used to net a number of minor figures associated with the Falier conspiracy. Convicted of speaking against the honor of the commune were Nicolo Greco from Castello, Nicoleto da Frixaturo, Nicoleto Gardesano, and Andrea Zafoni. Penalties ranged from a few months in jail for Nicoleto Gardesano to five years for Nicoleto da Frixaturo to the cutting out of Nicolo Greco's eyes. This variety of penalties suggests the broad areas of complicity that could be subsumed under the nebulous crime of speech against the commune. It is also a microcosm of the extensive use of this criminal category during the century under study. The charge could be brought to eliminate those who threatened the government or applied for a specific purpose. In its general application, prosecution for crimes of speech was used by the nobility to stifle dissent and impose an orthodoxy of expression upon Venetian society.[18]

A prominent feature of this orthodoxy was the personification of the commune and its nobility. The honor of the commune was interpreted and defended by the nobles, who were the individual parts of its collective personality. Speech against the commune was perceived as a violation of communal honor and thus as violence against the commune's person. It was just as real as violence against the honor of any one individual, and perhaps more dangerous. Honor played a central role in the perception of crimes either against an individual noble or against all nobles as personified by the commune. Although individually and collectively the nobility was a group of merchants and bankers, values like honor played a crucial part in their perception of reality. As a consequence, both individual nobles and the commune as a whole often responded in strikingly similar ways to insults. There was one fundamental distinction, however: the commune responded *as* the law, whereas the individual noble often responded from outside the law by resorting to violence.

Verbal Violence against Individuals

The noble who retaliated stood outside the law because the commune sought to protect society from the ravages of individual violence by righting such affronts to honor through the courts. The nobility had a deep respect for the divisiveness of words, as can be seen in the case of Blasio Malipiero and Saraceno Dandolo. Being nobles, both men were members of the Major Council; they had become involved in a heated debate about whether another noble, Pantaleone Barbo, should be granted a *gratia*. Dandolo argued strongly against it and Malipiero in its favor. In the judgment of the Avogadori, debate slipped into the realm of the unacceptable when Malipiero began to insult Dandolo personally. As a result, the Forty fined Malipiero 100 lire di piccoli. This is an interesting case because Dandolo represented a more socially important family than did Malipiero. The Dandolo family consistently occupied prominent positions in the trecento, whereas the Malipiero were of lesser prominence, only occasionally holding major offices. Malipiero, if he reflected cooly on his situation, was probably content to pay the fine for his insult to Dandolo's honor and end the matter. Whether Dandolo was appeased by the judgment is uncertain, but the politically sensitive Avogadori and Forty felt it wise to restore his honor in the courts, especially since the insult was made in a public manner before the Major Council.[19]

Most of the cases of insults among nobles heard before the Forty had a public context. The Ten occasionally heard other cases from other sources, but the main area of concern remained public speech. Two factors account for this concentration on the public sphere. First is the matter of public knowledge: a private insult, unless reported, would tend to be resolved privately. The assault records show that this was a regular option. Second, public insults were much more damaging in a society where honor was important and an affront could foment divisiveness. The chroniclers' accounts of the background of the Querini–Tiepolo conspiracy are instructive in this regard. Most chroniclers fix on moments of petty public insult and clearly find them as significant in the formation of the factions that led to the attempted overthrow of the Gradenigo regime as the crucial political and social differences. These insults may seem insignificant in comparison to the rejection of a war policy or the Serrata; but to contemporaries both were important. A petty insult provided a public event upon which factionalism could be built more readily than abstract considerations of government policy. In the end, it may have been the latter that pushed men to action; but in the context of the premium placed on honor, the insult was not underrated in its capacity to divide the nobility into factions.

Verbal Violence against Communal Officials

Another crucial area of verbal violence consisted of insults to officials of the commune. These were the speech crimes with which the Forty was primarily concerned. Insults to officials were seen as attacks upon the communal honor in the persons of the officials who represented the state. This identification of the state with its officials is indicated by the frequent references to verbal attacks on officials as crimes not only against persons but also against the honor of the commune. In cases of nobles attacking important men, these crimes often involved attempts by the powerful to override the state by insulting and threatening officials of lower social rank. Such tactics must frequently have been successful, but prosecution for crimes of speech at least offered a vehicle for limiting such abuse. If nobles could have been forced by legal means to treat the authority of the commune with respect, an important advance in communal operation would have been made. It is clear from these attempts to prosecute speech crimes, however, that the nobility as a group was aware that respect for communal authority was desirable. It is equally clear from the records of prosecution that as individuals nobles often followed the passions of the moment when they found their immediate desires thwarted by communal authority. Finally, the prosecutions were used in an attempt to control the factioning of the nobility that could be caused by violent verbal encounters between noble communal officials and prepotent nobles.

Many other factors could doubtless be advanced for the concern with insults to communal officials, but these reasons include the primary areas of perception. Attacks on communal honor in the form of verbal attacks on communal officials were the substance of most of the cases that involved members of the lower classes. These cases usually originated during some exercise of governmental authority that brought communal officials into contact with workers or marginal people. Simon da Vicenza, for instance, insulted a *famulum* of the Camera Armamenti, and by implication the commune, because he did not want to pay the amount the official claimed he owed on a fine. The Forty ruled that Simon must pay 40 soldi di grossi or spend fifteen days in jail. This was a relatively minor penalty for a mundane affront to a petty official and to the communal honor, but the fact that the Forty took the time to hear the case reveals the degree to which the nobility wished to enforce acceptance of communal authority, even at the level of speech.[20]

Noble officials were also verbally abused, generally as heads of police councils or as judges on communal courts. Normally the situation was similar to the case of Simon, but nobles were in the positions of contact. A parallel case involved Nicoleto Desiderato and a minor noble official, Bernabas Zorzi, who was trying to collect a fine from Nicoleto. Bernabas demanded the money, but Nicoleto claimed that he owed nothing and went on to characterize Bernabas as a robber. Although the fine was only 20 lire di piccoli, the remark was prosecuted by the Forty, which meant serious attention by the Avogadori di Comun and a trial before a large group of the most important men in Venice.[21] Occasionally, violent words led to more substantial penalties. The records do not relate what he said, but Zonta Bonifati must have given a serious insult to a representative of the Consoli dei Mercanti, who had ordered him to appear before the council. He was fined 800 lire di piccoli for his harsh words. Whether the penalty was large or small, the nobility was clearly intent upon preserving public officials from verbal assault.[22]

The state was equally zealous even if the verbal attack came from a noble, which, given the statistics discussed earlier, was likely. Lorenzo Vidal's problem with the Cinque alla Pace provides a typical example of noble prepotency. When Pietro Pisani, an official of the Five, took Lorenzo into custody for an offense, he was insulted by Lorenzo, who "dixisse certas vilanas" against him and his colleagues. For his insults, Lorenzo was given an extra two months in jail.[23] Such cases were extremely common. Nobles tended to see themselves as powers beyond the law because they were accustomed to being the law's controllers rather than its victims.

A case that failed provides a final example. During the summer of 1349, Loysio Bedheloto and his friend, the noble Mapheo de Mezzo, were stopped at the Rialto in a routine search for weapons by a patrol headed by the noble Giovanni Bondemiro. Mapheo was unhappy about the delay and objected to the search although it was fully legal. Finally, according to the case brought against him in the Forty, he spoke out insultingly against Giovanni.[24] One can easily imagine the scene: de Mezzo and his friend at the Rialto, the hub of Venetian economic activity, going about on important business when suddenly a patrol calls them up short and begins to search them for weapons. De Mezzo probably supported the continuation of the laws and patrols, because he thought them necessary to the security of his own status and business activity. But he was a noble, and he and his friend were no threat to Venetian order. Bondemiro, however, was not operating according to this logic, and de Mezzo insulted him. Other scenarios could be reconstructed for this crime because the records give no details beyond the search and a report of the insult; yet conflicts must often have arisen in a similar manner. The desire to control closely a society where violence was perceived by the nobility as a constant threat, not only to individuals but to the economic and social function of the state, came into conflict with a noble's sense of self-importance and honor. These speech crimes, one might contend, reveal an inner conflict in the psyche of the elite between noble ideals of honor and bourgeois ideals of order. Noble honor, which did much to limit violence by restricting its range in feudal society actually heightened the level of violence in the context of Renaissance society.

In the case of nobles, insults to officials could be threats designed to force them to back down in the face of superior power. From the records, it is impossible to distinguish these cases from simple insults, but they do exist. The best example is the case of the noble Francesco Venier discussed earlier. Francesco and his brother Lorenzo learned that the Signori di Notte were planning to investigate the death of one of their slaves because of suspicious wounds on his body. They then insulted and threatened one of the Signori, Pietro Michiel. Behind their harsh words was a desire to apply pressure so that the investigation would not proceed. Rather than being intimidated by pressure, Michiel brought the matter before the Forty who fined each of the brothers 100 lire di piccoli.[25] Given the nature of such threats, it is difficult to estimate how frequent they were. Coming from an important family, Michiel was probably secure enough in his position to resist the pressure. Lesser nobles or officials faced by a threat from the more powerful may have backed down. The frequency of reported cases or of cases that suggest such a threat indicates that threat and bluff were a normal part of noble contact with communal authorities.

The Significance of Verbal Violence

Some understanding of how seriously the nobility viewed crimes of speech can be gauged by the penalties imposed by the Ten and the Forty. The average penalty for crimes of speech in 220 cases was 21.6 points (based on the scale established in Chapter 3). That corresponds to a little more than one year in jail or a fine of about 216 lire di piccoli. Ten cases that involved corporal punishments were not included in the point averages; but corporal punishment was generally more serious than a year in jail or a fine, and one can assume that 21.6 points represent a minimum. As might be expected, the most popular form of corporal punishment was cutting out the tongue. This was used in four of the ten cases.[26] Beating and branding were the next most common, with two cases of beating and one of beating and branding.[27] Finally, there were two cases of spending time in a *berlina,* and one of cutting out both eyes of the criminal.[28] Although being beaten or branded and spending time in a *berlina* were probably less exacting than a year in jail, five instances of corporal punishment were considerably more severe. Still, corporal punishment was unusual: as noted earlier, Venetian penology had reached a stage where jail sentences or fines were more popular.

Of the 220 noncorporal penalties, 33 involved some period of banishment; 112 involved fines; and 103 involved time in jail.[29] The goal of the Venetian nobility was to control speech and the formation of factions; and penalties had therefore to be significant but not destructive. Mutilation was avoided because it eliminated men from the work force and created needless antagonisms. Part of the myth about Venetian justice may stem from the genuine restraint exercised by the commune in respect to corporal penalties; but this restraint was less concerned with an abstract sense of justice than with the wise investment of penalties. An occasional ritual mutilation, with all the gaudy publicity the commune could muster, provided a lesson; but in most cases, the quieter pressure of jails or fines sufficed.

Eight of the ten sentences of mutilation were meted out by the Ten, including all five of the serious mutilations. Being more concerned with public security, the Ten was inclined to use the stern warning of public mutilation more often. For example, in the case of Marco Rizo, who called on the people of Venice to help him throw the nobility in jail, the Ten responded with a typical public mutilation. Rizo was to have his guilt and his penalty proclaimed at the Rialto; then his tongue was to be cut out publicly, and he was to be banned perpetually from Venice and all its territories. If he ever returned to Venice, and this was presumably read at the Rialto as well, he was to lose both eyes and be rebanned. Such penalties periodically made the danger of speaking against the nobility clear to all.[30]

Although governments can be as violent as, or more violent than, the acts they define as criminal, in the area of speech, restraint was the more usual approach in Venice. The figure of 21.6 points, a stiff average penalty, does not reflect the actual distribution of penalties. More than half the penalties fall under 10 points. This is conveyed by the now familiar pattern of penalty distribution, the reverse J-curve. A few cases were severely penalized, but the elite generally responded with moderation: Although speech crimes were dangerous enough to be judged by some of the most powerful men in society, they generally required only a warning in the form of a short jail sentence or mild fine.

What distinguished the thirty or so serious cases from the rest were either the social gap between the lower-class assailant and his upper-class victim or an aspect of the crime that seemed to threaten the nobility or the commune. The highest penalty for a speech crime against a worker was 7 points; the highest penalty for such a crime against an important man was 80 points. When the nobility was victimized, the penalties spanned the whole range of points, but most penalties were quite severe.

Most of the more serious crimes were heard by the Ten. In only two cases were penalties of more than 100 points given by the Forty.[31] This is to be expected, because the Ten was responsible for crimes that seemed most to threaten the state. A breakdown of penalty averages by council proves this point: the average penalty in 135 cases before the Forty was 11.6 points; the average penalty for 69 cases handled by the Ten was 41.0. Although there was no clear dividing line between the work of the two councils (both could and did try cases of speech crimes against the commune and against individuals), it is apparent that the Ten, as the more important council for such matters, heard the cases that were perceived as most dangerous.

The Ten's principal responsibility was to check conspiracy and the formation of noble factions. These were the main fears of the nobility in relationship to the violence of speech. When speech created factions or attacked the nobility, it did violence to the social order represented by the Serrata. Implicit in this was a fear both of internal factions and of subversion from below. Fear of factions does not preclude a fear of the lower classes; and although the orthodox view of trecento Venice has tended to minimize social tensions, the records of prosecution for speech crimes reveal a vigilance against this danger, especially on the part of the Ten. If any doubt remains on this, one merely has to examine more closely the prosecutions of the Ten for speech crimes. The Ten heard 21 cases clearly against important men and nobles and 41 cases clearly against workers and those below. Although nobles were brought before the Ten at a high rate, the council followed the actions of the lower classes as well. If lower-class antagonisms were not feared, it is hard to understand why the Ten with its vital responsibilities wasted time and harsh penalties on workers and marginal men when the Forty was able to handle petty crimes.

The nobility's perceptions concerning the violence of speech are clear. Behind the rhetoric about honor of individuals and the state lay an awareness of the divisive potentialities of speech. They sought to eliminate this divisiveness in the public sphere. The Forty concentrated on insults to individuals and communal officials, which threatened the orderly operation of the commune or encouraged revenge on the part of insulted individuals. The Ten dealt with the more dangerous aspect of speech crime, which threatened to divide the commune along class lines or promote factions within the nobility. Each of these dangers was perceived as part of the violence inherent in the spoken word, and this made the nobility willing to strain their technology of government to secure some control over speech.

Chapter IX

ASSAULT

The Context of Assault

The pattern of assault crimes recorded by the Avogadori di Comun resembles the pattern already encountered for speech crimes. Unless they are read carefully, however, the figures are rather misleading. The Avogadori and the Forty actually dealt only with a limited range of assaults. Their elaborate procedures were far too cumbersome for the numerous *rixe* and *brige* (fights and brawls) of the Venetian streets. The primary responsibility for this day-to-day violence was placed in the hands of patrollers, especially the Cinque alla Pace, who dispensed summary justice in the streets for most petty brawls. A statistical analysis of this level of violence is impossible because records no longer exist, but the *gratie* registers reveal that such crimes were common. They appear to have been so common that the Cinque alla Pace could not handle all this violence by themselves, and well before the trecento the patrols of the Signori di Notte were also authorized to control *rixe* and *brige*. Later the Capi di Sestiere also joined this core of patrollers; and during the fourteenth century each group's numbers were periodically augmented in order to meet the problem of keeping order in the streets.

The rhetoric that accompanied these expansions of the city's patrolling forces provides testimony about the disruptive nature of petty assault throughout the period. In 1360, the Signori di Notte complained that the eight special *custodi* maintained at both the Rialto and in San Marco were insufficient to protect the peace. In the statistics, these two areas stand out as the dominant areas of violent activity. Together, they accounted for 37 percent of all crimes studied, the Rialto contributing slightly less than 17 percent, while San Marco reported slightly more than 20 percent. To preserve the "order" of these two "primary areas," which meant literally to stop "brawlers and other criminals," the Signori di Notte were given twelve well-armed *custodi* for each area.[1] A similar rationale was given for an earlier series of reforms of the Capi di Sestiere initiated in 1328 by the Council of Ten. The goal was to preserve the order of the city, especially in cases of brawls.[2] Examples of such rhetoric could easily be multiplied: almost every augmentation of patrols was justified by the need to eliminate petty violence in the streets.

In 1349, concern over street violence prompted the commune to pass an unusual measure empowering every communal official with a license to carry arms to act as a patroller of the streets. The rationale was to limit "brawls and blows." According to the order of the Major Council, "All officials including scribes and lesser officers, who have because of their office the right to carry arms, when they encounter such cases (such as the above *rixe*) they not only may but must break them up and impose penalties just as the Signori di Notte, Capi di Sestiere, and Cinque alla Pace." As a result, virtually every official of Venice was empowered, even required, to suppress fighting in the streets.[3]

At least some officials took this charge seriously although the outcome could be dangerous, as is demonstrated by the case of a minor official of the Officiali al Dazio del Vin. One night he came upon Antonio da Ferrara, called Tonso, beating a prostitute in a street near the Rialto. He stepped in to break up the fight, either from loyalty to the commune, desire for a part of the fine, or sheer gallantry; but Antonio slashed him across the face with a bread knife. Although blood flowed freely, the official was not seriously hurt, and Antonio was fined only 25 lire di piccoli and sentenced to less than three months in jail. It is significant that the assault on the communal official was handled by the Forty and the Avogadori, even though the original fight between Antonio and the prostitute was passed on to the Cinque alla Pace. Although the latter was not serious enough to warrant the attention of the Forty, the former was.[4]

For nonpolice officials empowered to break up *rixe*, there must have been tension between the desire to avoid potentially dangerous situations and the desire to collect the portions of the fines that went to arresting officials. It was likely to be a dangerous business, and the records of the Avogadori indicate that nonpatrolling officials either were cautious in choosing to interfere in brawls or tended to opt for safety over profit: almost all the victims of assaults growing out of attempts to break up street fights came from the regular patrolling forces of the city. Nevertheless, after 1349 all officials with arms licenses were theoretically responsible for helping to keep peace in the streets. Controlling violence was clearly important to the nobility, even though the extent and social breakdown of such activity cannot be gauged.

In any event, the Avogadori and Forty heard a large number of assault cases: 677 were processed, of which 569 were successfully prosecuted, according to the surviving records from the trecento. The decision to use the complex procedures of the Avogadori and the Forty instead of the direct and swift justice of the patrollers indicates the types of assault the nobility viewed as more serious threats to the order of society. This becomes clearer when the main categories of assault heard by the Forty are identified. By far the largest number of cases involved assaults on officials on communal business: patrolling, collecting fines, arresting criminals, or overseeing guild activity. A second area included assaults growing out of litigation before communal courts. Finally, a small group of assaults had dangerous social overtones: sailors attacking their masters in the streets or workers attacking an employer. In all these cases, the nobility saw the problem as more than a simple brawl.

Assault on Communal Officials

In order to protect the officials of the state from violence, even words against communal officials were punished as attacks upon the honor of the commune. If threats and insults violently disrupted the operation of the government, physical violence obviously did so as well. If they did not meet with retaliation, attacks upon officials could bring the commune's control of the city to a halt, especially in a society where even the nobility was unwilling to have its violent tendencies limited by its own state. The Forty consequently regarded this area of assault as threatening enough to warrant careful attention.

Assaults on communal officials also provide an unusual index of the contacts with government that were most objectionable to the people. There is no question that police patrols lead the list by far, their visibility and the nature of their work making them obvious targets of popular violence. Of 311 attacks upon communal officials, 37.9 percent involved police patrols. The Signori di Notte lead the list with 13.5 percent of the victims; the Cinque alla Pace are next with 11.3 percent; and the Capi di Sestiere come third with 9.0 percent. The next largest group are judicial officials, who were victims of 15.4 percent of the attacks. Guild officials and communal officers in charge of guilds come third, with 11.6 percent of the total. The last identifiable group with any sizable proportion of victims are officials who oversaw foreigners living in the city, with 5.1 percent of the victims.

Assaults by nobles were also focused on police patrollers—47.7 percent of 65 assaults upon communal officials. Interference by the police was likely to provoke violence from members of the nobility even though the nobility was responsible for the legislation that made these patrols a prevalent part of Venetian life. Because the officials responsible for guild affairs and foreigners seldom interfered with nobles, they were victimized by only 3.1 percent of such assaults. The courts were the only other area where nobles committed a considerable number of assaults, 18.5 percent of their total. No one court was singled out for abuse, but courts concerned with merchant affairs and the Giudici di Petizion were leaders.

The primary victims of worker assault were also the police—35.6 percent of 118 assaults were directed against police officials. Evidently workers were slightly more predisposed to accept police interference than were nobles. Guild officials were a distant second, accounting for 16.7 percent of the victims, and court officials accounted for 16.7 percent of the total. This last figure is a bit surprising; but as noted earlier the civil courts did have an impact on at least some workers, interfering occasionally even in family affairs.

Assault on Police

The police were constant victims of assault because their patrols came into regular contact with the people. There are many power struggles in an urban environment, but perhaps the greatest potential for violence comes where the force of government directly impinges on the everyday life of the citizens. The job of protecting the commune's position at this point of contact was important enough to warrant the involvement of the Forty.

A typical case involves a *custode* of the Signori di Notte, one Pietro Sartor. Near his home, Pietro searched a suspicious-looking noble named Jacomelo Emo for illegally concealed weapons. Somehow Emo had managed to hide a heavy sword on his person, but Pietro had little trouble finding it. As he was taking the weapon, Emo snatched it back and hit Pietro, as the documents record, in indignation about being searched (and also, presumably, because he was upset at being caught). The blow drew blood and left Pietro seriously wounded. The Forty fined Emo 200 lire di piccoli for the assault. For carrying a concealed weapon, he was fined separately by the policing body responsible for the arrest. It was not a particularly expensive fine for a noble, considering the crime.[5]

In such cases, the desire to protect communal officials was mitigated by a sense of social hierarchy that made the crime less serious for a noble. This generalization is supported by an interesting case involving foreign nobles, which demonstrates a similar social distinction. Rizardo, count of San Bonifacio, and the noble Phylipo da Peraga were stopped one night in a boat with some of their servants by three *custodi* of the Signori di Notte. The *custodi* intended to search the nobles for weapons but found themselves under an attack led by Phylipo. Two *custodi* were wounded and one escaped more serious injury by being knocked into the water as they were routed by the foreigners. The culprits were eventually apprehended, tried, and found guilty of assault upon communal officials. Phylipo was fined 300 lire di piccoli and Rizardo 100 lire di piccoli. The impact of this fine on Phylipo is to some degree indicated by the fact that he had little trouble raising the money almost immediately, even though he was a foreigner. He paid the fine the next day and was a free man, presumably a bit more wary of Venetian customs but none the worse for the incident. His servants, who were merely following their master's lead, did not fare so well: both were sentenced to two years in jail.[6]

The contrast is strong—the noble perpetrator going free the day after the trial only a little poorer and a little wiser and the servants spending two years in jail. Perhaps Phylipo's status as a foreign noble contributed to his lenient treatment, but it remains true that most nobles who committed assault were fined, whereas non-nobles were more regularly sent to jail. This suggests a certain tolerance toward assaults on communal officials by nobles, at least on the part of the Forty. Perhaps the attitude can be traced to the ability of the members of the Forty to identify with such criminals, especially in cases where non-noble patrollers interfered with the activities of fellow nobles. Although the nobility was striving to protect its order from violence, it simultaneously tended to resent lower-class interference in its affairs, especially in carrying concealed weapons.

The general statistics on penalties imposed by the Forty for assaults by nobles support the impression that these factors were at work. In all, 122 nobles were successfully prosecuted for assault, but only 34 received jail sentences. There were 100 fines and 2 banishments but no instances of corporal punishment.[7] Of the jail sentences, 26 were for six months or less; and no sentence, even when the victim was close to death, involved a jail sentence of more than two years. In contrast, workers spent time in jail in 131 out of 201 cases, 49 sentences involving at least a year in jail and some ranging up to six years. Corporal punishment, unknown for nobles, was used in 17 cases. Finally, a comparison of penalties as a whole confirms the pattern of leniency for nobles. The average assault penalty was 26.5 points for marginal people; 20.5 points for workers; 21.8 points for important people; and 16.0 points for nobles. Because the smaller penalty figure for nobles includes many painless fines and the other figures include a large proportion of jail sentences, the disparity was even greater.

Implicit in these sentences is the perception, whether conscious or not, that assaults by nobles, though a nuisance, were rarely a threat. The noble policy makers seemed to see them as matters of style, not as attacks upon the authority of the commune. Although these assaults were considerably more violent than speech by modern standards, the latter had a greater potential for creating factions. As a result, speech crimes by nobles were punished almost as severely as assault, with an average penalty of 13.4 points. Assaults against communal officials by nobles warranted serious attention by the Forty but not serious penalties.

Assaults on communal officials by lower-class people were a graver concern. Such aggression against communal authority, even against its lesser officials, disrupted the smooth function of the state and could lead to more serious resistance. The case of a worker named Matheo Solsa is typical. When he was stopped by a *custode* of the Signori di Notte, he struck out with an illegal weapon and felled the *custode* in a pool of blood. The Forty sentenced Matheo to six months in jail and a fine of 100 lire di piccoli, one-third of which went to the victim, a relatively restrained penalty.[8]

A more serious crime in the eyes of the Forty involved a gold worker named Michaleto Zusto and his friend Pietro Zentil, who attacked not only two *custodi* but also one of the noble Signori di Notte, Antonio Pisani. Pisani was patrolling with his two *custodi* in Dorso Duro, near "the bridge of the Franciscans which is across from the apothecary shop of Ravagnini." They came across Zusto and Zentil in the street with drawn weapons and called for them to stop and hand them over. The two friends attacked instead and escaped leaving one *custode* bleeding in the street. It would probably have been easier for them to pay a fine to the Signori di Notte for having drawn weapons because the Forty sentenced them to three years in jail and perpetual banishment if they surrendered voluntarily within a month. If they did not, their jail sentence would be doubled and they would be fined 500 lire di piccoli each. This harsh penalty at best meant life banishment for the criminals. It also reveals a common tendency in the Forty's actions against violent crime: violence against communal officials was more serious than normal violence, but violence against noble communal officials was graver still. Neither was acceptable, but the severe penalties for the latter are further evidence of a highly developed sense of class distinction.[9]

Assault on Other Officials

The collection of fines and the confiscation of goods by the commune also led to violence against communal officials. The context of this violence can be seen in the case of Marco and Zanino, sons of the deceased Vitti da Verardo. The Consoli dei Mercanti came to their house to catalogue their goods in order to pay off creditors. The Consoli brought one of the major creditors with them, Pietro Simoneti, who was apparently given first choice of the goods to be confiscated. It is easy to understand how this situation could lead to violence. The conflict was set off when Pietro decided to take some books that Marco did not want to give up. It was a minor confrontation, with only a bit of pushing and shoving and a slap for Pietro from Marco. But the Forty reacted strongly. For the slap and for interfering with the Consoli dei Mercanti, Marco was sentenced to six months in jail and a fine of 100 lire di piccoli which would be doubled if it was not paid within three days. Zanino, who had only interfered with the Consoli dei Mercanti, spent a month in jail and paid 25 lire di piccoli.[10]

A good contrast comes from a similar crime involving the nobleman Moreto Baseggio. Moreto lost a case before the Giudici al Forestier to Catarina, widow of Bartolomeo da Vicenza. When a communal herald, Antonio Petri, was sent to collect certain goods confiscated by the court, Moreto met him at the door with a knife and stabbed him although he did not draw much blood. Rather than face a trial, Moreto fled; but the Forty proceeded against him with remarkable restraint. After he was declared *in contumacia,* the court ruled him guilty as accused, fined him 80 lire di piccoli, and ordered his wife to pay. Although the crimes of Moreto Baseggio and Marco da Verardo were similar, perhaps Marco's actions being less violent, the nobleman fared better, as was normally the case in parallel crimes.[11]

Moreto's actions after his moment of violence were also typical of the nobility. The penalty turned out to be small, but stabbing someone was always a dangerous matter because if the victim died the commune could act with vigor even against nobles. The wisest course for those with the means was to leave Venice for a time to see what the penalty would be. If the victim survived and the penalty was light, one could pay the fine and return. If the penalty was too severe, one could remain in exile and negotiate for a *gratia* to make return possible. Ironically, escape was also the course taken by those at the bottom of society. Instead of facing trial, they often fled to other cities. They had little hope of being able to afford fines or obtain *gratie,* however, and even a small penalty meant life banishment.

The Forty gave two other areas of assault on communal officials its serious attention, those involving guilds and those involving grain distribution. Communal dominance of the guilds is revealed by the careful watch the Forty kept over assaults on guild officials. A dyer named Zanino Fanutio, who hit the *gastaldo* of his guild, found his case tried before the Forty. Zanino had attacked the *gastaldo* because he ruled that his dying was not up to standard. The fine was only 50 lire di piccoli, but the significance of the Forty's intervention was clear. This crime was not a minor personal matter but an event that warranted the attention of one of the major courts of the commune. In the eyes of the Forty, guild officials were as important as communal officials. That attacks on guild officials were treated like attacks on regular public officials is one more indication of the domination of guild organization by the commune.[12]

Communal officials were not alone in their attempt to control petty violence; as quasi-public authorities, guild leaders also tried to keep peace among their members. Official records of such activity do not survive, but the guild capitularies make it clear that this was a responsibility of their officials. It is difficult to judge how seriously the responsibility was taken, however, because it was often exercised by the regular policing bodies. The *gratia* records are full of *rixe* and *brige* between guild members penalized by the Cinque alla Pace, the Signori di Notte, and the Capi di Sestiere rather than guild officials. Still, the records of the Avogadori and the Forty reveal that the guild system was functioning at the same time. In 1367, a cheese seller named Gregorio was fined 100 soldi di piccoli by the *gastaldo* of his guild for hitting another guild member. Angered by the fine, Gregorio attacked the *gastaldo* with a bread knife and stabbed him three times but did not inflict serious damage. The Forty put Gregorio in jail for four months and fined him 25 lire di piccoli.[13]

One other area of public authority that caused friction was the program of communal grain distribution. It is ironic that a program aimed at least in part at keeping the lower classes content was a source of so much violence against communal officials. The rationale for the program was that famine, a main source of unrest, could be avoided by stockpiling grain and distributing it in times of need, presumably at a price that allowed the workers of the city to keep eating and working. On the face of it, the program might be viewed as the enlightened product of a benevolent merchant capitalism; but apparently there were flaws in the system, including a strong resistance to the commune's prices that was often accompanied by violence.

The nature of the problem is illustrated by the trial of Cristoforo Trentavasi and Antonio Torta. Cristoforo, the more active of the two, had attacked Benasuto Taiapetra in San Barnabe with drawn weapons and wounded him four times. Benasuto suffered the attack because he was a special official appointed by the Capi di Sestiere to collect outstanding debts for grain distributed in the sestiere of Dorso Duro. As such, he was clearly not a popular man. Grain distribution angered the people because the nobility seemed intent on making a profit from this service.[14] The Forty reacted with unusual severity: Cristoforo, who had escaped, was banished perpetually from Venice and all subject territories. Moreover, a reward of 200 lire di piccoli was offered for his arrest. If captured, he would have his right hand cut off, spend one year in jail, and be rebanished for life. Clearly, Cristoforo's crime appeared much more serious to the Forty than regular assault.[15]

The concern of the Forty about violence against officers of the state provides a convenient measure of the areas of friction between the government and the people. Friction was most likely to occur where the government interfered routinely with daily life, as in police patrols, or where the interference was least appreciated, as in the collection of fines, debts, or payments for grain. Conflict in these areas is not surprising: except for grain payments, these are normal areas of friction between ruled and ruling. What is surprising, however, is the sophistication of the Venetian nobility in developing a subtle vision of society that found such crimes unusual and deserving of special attention. They were not sufficiently threatening to the state to interest the Council of Ten, but they threatened the authority of the commune through its officials and therefore merited more elaborate and politically sensitive hearings than the Cinque alla Pace could give.

Assault and Litigation

The interest of the Forty in assaults growing out of litigation is another aspect of this same ranking process. Once more, the motive was to ensure the orderly function of communal authority. Violence could disrupt the thin veneer of order that the elaborate Venetian court system tried to maintain, especially in monetary and mercantile matters. One of the crucial advantages that a Renaissance city offered, beyond its well-discussed concentrations of labor and capital, was a bureaucratic structure that guaranteed a certain order and security for economic transactions. The Venetian nobility understood this; and although their courts were not centers of enlightened justice in the modern sense, their substitution of legal force for naked force was better suited to the developing technologies of trade and monetary transaction. For this bureaucracy to work, however, the process had to be protected from the older, more direct ways of handling disputes, ways that involved pure force.

For the Venetian nobility, assault during litigation was a typical type of violence, demonstrating once again the split in the noble psyche between adherence to its own order system and willingness to fall back on violence when that system did not work to its satisfaction. Although numerous examples could be cited, a typical case involved the nobleman Antonio Bon, and Florentia, the wife of Righi ab Aqua. Florentia was a witness against Antonio before the Giudici del Mobile. Antonio tried to keep her from testifying with both verbal and physical intimidation, but Florentia not only gave her testimony but also filed a complaint with the Cinque alla Pace. Not having learned that he was dealing with a determined woman, Antonio returned to her home and beat her again. As a result, the case was passed on to the Forty, which fined him 50 lire di piccoli in addition to whatever fines the Cinque alla Pace would levy. The fine was small, but the Forty thus showed its disapproval of Antonio's behavior. The case is suggestive, because Antonio's actions seem to indicate that he was so confident of his ability to intimidate a non-noble that he paid little attention to what was actually happening as a result of his badgering and threats. In the end, his loss was minimal; but this example raises questions about the extent to which litigation was not pursued because of threats and pressure. The records of violence already show a high level of criminality among nobles, but if they also managed to prevent many witnesses from testifying, their proclivity for violence may well have been virtually Florentine.[16]

When two nobles were involved, the Forty's response was more exacting. In a case that ultimately involved a substantial cross section of the Venetian order-keeping establishment, Donato Vitturi testified before the Giudici di Petizion against Francesco Contarini called Rizo. Francesco lost his temper with Donato and accosting him in the street gave him two blows over the head with an unnamed weapon. The wounds were so serious that the Signori di Notte were brought in to take testimony on the assumption that the assault would soon become a murder. Donato, apparently still a young man, managed to pull through; and the Signori di Notte returned the case to the Cinque alla Pace, who fined Francesco 200 lire di piccoli. But the Forty was not satisfied with this and ruled that the case be brought before them and retried. In the end, it decided that Francesco should pay 300 lire di piccoli, a penalty well above the average.[17]

More was at stake in this case than protecting the system of litigation. Francesco's attack on a Vitturi, a small but important trecento family, could have opened a serious rift in the nobility. Even though the Forty did not add significantly to the previous penalty, by reviewing the case the judges gave it a certain dignity and standing. The Vitturi family would have perceived the fine levied by the Five against its attacker as a technical response from a limited body of officials; but a fine imposed by the Forty was a penalty that reflected the serious judgment of a large group of important nobles. In this context, the perceived distance between the two fines is greater than 100 lire di piccoli.

Not even the family structure of nobles was safe from the violence that could arise from litigation. Jacobello Boldù's father left no written will. This oversight led to litigation with his stepmother over the estate. During the course of it, Jacobello became so angry that he stabbed the woman several times in the house they shared. The Cinque alla Pace stepped in immediately; but when the larger issues became apparent, the Forty took over the case. Jacobello fled, as nobles were inclined to do in these circumstances, to see how serious his penalty would be. The Forty ruled that he should pay 300 lire di piccoli within one month; otherwise it would order his capture, and a six-month jail sentence would be added to his penalty. For Jacobello, it was not a difficult choice: he paid the fine and presumably returned to his litigation.[18]

An important procedural point these cases reveal is the fact that the Forty routinely took cases out of the hands of the Cinque alla Pace. The mechanism for this was a combination of a regular review of cases by the Avogadori, who were responsible for seeing that significant cases were forwarded to higher courts, and the social and political contacts of the members of the Forty itself. It may be that less significant cases arising from litigation were left with the Cinque. Assaults on officials appear to have been a clear area of the Forty's responsibility; and there is little evidence that they were taken over from the Cinque. Assaults relating to litigation, however, belonged to an ambiguous area where the Forty intervened regularly but not in every case.

At times the Forty intervened in cases of this type that did not involve nobles. In 1351, it took over a case from the Cinque alla Pace in which Nicolo Galinarion had badly beaten Luca Marcella in the streets of Venice. Luca had testified against Nicolo in a rape case, and the assault was prompted by his testimony. The Forty ruled that Nicolo spend three months in jail and pay 25 lire if he turned himself in within fifteen days. If he did not, his stay in jail would be extended to six months. The Forty allowed the Cinque alla Pace to impose whatever penalty on Nicolo it deemed appropriate for carrying the arms used in the assault. Rape was not a serious crime, and there is no indication that these people were of special importance, but still the Forty intervened.[19] Thus, although the Forty did not take up every case of violence that resulted from litigation before communal courts, it intervened regularly even when the people involved were socially unimportant. If people were enough a part of society to participate in litigation, they warranted the special attention that the Forty could give.

Special Types of Assault

The nobility felt that special attention was also due to assaults that crossed status lines in a threatening manner. This is a nebulous category, but one that yields information about noble perceptions. Attacks upon communal officials and attacks upon opposing litigants are easily defined; but attacks upon social superiors, employers, or former communal officials all fall in a gray area that reveals a developed social awareness. There are no typical examples of such crimes because each case reveals a separate aspect of the upper-class concern about violence. Still, a paramount theme is the danger of violence from the lower classes, a fear on the part of the nobility that once again suggests the presence of class tension.

In an example involving a segment of the Venetian work force with a great potential for disruption, three sailors attacked a noble who had been an official on a ship of the fleet on which they had served. With apparent premeditation, Nicoleto Stornado and two companions attacked Pietro Balbi as he was leaving church and stabbed him with a sword. The Forty clearly regarded this as a grave crime: Nicoleto was given two years in jail and his accomplices were given a year each; all were banished perpetually from Venice and all its territories. In a move unusual for assault cases, even those heard by the Forty, their guilt and penalties were ordered to be publicly proclaimed.[20]

Public proclamation was reserved for murder, major crimes against the state, or especially troublesome crimes where a public example seemed necessary. The dangers inherent in Nicoleto's assault are obvious: if sailors were permitted to take violent revenge against their superiors for their grievances, the discipline of the fleet would be in serious jeopardy. The publication of the strict penalties following trial before the Forty emphasized the gravity of the offense.

Other disorders by sailors also warranted the Forty's attention. In 1342, three sailors ran amok, stabbing people at random. The Avogadori decided that the matter was a serious threat to the peace of the city and deserved a hearing before the Forty. The penalties were severe: each was to lose a hand and be banished perpetually from Venice. If any of them returned, he faced life imprisonment. Only two of the sailors had been captured, but the sentence was the same for all three.[21] These crimes and their penalties were also publicly announced as a warning to sailors and other workers that the state would not tolerate such violence.

The Forty also acted with severity in cases of assaults for pay. These crimes were clearly disruptive and dangerous, but the courts seemed to be equally troubled by their cold-blooded motivation. Assault was a matter of passion or uncontainable emotion. Although this did not make it acceptable, it often evoked an empathy based on the understanding that unconsidered violence could on occasion explode within every man. Assault for pay, however, turned emotion into a money-making venture, and this the nobility could not accept—especially on the part of those who took the pay. The man who hired someone else to do the deed for him retained the motive of passion, but the cold-blooded execution of the act was highly disapproved.

The case involving two sailors and a cloth worker discussed earlier illustrates these attitudes. In another case, a noble, Morosino Morosini, quarrelled with a priest of the Querini family named Bertuccio. Both families were among the most important in Venice although the Morosini were more numerous. Perhaps this was why Morosini decided to settle his grievance privately through the use of paid ruffians. There is little indication that murder was the objective: Morosini's men merely wounded Bertuccio and fled. The Forty reacted strongly. At first, only one of the three was caught; he was sentenced to four years in jail and his guilt and penalty were proclaimed at the Rialto. A second culprit was never caught, but he was sentenced in absentia to six years in jail followed by perpetual banishment; he probably chose a self-imposed banishment to avoid the jail sentence. The third man was caught by a patrol of the Cinque alla

Pace. He lost his right hand and was perpetually banished. His guilt was also proclaimed at the Rialto.[22]

Few such cases were reported to the Forty; and murder for hire was also relatively rare, as is discussed later. Both occurred, but the mentality of those who had the means to hire violence, especially at the level of assault, usually encouraged them to express that violence themselves. The predilection for immediate violence accords with the mentality of the Venetian nobility and explains to a degree the stricter punishments the Forty and the Signori di Notte meted out for crimes of violence without passion. It may also be true that members of the nobility who did not wreak personal vengeance found a more secure satisfaction in using the state rather than a hired hoodlum as an agent of vengeance.

The Forty also intervened on those occasions when a longstanding disagreement threatened to disrupt the commune with feuding and vendetta. The documents seldom describe the context of such violent acts, preferring to concentrate on those immediate antecedents that explain the passion of the crime. In one interesting case, there was a feud between two relatively substantial men, Nicoleto Zeno, a worker in gold, and his neighbor in the *contrata* of Santa Marie Nova, Nicoleto da Quaterno. The feud reached a climax in the early summer of 1378 when Zeno attacked his neighbor in a boat on his way to the mainland with a bow and arrows. It is hard to understand how Nicoleto avoided being killed, because Zeno hit him with twelve arrows before he was stopped. The Forty sentenced Zeno to a fine of 200 lire di piccoli and three months in jail. He must have been a substantial gold worker: he paid the fine the day it was levied and began serving his sentence.[23]

At the level of the nobility such divisions would have been much more dangerous to society. But criminal records and even chroniclers writing after the Querini–Tiepolo conspiracy make little reference to splits in the nobility that led to violence. Faction, though feared, was significant more in terms of political power (and perhaps eventual revolution) than in terms of assault; there was little sense that such divisions would be fought out in street violence. There might be moments of symbolic street violence, but feuds would be resolved only in more meaningful conflicts. The myth of Venice may have discouraged chroniclers from admitting the existence of these problems, and the criminal records, focusing on immediate events, fail to probe for deeper implications. But in this instance, the myth and the documents ring true. For the Venetian nobility, violence was seldom a means to any end beyond immediate gratification; it was a style of life, not a struggle for position. The Serrata had already defined social position. State violence might be needed to defend that position; but councils like the Forty and Ten watched carefully to see that it was not threatened by violence from within. In effect, control had become so sophisticated that violence within the nobility lost most of its function and became a minor diversion—a matter of honor. Carefully monitored, it disrupted society but had little potential for overthrowing society. This transformation of violence among nobles into an annoyance rather than a revolutionary force placed Venice in a uniquely secure position in the Renaissance, even though fear of such violence remained a norm for the ruling class.

The assaults handled by the Forty were occasionally of a more trivial nature. One case involved two teachers who quarreled over students. Magister Balsamo, straying from the path of reason, attacked his worthy intellectual opponent with an unnamed weapon, wounding him and leaving him in a pool of blood. Realizing that this attack was not likely to improve his teaching reputation, at least with communal officials, Balsamo then chose the wandering life of the early prehumanists, leaving the city and his students to his wounded colleague. The Forty ruled that if caught he would be fined 50 lire di piccoli and spend three months in jail. The case was no threat to the commune, but it caused enough scandal for the Avogadori to pass it on to the Forty.[24]

Assault on Clerics

The last category of assault tried by the Forty involved members of the clergy. This was a perennial problem in trecento Venice, as even a cursory reading of the records of the Major Council reveals.[25] The Forty did not handle all such cases, merely those that appeared disruptive or politically sensitive. A brawl involving some minor cleric was little more significant than any other *rixa*, but certain brawls had social, political, or even economic implications. An attack upon a cleric from the household of the Patriarch of Grado, an important local power, illustrates this. Donato Buscharino, a Venetian of unclear station, attacked and wounded the patriarch's man while aiding in his brother's escape from ecclesiastical captivity—his brother was a priest. The crime was mixed, and the Forty tried Donato both for insulting the patriarch and for assaulting his man. This crime warranted more of a response from the government than a regular assault to demonstrate from a wide base and in a serious forum that Venice did not condone such flouting of ecclesiastical authority. The Forty was the ideal medium for the political message, and it gave the proceedings a seriousness that was likely to assuage the dignity of the patriarch.

Of course, Venice often defied church authority, but in this case there was nothing to be lost by a show of righteous indignation. Donato was fined 100 lire and given a six-month jail sentence. In addition, he was forbidden to approach the patriarch's residence when the latter was in the city, under a penalty of 25 lire di piccoli for each time he was caught in the area. Donato had already fled the city, and the Forty gave him fifteen days to surrender before the jail term would be doubled. Although the penalty was not much stricter than others for assaults tried before the Forty, the forum itself gave the correct political dignity to the case. Further, prohibiting the criminal from entering the area where the patriarch lived provided a sage personal touch. The commune was saying it would do its best to see that this sort of petty annoyance would not recur.[26]

The Forty was not always so concerned with attacks on clerics, especially when nobles were the assailants. Attacking monasteries and nunneries seems to have been a sport for young nobles; and the Forty, though consistently stepping in, was inclined to penalize this youthful excess with lenience. In 1333, Poluccio Soranzo, Blaxio Bredani, Andrea Bredani, and Nicoleto Morosini, all noble youths, broke into a convent where they insulted the abbess and others and caused many injuries. The Forty proceeded with all its dignity, but brought forth only a token penalty. Soranzo, the leader, was fined 50 lire di piccoli, the others 5 lire di piccoli each—small change for young men of their station.[27]

The ambiguity here is significant: the crime was considered serious enough to bring to the Forty's attention but not serious enough to justify stern measures. The result was a kind of protective upgrading of the case; for if it had been judged technically by the Cinque alla Pace, the penalties would have been more exacting. In general, the penalties for gang rowdiness by noble youths were quite mild although there are few reports of such activity beyond mention of groups causing minor disorders in the streets at carnival time or a rare spectacular crime. Noble youths did form gangs, but the records of violence reveal little about their activity. The nobility probably considered most of these excesses too unimportant to demand the attention of the councils whose documents have survived. The exceptions occurred when the violence crossed political or social boundaries or when it became too great. The assault on the nunnery is an example. Even though the crime was not sternly punished, it required a more formal response than could be given by one of the lesser policing bodies because it injured another power center in society—the church.

When clerics involved in the economic life of the commune were assaulted, the Forty seemed more inclined to protect them with stern penalties. In the fourteenth century, a cleric who could read and write was still an important asset to society. Along with secular notaries and lawyers, he was a technician of the revolution that first made capitalism possible—the "contractualization" of personal relationships. His ability to manipulate the written word and to record transactions was essential to the development of an efficient profit-making society. Although Venice was making an effort to discontinue the use of clerics as notaries, they were still very active, even as low-level communal officials. The case of presbyter Jacobi illustrates the value of their skills for Venetian society. His titles make him sound like a proto-Renaissance man, even if he was a cleric: "provincialis, Archipresbyter Torcellansis, olim scribe ad Officium Advocatorum Comunis et nunc ad Officium Superconsulum." He was attacked by three men, two of them petty officials of the Auditori Vecchi. Their motive is not clear, but it apparently involved a dispute about communal business. In an unusual move, the doge and his councilors, as was their prerogative, ordered the Avogadori di Comun to prepare the case for the Forty. The Forty sentenced the leader of the assault, Pietro Bono of Treviso, to three years in jail to be followed by banishment for life. It also ordered his crime and penalty announced at the Rialto. An assailant who escaped, Francescino Collegario, was to receive the same penalty as Pietro if captured; and a reward of 50 lire di piccoli was offered. The final culprit, apparently only a minor accomplice, served six months in jail and was perpetually deprived of all communal offices.[28]

Certain clerics were integrated into the economic life of society and thus as susceptible to a wide range of attacks as any other group in the population. Many of them were set apart, however, because they represented more serious political, social, or economic concerns. When this was so, the Avogadori and the Forty took action to protect the interests of the commune and to give the proceedings an air of considered importance.

The Significance of Assault

The outstanding feature of all the prosecutions for assault by the Forty is the relative restraint of the penalties, especially for assaults that came close to murder. The mutilations of the medieval world were far distant from penalties that averaged 24.8 points for all assaults of a serious enough nature to be brought before the Forty or penalties that averaged only 16.0 points for the nobility.

The Forty also established a division within the category of assault. On the basis of an initial subjective reading of the data, it was assumed that because the Avogadori made such a careful record of whether or not blood was shed in an assault, the spilling of blood marked a perceptual dividing line. A second separation was assumed to divide cases of bloodshed from those where the victim was in danger of dying. Analysis of the data, however, reveals that this threefold distinction was not accurate. Bloodshed was the only significant dividing point for ranking the seriousness of assault cases. The validity of this division is supported by the early legislation of the *Promissio Maleficorum,* where assault with a weapon that drew blood was treated as a more serious crime than mere assault.[29]

In the fourteenth century, the weapon was not so crucial as the fact that blood was drawn. Of course it was usually easier to get blood flowing with a weapon, but a determined man with his bare hands could often cause an "effusione sanguinis"—the phrase used to describe a situation where enough blood had been shed to distinguish a crime of bloodshed from a bloody nose or lip.

When assault cases are divided into these two major categories, significantly different profiles of the penalties become visible. The average penalty for assault without bloodshed was 11.9 points for 281 cases. This penalty is not only low but also significantly below the average penalty for crimes of speech. Perhaps a factor of diminishing concern is operating here. Crimes of speech, to justify interference at all, had to imply the threat of more serious disruption to follow; but petty brawls, even those singled out for attention by the Forty, were part of a steady level of violence that the nobility accepted and avoided exacerbating through harsh penalties. Although illegal, an occasional fistfight was more acceptable than harsh words that threatened more.

In contrast, assaults where blood was shed were far more serious, carrying an average penalty of 40.0 points for 237 cases. This is equivalent to about two years in jail or a fine of 400 lire di piccoli. Even this is not especially harsh considering that it is the average for the most serious type of assault heard by the highest regular court that judged these crimes.

Blood, or the lack of it, was not the only factor in the Forty's perception of crime. These judges were politically and socially sensitive, also taking into account the social relationships, political context, and power realities of a case. Technical questions of jail capacity were a further limitation upon the size of both fines and jail sentences. By themselves, however, these factors are not enough to explain the low penalties for middle-range violence. As the discussion on murder shows in greater relief, crimes of passion were considered less serious than crimes of self-interest. Man was regarded as a passionate and violent creature (though perhaps for different reasons among the nobility than at other social levels); and a certain level of violence was accepted as normal. Violence had to be kept under control, but there was little notion that stricter punishments would reduce the violence of passion. Punishment for all violence was the goal—in order to control less passionate forms of violence and provide a legalized form of vengeance that would keep passion from becoming vendetta. At best, perhaps, the certainty of punishment would somewhat improve the situation.

The Venetian nobility did not believe that rational considerations like weighing the possibility of severe punishment would deter people from committing crimes that were perceived as explosions of passion. Men did not yet think themselves cooly rational enough to be stopped by such logic. Jacobo Tiepolo, who was responsible for the great thirteenth-century codification of Venetian law, summed up this attitude in the introduction to the *Promissio Maleficorum* with his call for "unceasing vigil" as the best method for controlling crime.[30] This vigil was considerably extended in the fourteenth century by an increase in police patrols to control violence in the streets. At the same time, the stern penalties for assault advocated by the *Promissio* were ignored in practice by the Forty.

Chapter X

RAPE

Rape and Changing Sexual Values

Violent sexual crimes—rape, attempted rape, and sexual molestation—are strictly speaking no more than a special subset of assault.[1] But "no more than" is a crucial qualifier because the distinction a given society makes between violent sexual crime and assault in general helps to reveal the sexual values of that society. One might even argue that this distinction provides a rough measure of the strength of sexual taboos in that society. If this is true, Early Renaissance Venice was a city where the traditional Christian sexual mores of the Middle Ages had lost much of their weight. The penalties for sexual assault reveal that it was perceived as a minor crime.

This is not the usual interpretation of the strength of sexual taboos in the cities of Early Renaissance Italy. Rape has traditionally been associated with such major crimes as homicide and treason.[2] Perhaps Venice was an exception, but historians have not treated it as such. Stanley Chojnacki, in a pioneering article on violence, concludes that for rape in fourteenth-century Venice "the penalty was very heavy."[3]

In fact, sexual criminality in general—and rape in particular—were viewed as minor offenses against the victim and against Venetian society.[4] The explanation for this is at once simple and complex. On the level of facile generalization, one might say that the urban, mercantile environment of Venice made it impossible for family or society to enforce certain traditional taboos. The population was sexually unstable: husbands were frequently away with the fleet, and young men were attracted from the mainland by the city's promise of labor and riches. These circumstances created dangerous fluctuations in the male–female ratio. Add to this the urban custom common to most of northern Italy of late marriage for males to inexperienced young females, which created difficult sexual tensions both before and after marriage, and one has plenty of motives for the frequent transgression of taboos.

More subtle factors also help explain the disappearance of parts of the sexual taboo, a primary one being the social composition of Venetian society. Sex crimes directed against lower classes were treated with great leniency by the nobility. First, women were less important than men and assaults against them were considered a lesser matter; and second, lower-class women were markedly less important than other women and their sexual victimization was accepted by those who enforced the laws. In this climate, traditional taboos were so easily violated by the nobility that they became difficult to maintain. They may even have been discarded as a form of emotional self-defense against the sexual aggressiveness of the powerful.

Many examples have already been presented of this sexual exploitation, and the records are filled with others; but one case in particular illustrates perfectly the acceptance of the sexual power of the nobility by the lower classes. Three young rapists, all carpenters, conspired to rape a young girl without beating or threatening her and gained their objective by claiming to be nobles from the large and powerful Morosini family. In their prosecution before the Forty, their lie was mentioned as though it was the equivalent of a threat or beating, constituting the duress that made the crime rape. This attitude implicitly reveals the sexual power of the nobility, which combined with the conditions of urban living to loosen the sexual taboos of the city.[5]

The Significance of Rape

The weakening of sexual taboos is most clearly evidenced by the moderate penalties for rape and attempted rape imposed by the Forty throughout the period.[6] Calculations based on the point scale established earlier show that the average penalty for 269 successfully prosecuted rapes was 22.6 points and the average penalty for 109 attempted rapes was 22.8 points. The average for attempted rape seems to be an anomaly, but its virtual equivalency with rape is linked to another important factor in such penalties. In the eyes of the nobility, there was much more to these cases than the sexual molestation of a woman. The amount of force used; the violence used to enter the victim's home; the age, social, and marital status of the victim; and the social status of the culprit—all played a role in the size of the penalties imposed. These variables were largely independent of the success of the rape itself.

Dropping thirteen rape cases with exceptional penalties from the total lowers the average penalty for rape to 17.2 points; similarly, dropping nine attempted rapes lowers the average penalty for this crime to 15.1 points.[7] This implies that the typical jail sentence for both crimes was considerably less than a year. In fact, the median penalty for both crimes is just slightly above 10 points, i.e., six months in jail or 100 lire di piccoli. When one considers that these penalties often covered other crimes committed in conjunction with the sexual crime, one has a clear view of just how low the status of the taboos had sunk. Rape and attempted rape were not major crimes at all in the eyes of the nobility; they had become petty offenses of little consequence to the commune.

This interpretation appears to be contradicted by the fact that the Forty, a body with so much political and social power, was given responsibility for these crimes. It seems odd that the council entrusted with such sensitive matters as assault on state officials or foreign dignitaries should waste its time hearing sexual crimes. In fact, it is apparent from the records that the judges of the Forty did so with little interest, merely because this was part of the traditional responsibility inherited from the previous century, when sexual crimes were considered more serious. The briefs for sexual cases are much shorter than the briefs for other cases, and they usually contain little detail, as if there was little worth reporting in such crimes.

Another reason the Forty retained jurisdiction may have been to achieve a safe consensus in decisions where guilt or innocence were, in the eyes of a male-oriented society, difficult to prove. Rape was often a subjective matter, and the Forty, which had more than forty members, could at least give a more representative decision in difficult cases than could a smaller body. This was especially important in cases where both victim and assailant were nobles and the crime assumed a significance far beyond its sexual dimensions. Finally, because rape was theoretically a more complex subset of assault, it belonged to the council that heard other complex cases of assault that stopped short of murder.

In reading the records of these cases, one is struck by the small role played by the description of the physical violation of the victim. The act itself is usually described in a few formulaic expressions, such as "cognovit carnaliter per vim," or some variation on that phrase that conveys little of the physical brutality of the crime. Other antiseptic formulas include, "fornicationis per vim," "forcia," and "violasse per vim." Such reticence can hardly be attributed to prudery because parallel documents describe with elaborate detail the physical aspects of homosexual and bestial encounters.[8] Rape was just not important enough to merit close scrutiny. Perhaps a certain reticence in the records also made it easier to impose a mild penalty.

When a more complete description is given, it usually applies to an abnormal case where stiff penalties were handed down. For example, a small trader named Nicolo had enough wealth to hire a young girl of twelve to help his wife with housework. In an attempt to take advantage of the girl, he sent his wife on an errand; then, the records say, "he grabbed the girl violently, putting one arm around her shoulders, and holding her hands, began kissing her. Next he threw her on the floor, lifted her clothes up and got on top of her, trying by force to corrupt her." The girl fought and screamed, and Nicolo finally abandoned his effort. Although it was an unsuccessful attempt, the penalty was still considerably above the norm—one year in jail and a fine of 25 lire di piccoli.[9] Nicolo's crime was especially serious because it was directed against a *puella,* a girl who had not yet reached puberty. Most of the cases that bother to record the physical nature of the crime deal with *puellae* and reflect an enduring strong taboo against sexual advances toward children.[10] When the victim was not a *puella,* the actual crime was usually masked behind bland formulas that matched the bland penalties imposed.

Violence and Resistance

The bland formulas, however, do refer formally to the violence of the crime. It is "cognovit carnaliter per vim"; and although this phrase has the ring of a forced handshake, the element of force is still identified. Nevertheless, the main reason for the reference to force was the need to support the contention that the case was one of rape, not one of adultery or fornication, always a problematic aspect of rape cases. Apparently, the all-male Council of Forty often had doubts about the level of participation or cooperation of the victim. Thus although "cognovit carnaliter" was used interchangeably with "fornicationis" or "adulteria," the addition of "per vim" or some other modifier that implied violence to any of these made it a more serious crime.

If possible, the cases prepared by the Avogadori did go into some detail about the resistance, usually verbal, put up by the victim. In a strange coincidence with modern antirape tactics, many fourteenth-century women are reported to have yelled "fire" rather than "rape" to summon assistance from their neighbors or passersby. In 1360, Donata, wife of a builder, was attacked in her own bed. She screamed, "fire, fire!" causing the house to awake; her assailant then jumped out of the window into a convenient canal and swam off. He was a neighbor, as was often the case in such crimes, and easily apprehended.[11] A similar case showing continuity of the practice involved Catarina, wife of Jacobo Darmo, and her mother Lucia. In 1400, the women were at home when they were attacked by three men who broke down the door of the house. They put up a fight and screamed, "fire, fire!" This time the document gives the actual words in dialect, not bothering to translate their screams into Latin, "fuogo, fuogo"; and once more, the trick worked. Their attackers fled as neighbors arrived to put out the fire.[12]

Women sometimes resisted with more than screams. Zaneta, a young wife five months pregnant, defended herself so strongly from a wool worker carrying a sword, even after she was seriously wounded in the face, that the Avogadori paid her their compliment of referring to her self-defense as "viriliter" (manly). The Forty dealt out a severe penalty to her assailant. It is an exemplary case because so many factors entered into the penalty besides the attempted rape. First, Zaneta was five months pregnant, and an attack of any sort on a woman in this condition was serious. Second, her home had been broken into. Third, she was recognized as a "young woman . . . of good condition and reputation," which was reflected in her spirited defense against her assailant. Last, and perhaps most important, her assailant hit her in the face with a sword, a blow that must have been disfiguring. For the Forty, this made the crime much more than a simple attempted rape. The culprit was taken to the *contrata* where he and the victim lived as neighbors; he was beaten around the neighborhood then brought before her house and branded three times on the face, a symbolic disfigurement reflecting his destruction of his victim's beauty. After this, he was led to the Rialto where his guilt was proclaimed. He was then jailed for a year, after which he was perpetually banished from Venice and all subject territory.[13]

Although Zaneta's struggle was unusual, at least according to the records preserved, in proving a case of rape before the Forty some evidence of resistance was important. The case of a certain Francesca, daughter of Bartolomeo, reveals this. Francesca had been abducted and raped by Nanino Antelini with the help of two accomplices. The tables were turned on Francesca when she was accused, probably by her assailants, of assenting to the crime with "great damage to her father, mother, and brother." It was to the advantage of the assailants to establish this point because the victim's cooperation transformed the crime (high-sounding rhetoric aside) into the less serious matter of fornication. The case against Nanino and his helpers was carefully argued by the Avogadori to disprove the point. They stressed the force used in the abduction, the use of weapons, and the cries for help by both the girl and her mother. Again, the women called "fire, fire!" rather than "rape," but this time to no avail. The girl was carried away from Venice, raped several times, then returned home. The Forty accepted these signs of force as proving Francesca's case. They absolved her and gave Nanino and his helpers relatively stiff penalties. Reference to force was a crucial part of the trial brief, and resistance on the part of the victim helped significantly in establishing a strong case.[14]

Associated Violence

Beyond establishing the violent nature of the attack, the rest of the material in the Avogadori's brief, usually the majority of it, was concerned with matters that had little to do with the actual sexual assault. The reason for this concentration on subsidiary matters was, at least in part, to adjudicate other areas of violence that added seriousness to the crime. Because rape was so unimportant in itself, the concomitant factors, such as breaking and entering, threatening with a weapon, drawing blood, or abduction, added importance to the crime.

Breaking and entering was common, many women being raped while sleeping in their own beds, unlikely as that may seem. Paradoxically, if the assailant broke and entered for the purpose of taking anything but a woman, it was treated as an extremely serious crime, normally resulting in the mutilation of the culprit at least; but in rape, it merely added to the seriousness of a minor crime. A typical example of the way in which breaking and entering overshadowed the rest of the crime is a gold worker's attempted rape of a sailor's wife, who lived in the same neighborhood. The total description of the crime is, "he wished to violate her and at night he broke into her house by force." This taciturn account emphasizes the fact that the Forty was usually concerned with more than mere rape.[15]

In fact, when the rape occurred at the victim's home, the Avogadori described how entrance was effected. Usually it was by force, but some rapists were more subtle. One case, where workers claimed to be nobles to secure entrance, has already been mentioned; others entered as neighbors or friends; and some used power of another sort.[16] The noble Daniele Moro got into the home of Maria, a worker's wife, by claiming that he was there in an official capacity as a representative of the commune. He threatened that if she did not open her door she would be arrested. She let him in, he raped her, and he got by with a mild penalty. He was deprived of his communal office and fined 25 lire di piccoli. No restrictions were placed on future office holding, and the fine was a trifle for an important noble like Moro.[17]

Often a rapist entered his victim's home when she was out and hid in her room, often under the bed. This seems a singularly unlikely place to hide, but it is frequently mentioned in the records. The results of this strategy, however, were often more humorous than harmful. Bernardo Cimator hid under the bed of a business associate's wife while she was out. He waited and waited, but she did not return. Finally he got cold feet; but he was apprehended as he tried to sneak out of the room.[18] Hiding under the bed may have been a maneuver preferred by men who hoped they would be accepted as lovers rather than rapists. The culprit put himself in a dangerous situation because he had little control over who would enter the room with his victim. This tactic was also likely to be used in a crime that involved neighbors or associates who had information about the house and the best time to enter it. A case where acceptance was apparently anticipated involved the noble Raynucio Dandolo, a man from an important family. His chosen victim was the wife of a hat maker, who might have appreciated the attentions of a noble of good family. When he emerged from under the bed, however, he met with nothing but screams and resistance. After a half-hearted attempt to secure his goal by force, he fled.[19]

For some, the door was opened without the bother of breaking and entering. Men of wealth and power could often commit rape without the unpleasantness of breaking down doors or climbing through windows. Wealth and power have a force in themselves; but when doors are opened by such means, the criminal records are normally silent. Occasionally these well-laid plans were disrupted, giving a glimpse into an activity that must have been much more prevalent than the records indicate. In 1375, the noble Domenico Polani was not only welcomed by the mother of his victim, a young girl who had not yet reached puberty, he was also helped in the deed itself. It is not clear how the crime came to the attention of the authorities, but Polani was captured and the girl's mother fled Venice.[20]

A lesser man usually relied on a more direct and violent entrance into the home of his victim. This lower-class directness is exemplified by a young man identified merely as Leonardo, son of Marco, who one summer night presented himself before a neighbor's house on the Giudecca, completely nude but armed. He broke in and tried to rape the daughter of the house, wounding those who interfered. The Avogadori's brief has so many details about his direct assault that it never clearly specifies whether the attack attained its goal. Evidently that was a small matter compared to the outrageousness of a naked, armed man terrorizing a whole household in the pursuit of a sexual victim.[21]

It is difficult to measure how much breaking and entering concerned the Forty because so many other factors were involved in these cases as well. One indication comes from a case that did not even make it to the level of attempted rape. In 1385, a builder named Cristoforo, who originally came from Verona, earned the dubious distinction of being the only male in the records who failed not only in his rape but also in his effort to break into his neighbor's house to make the attempt. A rather sad criminal and ironically a rather sad builder (one expects men who build homes to be able to destroy them), Cristoforo was sent to jail for four months for his failure.[22] This is a penalty of about 6.6 points on the scale set up earlier. If the penalty is at all representative, it means that in rapes where breaking and entering was involved, or in more than three-fourths of all cases, the penalties were overvalued by about 6.6 points. This would reduce the average penalty for successful rapes to 12.2 points. The statistic is inexact, but it suggests how minimal a crime rape could be when penalties are adjusted for breaking and entering.[23]

A rape did not always occur in the victim's home. In a significant number of cases, women were attacked in the streets or in boats or abducted. Abduction definitely added to the seriousness of the crime in the eyes of the Forty. Often, the woman was merely taken to the offender's home and kept there. Two millers, Vendramino and Jacobino, who worked at the Molendina Stenchi, kidnapped Agneta, a young girl who was living with Dardi Cancharello, a governmental official. They carried her off to the mill and raped her. The Forty reacted sternly to the crime, which in addition to the kidnapping and rape had been directed against a communal official. Both men were sentenced to four days in a *berlina,* five years in jail, and perpetual banishment from Venetian territory.[24] This was an extreme penalty, but the opposite may be seen in the rape of Anna, slave of Michaleto Dolfin. The Avogadori claimed that the noble Checo Duodo carried her off to a vacant house he owned and there raped her. The Forty, however, absolved the nobleman.[25]

A case with less social distance between victim and culprit provides a better model. A servant, Antonio da Cernia, raped a certain Elizabeta, a slave. Several of Antonio's friends, all servants themselves, cooperated to carry Elizabeta off to Antonio's lodgings. After the details of the abduction, the rape seems almost incidental to the Avogadori's brief; but Antonio, along with Facio da Ferrara, Bolezino da Bologna, and Martino Furlano, were convicted for rape and abduction and sentenced to short jail terms (three to four months) and small fines (25 lire di piccoli). Abduction heightened the seriousness of the crime, but other factors such as the relative social equality between victim and culprit were probably more important in the final penalty.[26]

Beating or wounding a victim was also stressed more than the rape itself. This aspect of the crime followed the distinction identified in assaults between beatings that drew blood and those that did not. The descriptions of beatings use the same formulas as the assault records. When Zanino Zen attacked Alegreza, wife of a boatman, not only did he rape her but he also wounded her and her mother as well. The rape was, as usual, barely mentioned; but the blows landed and the damage done to mother and daughter were carefully and completely described. Alegreza was wounded by a knife slash on the left arm "cum effusione sanguinis," and her mother was beaten and slashed above the left eye, also "cum effusione sanguinis." The Avogadori reported the physical nature of the wounds with great care but left the rape as a distant abstraction. The prosecution's case centered more on the bloodshed than on the rape of Alegreza. If caught, Zanino was to serve one year in jail. A reward of 25 lire di piccoli was offered, which Zanino was required to pay himself (an interesting technique used by the Forty to reduce the cost of justice) before he began serving his jail sentence.[27]

Leaving the rape aside, Zanino's penalty for the assault alone seems quite restrained in comparison with the norms established earlier for assault cases. This was typical of cases involving sexual crimes: something about them made the whole less serious than the sum of its parts. It is clear that factors like breaking and entering, abduction, or assault all added to the seriousness of the crime; but even so, the penalties remained well below the level associated with these separate offenses. Perhaps the best example of this is the area of rape plus theft. Theft was usually punished by mutilation or death, but theft in conjunction with rape was perceived as a much less serious crime. In 1373, a notary named Bartolomeo broke into the house of Thomisina, raped her, and stole a purse containing 4 ducats and 28 soldi di piccoli. If he had only stolen the purse, he would by law have been mutilated at least.[28] Fearing the worst, Bartolomeo fled the city; but instead of mutilation, he was given a sentence of a year in jail and a fine of 100 lire di piccoli, a punishment of 30 points. For rape, it was a stiff response; for robbery, it was a token penalty.[29]

Examples could be multiplied. In 1350, Pietro Sanuto, a noble relative of Marin Sanuto Il Vecchio of crusading fame, launched his own little crusade against Penina, wife of Marco dalla Stava. He not only succeeded with his rape but also carried off 70 ducats in spoils as well, a crime which in legal theory required hanging. Instead, the Forty instructed him to return the 70 ducats and pay an additional fine of 50 ducats. This was a stiff fine for rape, but much milder than hanging.[30]

What took place in these cases to create this perceptual myopia? Why were these serious crimes less serious when committed in the context of rape? There are several likely factors. First, rape was so unimportant, seen almost as a boyish prank or indiscretion, that its associated crimes were similarly discounted. As a consequence, the penalties were not designed to control robbery or assault; they were aimed at rape, although the concomitant acts added to the seriousness of that offense. In other words, the Forty believed that it was dealing not with robbers or serious assailants, but with rapists who were "forced" by the situation—carried away by the passion of the moment—to be more criminal than the rape implied. It is significant that most rapist-robbers tried by the Forty were members of the upper classes, who had little need of their spoils and were not, in the eyes of the nobility, likely to threaten society with their need to rob.[31] A second factor, closely related to the first, is that rape was viewed as a crime of simple passion. Passion tended to purify the crimes associated with it. Passionate sexual violence, although not socially acceptable, was a comprehensible and nonthreatening part of the nobility's world. Even in conjunction with assault or robbery, rape interfered little with the essential order of that world.

Types of Rape

Rape was also perceived to have five separate degrees. The distinctions were based not upon social position, which provided another whole range of subtleties, but upon the stage a woman had reached in her life cycle. At least four stages can be discerned in the records of rape crimes: a presexual period, lasting until the age of twelve, during which a girl was referred to as a *puella;* a short intermediate period when a woman was of marriageable age and perhaps most sexually dangerous; a period of marriage; and finally, for those women who lived through the childbearing years and survived their husbands, a period of widowhood. A fifth status for women with implications both for the cycle of life and for social position comprised those married to the church as nuns. Nunneries were not only spiritual havens for the committed; they were also places for women who for economic reasons did not otherwise fit into the regular life cycle.[32]

Rape of Children

Although the violence of rape was not regarded as particularly serious, there were stages in a woman's life when it was dealt with more harshly. Female children were not viewed as little adults, as Aries has theorized about premodern childhood; and their victimization was much more serious than the rape of other women. For 42 rapes of *puellae,* the average penalty was 43.3 points, more than double the norm for all rapes. Furthermore, as noted earlier, the rape of children was the one category where the Avogadori went into detail about the crime itself.[33] In the Forty's view, it was a reprehensible sexual act. Implicit in this is a belief in the sexual innocence of children under a certain age, which again cannot be easily reconciled with Aries's thesis about children as miniature adults.

The rape of *puellae* also gives information about society's perception of the duration of this prepubertal age of innocence and indicates that it advanced slightly in the second half of the century. Before the 1360s, twelve was the maximum age of *puellae.* In fact, ages greater than this were not mentioned in rape cases, suggesting that the victim's age ceased to be a factor in the consideration of the crime once she had reached thirteen. From the 1360s, however, one finds occasional references to *puellae* of thirteen and in two cases, to *puellae* of fourteen. This apparent advance of the dividing age was not merely an upper-class phenomenon: Anna, a slave and servant of the apothecary Giovanni da Sabardia, was raped in 1401 by Rambaldo Rambaldo, and she was identified as a *puella* by the Avogadori, though she was already fourteen. This was not merely a mistake or a change in scribal convention. Although the girl came from the lowest social class, her attacker was given a six-month jail sentence and fined 200 lire di piccoli. The victim was to receive half of this to buy her freedom. The Forty saw this fourteen-year-old girl as an object of its sympathy, which seems paradoxical considering its attitude toward servant and slave girls a few years older unless the special innocence of being a *puella* is taken into account. It is possible that the distinction between a *puella* and a girl of marriageable age was a flexible one based upon the physical maturity of the girl. Nonetheless, it is significant that for the last years of the period under study the dividing age seemed to be getting higher.[34]

Age put an upper limit on the *puella* group, but it placed hardly any lower limit at all. Men were accused of raping or attempting to rape girls as young as four.[35] The youngest victim to have her rapist successfully prosecuted, however, was "six or seven."[36] There seems to have been little escalation of penalties as the victims got younger; they were viewed by the Forty as a group, and within it relative age was unimportant. The only distinction where age was a factor had to do with very young girls. Securing the conviction of those who raped or attempted to rape the very young was difficult—perhaps because such girls were too young to testify themselves and perhaps because the Forty was wary of attempts by parents to secure dowries through accusations of rape.[37]

An atypical case of the rape of a *puella,* which reveals the complexities of the Venetian sexual scene, involved Pietro Solario and his sister-in-law Catarucia, a nun who lived in a convent in Padua. Pietro first raped Catarucia when she was twelve, but the relationship continued after the crime. In fact, it continued after Catarucia became a nun; after Pietro's wife died; continued, in fact, until Pietro was arrested after the birth of five children to the illicit couple. In theory, Pietro's crime covered the whole range of heterosexual criminality in Renaissance Venice: he had raped a child, been an adulterer, committed incest, and violated a nun; and he had apparently done quite well until his crime came to light. Nonetheless, for breaking virtually every heterosexual taboo society had, Pietro's penalty was not overwhelming. If caught (for he had wisely fled the city), he was to serve three years in jail and pay a fine of 300 lire di piccoli, after which he would be banished.[38]

Most rapists of children were less versatile than Pietro, but they were still quite reprehensible in the eyes of the Venetian nobility. They profaned the innocence of childhood, and the Forty demonstrated a sympathy for the victims by punishing their attackers strictly and occasionally by providing dowries for the victims, an act of charity singularly uncharacteristic of that council. Of 167 unmarried victims of sexual assault in the period, only 41 received dowries; and by far the largest proportion of those were *puellae.* Dowries were received by 46 percent of the *puellae* attacked, while only 15.4 percent of the girls of marriageable age were so treated. The nobility was wary of creating a situation where an accusation of rape could become a form of blackmail of the rich. Nonetheless, the rape of a child was so serious that when it could be proved the judges were often willing to set aside a part of the fine—to be invested with the Grain Office or in government loans—to give the victimized girl a chance to marry.

For example, the noble Nicoleto Zorzi was accused of raping an eight-year-old girl, but the case was difficult to prove. Nicoleto was strongly suspected, however; and he was finally tortured by a *collegio* made up of two ducal councilors, one Avogador, and two Signori di Notte, to whom he eventually confessed. The use of torture on a noble accused of rape indicates immediately how seriously the Forty regarded Nicoleto's crime. His penalty was a fine of 500 lire di piccoli and six months in jail. One-half the fine was to be invested as a dowry for Nicoleto's victim. Eight years later, the girl married the son of a boatman, bringing with her a handsome dowry of 99 gold ducats and 25 soldi di piccoli.[39]

Rape of Unmarried Women

Although the rape of *puellae* was a serious crime, that of girls who had passed puberty was just the opposite. When a girl passed this magic age, the Forty abruptly perceived her sexual violation as a matter of little concern. An average penalty of 43.3 points for the rape of *puellae* drops to 16.4 points for the rape of unmarried girls of marriageable age. When childhood's innocence passed, much of society's solicitude for the victim also vanished. The Marquis de Sade argued that the rape of unmarried women should be a minor crime in society's eyes because the rapist "has done no more than place a little sooner the object he has abused in the very state in which she would soon have been put by marriage and love."[40] In this, he was not so radically insane as has been assumed; in the Venice of the Early Renaissance, he would have found his fantasy to be a common operating assumption. In fact, the Forty occasionally followed de Sade's dictum to a logical and medieval conclusion by offering the rapist the choice of paying a penalty or marrying his victim. Zanino Viscia, for instance, was offered three options after raping a laborer's daughter who was away from her home learning the art of dressmaking. He could either pay 40 soldi di grossi or spend six months in jail or marry the girl. If he chose the last option, he was also required to credit the girl with a dowry of 20 soldi di grossi.[41] Zanino could put the "object he . . . abused in the very state" of marriage, if not love. Medieval tradition and the cost of dowries were important factors in this judicial solution. It is difficult to reconstruct from the documents how the procedure actually worked. The parents or the victim probably indicated a willingness to marry the assailant, a move that would obviate the difficult problem of raising a dowry. It is possible that some of these rapes involved consent rather than violence.[42]

Too much should not be made of the continuity of this medieval tradition; the great majority of rapists paid so lightly for their crimes that marriage may have seemed to them by far the stiffer penalty. Nicoleto, who raped Cristina, daughter of Gerardo, was penalized 50 lire di piccoli.[43] The nobles Zusto Foscari and Mafeo Querini raped two young sisters, breaking into their house to do it. They were given one-month jail sentences.[44] In the context of such penalties, the Forty's attitude was clear; rape of girls of marriageable age was not at all serious.

This generalization must always be qualified by the fact that the rape of unmarried women was, and remains, a hard crime to prove in a male-dominated society. *Puellae* innocent of sexual knowledge could be assumed to be innocent victims; but once puberty was reached, the situation changed drastically; and young women had to be watched closely to be kept out of sexual trouble. The fourteenth-century moralist, Fra' Paolino Minorita, warned in Venetian dialect that when a girl reached the age of puberty "one must watch her carefully to make sure that she does not wander about . . . in order that she does not fall into evil." [45] One evil was sexual. The criminal records of fornication and adultery reveal that young women did in fact participate willingly in such activities. To a degree, moderate rape penalties may reflect uncertainty about the element of female complicity in the crime. The border between fornication and rape was hard for a male Venetian noble to define, especially when the victims were young women of marriageable age. Still, it is clear that the rape of an unmarried woman from the lower classes was considered unimportant.

Rape of Married Women and Widows

Rape of a married woman was a more serious matter. The average penalty for 153 cases was 21.8 points, far below the norm for the rape of a *puella* but considerably more than the average for the rape of unmarried women. Two factors seem to be involved. First, a married woman was a more valued member of society; she had proved her value and her right to a position in the world by producing a dowry that allowed her to advance to the full status of womanhood—marriage. She had therefore reached a state of importance that made sexual assault against her a graver crime. Moreover, by virtue of this state she had become a piece of property—an asset to her husband as a wife rather than a liability to her parents as a daughter requiring the sacrifice of a dowry. This state of value achieved through marriage once more transformed a woman in the eyes of the Forty.

A secondary factor was the belief that married women were slightly less likely than unmarried women to encourage sexual advances. They had no need to entice men into marriage; they had no motive to seek dowries through accusations of rape; they had no reason to make a charge of rape to explain their loss of virginity or their pregnancy. Of course, if caught in bed with a lover a married woman might claim rape, but on the whole the Forty felt more secure in dealing with rape of married women as a violent crime. As a result, married women, as *realized* women or more important women, were less likely to invite rape and therefore more protected than unmarried women.

Widows, although there are few cases in which they were clearly involved, occupy a middle ground in penalties, with an average of 18.7 points for 16 cases. Although this is not a large enough sample to provide a basis for analysis, it is suggestive. A widow apparently commanded respect although her importance had nonetheless been diminished by the death of her husband. There may also have been a fear of the mature sexuality of older women that contributed to lesser penalties.[46] One reason for the low level of prosecution for the rape of widows may be that they were found more commonly among the upper classes and were less likely to be attacked. Noble rapists had a large field from which to choose their victims, and they probably preferred easier targets.

Rape of Nuns

The rape of nuns was a popular diversion, especially for the nobility. However, it was a crime that had to be treated with caution as the Forty learned during the trecento. In the years before 1360, the convent of San Lorenzo had been a trouble spot for rape. It was a preferred target for young noble ruffians, who periodically clambered over the walls to rape the young nuns within, who were also of noble background. In 1360, the communal authorities were finally forced to admit that something was wrong at San Lorenzo when a minor noble named Moreto Boccassio and four friends, all but one of them noble, were caught in bed with five nuns. Two other nobles were caught at the convent as well, but they were accused of no more than stealing chickens. The obvious problem was that these young men had not encountered the kind of resistance that argued for rape. In the course of the investigation, the Avogadori learned that Boccassio had been a regular visitor to the nunnery, another fact that damaged the claim of rape. The case broke when three women, two servants and a slave, who had worked at the convent for a number of years, fled. It was revealed that these women headed a group of workers who had been arranging meetings between lovers and nuns for some time. The nobles who reportedly scaled the walls to rape innocent virgins had actually taken the saner approach of paying to enter through the front door to spend their nights with willing victims. Boccassio and his associates were punished with rigor, and the closely watched convent dropped out of the records of sexual crime for about a generation.[47]

Although this tendency for sexual relations with nuns to be fornication rather than rape makes it difficult to evaluate penalties, those penalties were generally stiff. In addition to the taboos involved and the desire to clean up the convents (which is also mentioned in contemporary documents), many of the nuns were of noble background. As noted earlier, sexual crimes against or with noblewomen were much more serious than crimes against lower-class women.[48]

Rape was a crime of many dimensions, so many that the physical nature of the sexual assault often seems a minor part of the Avogadori's briefs and the Forty's considerations. Breaking and entering, abduction, assault, and theft were elements that made the crime considerably more important than simple rape. Yet it is a strange reflection on the unimportance of rape that all these accompanying crimes themselves became less important in the context of the rape. Perceptually, rape also differed according to the age and status of the victim. When *puellae* were victims, the crime was serious; wives, though much less important, were more valued than widows; and, finally, unmarried girls of marriageable age were so little valued that the penalties for their rapes were minimal. Rape was not perceived as a major crime; and for unmarried victims, the state barely considered it a crime at all. It is no wonder that young nobles with the money to frequent prostitutes and the power to attract mistresses so often preferred simple violence to secure their gratification. Rape was more an excess of youth than a crime both in their eyes and in the eyes of their elders who assigned the criminal penalties. Sexual taboos that were still powerful in literature, sermon, rhetoric, and social theory had already been largely demolished in the unsettled urban environment of Early Renaissance Venice.

Chapter XI

MURDER

Two Approaches to Murder

The proscription of murder comes as close to a moral absolute as one can find, but a society may still condition perceptions of this violent crime. Early Renaissance Venice is a good example. Murder violated the deepest taboos and needs of Venetian society. It disrupted the family, the smooth flow of the economy, and the organization and control of the state. (Murder and robbery were the two most heinous crimes; homosexuality and counterfeiting were punished as harshly, but they were much less regularly prosecuted. Both murder and robbery usually resulted in either the serious mutilation of the criminal or his execution.) Within the context of this harshness, however, there were differences that reveal much about the nature of Venetian perceptions of violence and the organization of Venetian society.

An indication that Venetians made at least one major distinction in murder cases is revealed by the fact that although the Signori di Notte and Giudici di Proprio were by law responsible for homicide prosecutions, many cases were handled by the Avogadori and the Forty.[1] The basis for the division of cases between the two councils is not at first apparent, but to some extent it may have lain in the fact that the Forty was a larger, more politically sensitive body whereas the Giudici di Proprio was a smaller, more technically correct, legalistic group. Cases of political significance were usually heard by the Forty.

One example involved the planned assassination of Ubertino da Carrara, *signore* (ruler) of Padua, while he was visiting Venice in 1340. The leaders of the plot were Paduans led by Francesco Scrovegni (of the important and rich Scrovegni family) and Vitaliano Dente.[2] Together they hired Geminiano da Mutina, former servant of a doctor, to assassinate Carrara. Before the plot could be carried out, it was discovered by communal authorities and Geminiano was arrested. Dente, who was in Venice at the time, managed to escape. The Forty stepped in to handle the conspiracy because of the need for diplomatic subtlety and a communal response—a response that was both logical and diplomatically sound: Dente and Scrovegni, absent foreigners, were banned perpetually from

Venice. In this way, the facade of justice was preserved without the Forty in any way attempting to extend communal justice beyond its own territory. Geminiano, who had been captured in Venice, was sent to jail for three years, to be followed by perpetual banishment. The response was restrained but correct. The Forty maintained effective neutrality by mildly punishing a crime that grew out of factional strife in Padua without really identifying itself with one faction or the other. Justice was served with no loss to diplomacy.[3]

Although this case was closed to the satisfaction of the Forty, it was reopened by Ubertino da Carrara. Vitaliano Dente had fled Venice, but a relative of his, Lenuzo Dente, still lived there with the Querini family. Ubertino believed that Lenuzo was also involved in the plot against him, or perhaps he wanted to escalate the matter to the level of a family vendetta. Whatever the reason, in 1343 he hired two vagabonds and a barber to murder Lenuzo. Although the plot was elaborate and involved at least three other accomplices, it failed, and the three assassins and one assistant were arrested. Once more, the Forty demonstrated unusual political insight. The paid assassins, being men of "vile condition," were treated harshly as examples. Their eyes were cut out and they were banned perpetually from Venice and its territory. As the instigator of the plot, Ubertino was also liable to prosecution; but the prosecution of a foreign head of state was a delicate problem. The Forty's solution was politically sound: Ubertino was banned perpetually from Venice, and if he broke this ban he was to be brought before the Forty, who would decide at that time what would be done with him. A shrewd solution, this penalty was simultaneously everything and nothing. Perpetual banishment gave the appearance of severity, but if diplomatic necessity warranted, the Forty could as easily welcome Ubertino with open arms as throw him in jail. The penalty kept up the facade of Venetian justice without altering Venetian–Paduan relations at all; one is tempted to refer to it as a rhetorical penalty, which left Venice's options completely open in future dealings with the Carrara.[4]

The Forty enjoyed wide representation from the important families of Venice, plus the regular participation of the doge and his councilors and the advice of the Avogadori di Comun. It was much better suited to handle delicate diplomatic matters than the legally focused and socially isolated Giudici di Proprio. Nevertheless, cases of this type were rare; but although few murders involved diplomatic interests, the Forty handled almost one-fourth of all homicides. One might suspect that the Forty tried all cases involving nobles, but in fact both councils dealt with nobles. The Forty's cases did include a higher proportion of noble criminals than those heard by the Giudici, but this seems to be closely tied to a consideration separate from political and social sensitivity.

The division between the two councils essentially mirrored that distinction between passion and rational self-interest so crucial to Venetian perception of violence. This distinction has been mentioned before; but in the crime of murder, it has a vivid confirmation. Modern jurisprudence draws a related distinction between premeditated murder and unpremeditated murder, but the passion–reason dichotomy of trecento Venice was more wide ranging. A crime of passion might involve some planning, but the dividing line was whether or not it served the self-interest of the criminal or his family. Such a murder was a graver offense.

The passions, in contrast, were accepted because they were an inevitable part of life and their destructive powers were limited. For the Signori di Notte and Giudici di Proprio, murder was a crime of passion; and the elements of passion tended to be stressed in the testimony they took and recorded. They dealt with a kind of homicide that required both compassion and retribution but demanded no heightened political or social awareness. The Forty and Avogadori, in contrast, treated murders that served the interests of individuals or families. As such, these crimes required more careful attention and a strong response to offset the political and social dangers they implied.

Almost every murder heard by the Giudici di Proprio began as a quarrel that escalated to physical violence. The primary goal of the extensive testimony taken by the Signori di Notte, aside from proving guilt, was to determine the source of the emotion that led to the crime. A regular part of the confession of a criminal, in fact, was an explanation of that emotion. Although self-serving, it was important in establishing a case. This is apparent in the testimony concerning the murder of Pietro Tansuro by Nicolino Chavalerio and Bartolomeo della Cava. In his confession, Nicolino described simple passions: one evening in the *contrata* of San Gregorio Pietro and a friend came up to him and said, "Buona sera." Nicolino did not at first respond; then he gave a short reply that Pietro and his friend found lacking in courtesy, for they beat him up, Pietro holding him while his friend did the punching. No one witnessed the attack, and Nicolino was left bruised. The following Monday, after riding on the *traghetto* of Santa Marie Zobenigo, Nicolino and Bartolomeo again met Pietro. Despite the fact that he was alone, he attacked them with a sword. Nicolino and Bartolomeo defended themselves as best they could with the bread knives they were carrying. Bartolomeo was wounded; but the odds were against Pietro, who was stabbed several times and later died as a result of the brawl. The sequence that led to murder was simple enough, according to Nicolino's testimony: a recent quarrel growing out of a slight grew into a brawl with weapons that ended in death. Nicolino's story is obviously full of self-serving details. His report of the murder gave him the excuse of self-defense, and he claimed to be the wronged party in the first, unwitnessed beating.

But there are contradictions in his story. Foremost was the question of why Pietro, having already beaten Nicolino, would attack him again in the company of a friend. Surely it was unnecessary, given the previous beating, and unwise, given the odds. The Signori di Notte noticed this problem and took considerable testimony which established a different story from the one in Nicolino's confession. According to a number of women who had seen the crime, as well as Pietro, who lived long enough to give a deposition, Nicolino and Bartolomeo approached Pietro in the street, got him between them, and began beating and stabbing him. Despite the conflicting stories, the Signori di Notte could construct a fairly clear picture of the crime. Pietro's testimony about the actual attack, supported by the testimony of uninvolved bystanders, revealed that Nicolino and Bartolomeo were the aggressors. The emotional context of the case was an earlier brawl, the exact nature of which was unclear because no impartial witnesses could be found. The formula, however, was clear: words led to a brawl which triggered murderous emotions. This was the Signori di Notte's perceptual model for murder. Identifying this train of events seems to have been their chief goal in taking testimony. Each step in the formula was important both for proving the crime and for deciding the penalty.[5]

A host of motives could be involved in murder cases heard before the Signori di Notte, but they were less important than the emotional context. In contrast, the Forty was more interested in motives because they were the most threatening part of the crimes of self-interest that came before it. Murder motivated by sex illustrates this contrast: sudden jealousy was the usual motive cited by the Signori di Notte whereas cold-blooded planning to eliminate an unwanted husband or wife was the more typical motive of the Avogadori. When Bartolomeo da Ziliolo murdered his wife, the Signori di Notte secured a report on the emotional antecedents of the crime from Bartolomeo's brother who reported that Bartolomeo told him that one night when they were sleeping his wife said that she did not feel well and was going to go into the kitchen to light a fire. He thought nothing of it and went back to sleep, but later he thought he heard noises in the kitchen and called out, "What's happening?" His wife replied that she would come to bed in a moment, and Bartolomeo dozed off again. In the morning, he awoke to hear whispers and giggles ("murmare et zizolare") from the kitchen. Rather than say anything, he sneaked into the kitchen just in time to see a man escaping half-dressed out the door. He chased his wife's lover but was unable to catch him. He then returned, and in the ensuing quarrel, he killed his wife. The emotional model, activated by jealousy and rage, fits the context of the Signori di Notte: words led to a fight that ended with murder.[6]

The Avogadori's cases were different. When Cristina, wife of Zanino Volpe, and her lover, Donato Paxe, killed Zanino, their crime, although sexually motivated, was a model of self-interest in action. The crime was carefully plotted, the unsuspecting Zanino being murdered in his own home and his body quietly disposed of in an attempt to hide the deed. When the body was discovered, the culprits were brought to stern justice.[7] Here the emphasis was on the cold-blooded planning of the murder. No jealousy and little passion were involved; rather, a pair of self-interested lovers eliminated a husband with rational efficiency. Police patrols were no match for such rational crimes of self-interest, and society could not be monitored closely enough to prevent them. The only response that could hope to limit such violence, in the opinion of the nobility, was a policy of stern retribution by the state. The rational person who planned to use violence was promised that his crime would be treated so severely that the danger of punishment far outweighed any advantages to be gained by the violence.

Controlling these crimes seems to have necessitated a strategy of violence that was designed to balance self-interest against fear. The managers of this strategy, the nobles who sat on the Forty, apparently believed that this tactic would work only for crimes of self-interest, where a criminal was likely to calculate risk. In crimes of passion, policing rather than fear was the means for control. The responsibility for murders of self-interest thus fell to the Forty because it was qualified to give broader political and social weight to its deliberations on violence and the penalties to be applied. Further, because upper-class men were disproportionately represented in this category of crime, the Forty's authority was needed to make decisions as acceptable and nondivisive as possible.

Although both the Signori di Notte and Giudici di Proprio and the Avogadori di Comun and Forty dealt with a wide range of motivations for murder, the distinction between passion and self-interest meant that certain types of cases aggregated within each council. The Forty heard most of the cases involving paid assassins, murders committed during robberies, or exposure of infants; whereas the Giudici di Proprio heard cases growing out of drinking and gambling quarrels, street fights, and apparently senseless violence. Although homicides involving family matters, sex, communal business, private business, and vendetta were more ambiguous, in almost every case, the dichotomy between passion and self-interest accounted for the division of governmental responses.

Paid assassins, although a small proportion of the population of recorded murderers, were severely penalized by the Forty.[8] This form of murder was cold-blooded and potentially disruptive to society. In most other murders of self-interest, the victim had at least interfered with the criminal in some way; but murder for hire was strictly a mercenary arrangement. The murder of Semelino da Mosto, a Venetian noble and banker, gives a good picture of the character and danger of these crimes.

Zanino Soranzo, also a noble banker, wanted to have Semelino elimi-nated, apparently for business reasons. Rather than dirtying his own hands with the crime, he hired a local boatman called Blasio to do the job. Given the disparity in wealth between members of the nobility and those at the bottom of society, paying for crimes was both easy for criminals and dangerous to the state. Blasio received 100 gold ducats for the deed and living expenses for two years in Treviso. He proceeded too directly with the job, however, breaking into Semelino's home and dispatching him with a sword. Trapped in the house, he was rapidly apprehended in the ensuing uproar.

Although Blasio had been well paid, he still named Soranzo as his em-ployer, forcing the latter to flee Venice for life: wisely it appears, for the death penalty was imposed on him in absentia and a 400-ducat reward was offered for his capture. Blasio, paid to take the risks, also paid the price for the crime. He was taken by boat to the place of the murder, his guilt proclaimed by a communal herald. There his right hand was cut off and hung by a chain around his neck. His guilt still being proclaimed, he was then led to the *traghetto* nearby, hanged, and left for three days. Noth-ing was spared to drive home the message that crime for pay did not pay.[9]

Still, men were willing to murder for money, and for considerably less than Blasio received. Federico da Ferrara murdered a fur trader for 48 ducats.[10] Baldasera da Valaseno was paid only 6 ducats (plus up to 25 lire di piccoli for living expenses) for a similar crime.[11] The three Florentine assassins discussed earlier, who were hired to kill two fellow Florentines in Venice, received 100 ducats each.[12] Unfortunately, there are not enough cases where the amount paid for murder was reported to recon-struct a normal price for the crime, but it is apparent that the job could be done for less than 100 ducats right through the end of the century. This was not a small sum, but for the powerful of Venice it was no large invest-ment either, and this factor is what made the crime so dangerous. A noble could hire an assassin to eliminate his enemies, or even to kill people who were mere annoyances to him.

Paid assassins, as one would expect, were drawn from the lowest levels of society. Of twenty-eight paid assassins, nine were identified as work-ers, primarily boatmen and rowers; six more were marginal men; and the remaining thirteen had no listed occupations or social position. The dregs of society provided a ready pool of men desperate enough for money, or sufficiently inured to death, to murder for pay.[13]

Murder during the course of a robbery is more difficult to analyze, pri-marily because it was not reported often enough to fit the expected pat-terns of criminality. There are only twenty-six clear cases, accounting for only 6.1 percent of the total murders in the period. The problem is com-pounded by the fact that the Signori di Notte, who investigated most important robberies for trial before the Giudici di Proprio, included few details in their briefs of these cases beyond the value of the goods taken. Their murder briefs, in contrast, are detailed summaries of the testimony taken.

This difference can be linked to the penalties for robbery established in the *Promissio Maleficorum* and in later refinements of that code. These penalties were based upon the value of the goods taken and the number of prior offenses committed by the robber. Accordingly, the briefs intended to aid in prosecution and in the imposition of penalties paid little attention to violence. This perceptual myopia is mitigated by the fact that most robbery cases heard by the Giudici di Proprio ended with death sentences anyway, without recourse to the evaluation of violence. In fact, in terms of percentages the Giudici di Proprio gave out more capital punishment for robbery than for murder. This is an important indication of the relative perceptions of crimes against property and person. Property crimes were the dominant concern.

The Forty heard almost all reported cases of robbery that involved murder as well. The cases selected for special treatment were particularly heinous and uncharacteristic of the violence normally associated with robbery.[14] For example, Bishop Domenico Graffaro was murdered in his bed by two of his slaves and a servant, who planned to steal his rich jewels and accoutrements. The Forty responded brutally. The two slaves who committed the murder were taken by boat to the far end of Venice and then led over land to the home of the bishop, all the while with their guilt being announced. Before the bishop's home, their right hands were cut off and hung by chains around their necks. They were then led to the Rialto, their guilt still being proclaimed. There they were put on meat hooks and dragged to San Marco, where what was left of them was drawn and quartered and hung on view for several days. This penalty was typical of the extreme reactions of the Forty to this type of crime against masters and property.[15]

Equally serious was the Forty's response to a murder and robbery committed by a fellow noble, Tomaso Corner, in the only reported case of such a crime during the century. Corner and a priest, Jacobo Tanto, stole the jewels and silver entrusted to the priestly custodian of St. Mark's Cathedral and killed him in the process. It was apparently not a robbery of the treasury of St. Mark's, for the crime was committed at the priest's house in San Aponal. Nonetheless, many objects of value were carried off, and relations between church and state were seriously compromised by the deed. Corner escaped the city, but he was tried *in absentia* and banned perpetually. The Forty was deadly serious about punishing him, and it offered a reward of 4000 lire for him alive or 2000 lire for him dead. If taken alive, he was promised a ghastly end, not unlike that given to the murdering servants described above: Corner was to be taken by boat to the far end of Venice and then dragged by horses to the scene of the crime; there, he would lose his right hand, which would be hung around his neck on a chain. Last, he would be dragged by horses to San Marco and there drawn and quartered. The quarters were to be hung one on the road to Padua, one on the road to Mestre, one on the road to Chioggia, and one on the Lido. There is no record of Corner's return to Venice.[16]

Murder was a grave offense, but robbery and murder together broke all the taboos in which the Venetian nobility believed most strongly. Perhaps Corner's penalty was so extreme because he was not there to face it and thus it provided a good chance for the Forty to appear strict without actually carrying it through. In the trecento, nobles seldom committed such crimes. They did not need to rob. Officeholding, marriage alliances, and privileged status secured them many opportunities through legitimate channels to live well. The impoverished noble was a feature of a later age. Corner came from a family rich in connections, making his crime all the more serious because it seemed so unnecessary to his peers. For a person of his station, it was self-interest run wild, and it put the nobility in the worst possible light. Further, it created serious problems with the church. As a consequence, the Forty reacted strongly against the crime and its perpetrator.

Exposure of infants was another crime heard by the Forty. It was a crime of self-interest, but it was rarely reported and seldom proved. It is difficult to determine from the cases preserved just why the Forty heard the crime. Perhaps, as a larger body, it was deemed more capable of weighing the likelihood of guilt. The death of a baby born to Catarina, slave of Marco Tuloni, provides a case in point. Catarina was accused of killing her baby by throwing it into a canal. She denied this and continued to deny it under torture. The Forty was finally forced to free her because thirty-five members abstained on the vote for prosecution. Although few believed strongly that she was innocent, they felt that the case against her could not be proved.[17] Most cases ended in such inconclusive decisions. An exception occurred in 1329, when Anna, from Constantinople, was burned for killing her child. Perhaps it is significant that the child was a boy while most of the other cases involved girls.[18]

What stands out in these prosecutions is the strong chance one had of escaping successful prosecution for the exposure of unwanted children. Venice was well situated for this crime, because the canals and natural drainage of the lagoon by the tides made disposal of a body simple. How prevalent the crime was among the lower classes is difficult to assess. That the tendency to use exposure continued through the Renaissance is strongly suggested, however, by the emphasis given to foundling homes in Christian charity. The relationship between foundling homes and exposure has not yet been studied, but surely an important reason for establishing these homes was to provide an alternative to exposure.[19]

The average murder case heard by the Forty fell into no category other than the broadly defined one of self-interest. As noted earlier, the motivation could be similar in cases heard before both courts, but the dividing line was the dichotomy between rationality and passion. Of course, the two were easily confused and often co-existed, but the Venetian nobility took the care to distinguish. From its perceptual perspective, this care was warranted by the dangers inherent in crimes of rationality and self-interest.

In contrast, many of the cases heard by the Giudici di Proprio could be classified as senseless murders. This is partly a result of the emphasis placed on passion in the reports of the Signori di Notte, but to a large extent it reflects reality. A great number of murders, especially among the lower classes, were purposeless explosions of rage, developing out of seemingly trivial incidents. They arose from the deep level of frustration and alienation in lower-class life discussed earlier. Drinking, gambling, or minor brawls were all typical triggers for this violence. One aspect that should be underlined is the rapidity with which lower-class men moved from quarrel to brawl to death, a process that literally resembled an explosion: a minor incident released all the accumulated tensions of lower-class urban life and focused them on an immediate object-victim.[20]

A typical gambling and murder case involved a noble's servant, Nicolo da Padova, and the slave of a painter, Cristoforo Tartare. They were gambling in Campo Santa Marie Formosa ("ludendo ad zonos") when Nicolo decided to leave and began asking for the money he had won. As often happens in such situations, Cristoforo was unwilling to quit a loser and even less willing to pay. Words came to shoves and the men had to be separated by bystanders. Cristoforo almost immediately picked up a club and began chasing Nicolo. Nicolo drew a long knife and stabbed Cristoforo to death. In a matter of a few minutes, an unremarkable quarrel had ended in murder.[21]

Another variation on the same theme, this time involving drinking, occurred in the lodgings of a wool worker named Giuliano. He was drinking with a group of fellow workers. As the evening wore on, an argument began over who was the drunkest and who had been drinking the most. Suddenly, everyone drew weapons; and when the brawl was over, Giuliano lay on the floor dead.[22]

These explosions of passion were the expected context of violent crimes, especially murder. Man was perceived as an unpredictable and violent animal, and it was natural that society should be subjected to such outbursts. This acceptance of the inevitable was somewhat eased by the fact that the nobility seldom fell victim to such outbursts. The nature of the crimes suggests a certain level of familiarity (or at least informal contact) between victim and criminal. Although there was contact between the classes, little of it was informal and it was rarely familiar; thus the nobility seldom found itself victimized by such outbursts. Nonetheless, there seems to have been more to this acceptance of passionate violence than noble self-interest. The realization that such crimes could not be effectively controlled played a part as well. Even though the penalty for murder was usually death, members of the lower classes continued to explode into murderous violence. What could the nobility do but accept the fact that these were natural occurrences beyond the control of the rational organization of society. Arms could be monitored and curfews set; but only the lucky appearance of a communal patrol could stop such outbursts, and increases in patrols decreased the element of chance involved. In the end, patrols could only limit such activity; its elimination was impossible and, apparently, outside the conception of control.

The Significance of Murder

A reflection of this acceptance can be seen in the penalties given out for murder. Death was routine unless a degree of self-defense or extenuating circumstances could be proved. Still, there was a significant difference between the penalties handed out by the Forty for murders of rational self-interest and those imposed by the Giudici di Proprio for passionate murders. Although the records of the Signori di Notte do not always report penalties, in 93 cases, which is a good sample, they are preserved. Penalties imposed by the Forty are known for 118 murderers. They provide a revealing comparison. Murders heard by the Giudici di Proprio, primarily passionate, were punished by death in only 49 percent of the cases, while the self-interest murders heard by the Forty were punished by death in 85 percent of the cases.

A part of this contrast may derive from the fact that many of the murder cases heard by the Giudici di Proprio contained an element of self-defense that might serve as an extenuating factor in the penalties imposed.[23] A closer look at the actual penalties reveals that self-defense alone cannot explain the difference. Ritual executions—those that involved mutilation along with an elaborate symbolic panoply—were strictly the prerogative of the Forty. More than 60 percent of all penalties they handed down for murder called for ritual executions. In contrast, the Giudici di Proprio used only simple executions: hanging (35 percent of all cases), burning (1 percent, reserved for women), and decapitation (13 percent).

Ritual hanging was the most common symbolic execution used by the Forty.[24] It consisted of three basic steps. The criminal was taken, either by boat or through the streets, across the city and then back to the scene of the crime. There his guilt was proclaimed and he was mutilated, usually losing his right hand which was hung on a chain around his neck. He was next conducted back across town to the columns in San Marco, between which he was hanged. More severe variations included dragging the condemned to the place of execution behind a horse, hanging him with a chain, or leaving him hanging for a number of days.

A typical example is the hanging of Bernardo da Forli, convicted of robbery and murder. He was taken by boat to Santa Croce with a herald proclaiming his guilt, then returned by land to the place of his crime, where his right hand was cut off and hung around his neck. Finally, he was taken back to San Marco and hanged there between the columns. This penalty provided maximum visibility and psychological impact for its brutality. A sweep across the city, first by water and then back over land, must have attracted a sizable crowd, especially with a herald proclaiming the victim's guilt. The first mutilation, full of blood, pain, and symbolism, with the offending hand chained around the criminal's neck, must have made a strong impression even on a society habituated to public mutilation.[25]

It is often observed pejoratively that the crowds enjoyed these bloody spectacles, and comparisons are drawn between them and Roman games, football, or bullfights. But the ritual nature of such events has the capacity to focus the observer's attention less on the violence of the ritual than on certain transcendent emotional values. In a ritual execution, when belief in the myth of the state as giver of justice and protector of order is strong, the full impact of the brutality is focused on purification. When Bernardo's hand was cut off and chained around his neck, the focus was provided by the herald chanting the victim's violence. This provided the avenue of transference whereby the victim of the execution became—for those who believed—the other, the evil one whose mutilation and execution were not only just and acceptable but even liberating for society. Purified and returned to a state of goodness, the state and society were restored to a starting point where violence was under control. Periodic repetitions of this ultimate sacrament of the state meant periodic renewals and returns. Bernardo was the vehicle.

The ritual could change, but the message remained the same. After 1382, the penalty for homicide was changed from hanging to decapitation, reportedly because the nobility believed that hanging was out of style. The *parte* stated that murderers "ought to have their heads cut off . . . so they die as is done in the rest of the world."[26] But this brought little change to the format of ritual executions. The same formula was followed, with the substitution of chopping off the head of the victim between the columns of St. Mark's. In a fashion typical of the relaxed attitude of the Venetians to their formal legal declarations, as early as 1388 the Forty had returned to hangings for murder, although decapitation also continued. The first example of a return to hanging involved the perpetrator of the robbery and murder of Marte Tartare discussed earlier.[27] For cases that required even more graphic penalties, the Forty reserved drawing and quartering, the remains being hung for varying lengths of time in locations having special significance for the crime.

It is appropriate that with this discussion of ritual execution the analysis has returned to its point of departure. Nothing could be more fitting, because it is the ultimate metaphor for violence and its perception in Early Renaissance Venice. These moments of public transcendence through public violence were the place wherein reason met emotion in violence on several levels. For instance, they were an application of rationality to control violence, but the state had paradoxically selected the emotional medium of ritual to convey the message. They embodied a ritual that was wedded, imperfectly but well, to the bureaucratic structure of control. They were emotional moments reserved for the elimination of rational criminals while rational executions were reserved for passionate criminals.

Behind this lay a key paradox in the Venetian perception of violence. The rational violent crime, planned and executed for reasons of self-interest, was unnatural because it was based upon reason rather than passion; yet part of the essential nature of Venetian society was the denial of immediate passion in the pursuit of self-interest. As the Marquis de Sade pointed out for a later period, the pursuit of self-interest, when taken to its logical conclusion, could bring society to an end in violence, and the Venetian nobility perceived that as well. (Both de Sade and the Venetian nobles lacked the nineteenth-century liberal view of society which, to a degree, overcomes or overlooks this problem.) Thus, the Venetian nobility's vision of success contained the germs of social destruction. Whether consciously understood or not, this tension was reflected in the stern and ritualistic penalties reserved for self-interested crimes of violence.

Murder plays all the chords of Venetian violence: brutality and symbolism, passion and reason, state bureaucracy and state ritual. The perception of violence in Venice was as complex as the society it reflected, because it was determined by that society and its organization. Violence in Venice was not, in the end, a form of behavior alien to social organization; rather, it grew directly out of that organization and the perceptions that informed it. Perhaps violence was even society itself, seen through a glass darkly.

NOTES

Abbreviations

A.S.V. Archivio di Stato, Venice
Adv. Avogaria di Comun
Dieci Consiglio dei Dieci
M.C. Maggior Consiglio
M.C. Deliberazioni di Maggior Consiglio
m.v. more veneto

Introduction to Part One

1. "Tercio ostenditur ensis sive spata domini ducis, que post eum aportatur, ut doceantur de vindicta potencia et fortitudinis ducalis ad penas iudicentis incisione membrorum graviter infligendas." Jacopo Bertaldo, *Splendor venetorum civitatis consuetudinum*, pp. 12–13.
2. A.S.V., Adv., *Raspe*, Reg. 2, f. 246r (1355). As is the case in many primitive societies, the columns of justice may have represented the point where the divine enters this world.

Chapter I

1. Vittorio Lazzarini, *Marino Faliero*, p. 171. For the claim that the object was to "cut to pieces" the members of the Major Council, see Correr, MS Cicogna 1180, f. 690r. This chronicle is generally attributed to Daniel Barbaro, but internal evidence suggests that the material from the fourteenth century comes from an earlier source little influenced by humanism and propatrician sentiment.
2. Lazzarini's discussion of the conspiracy limits the first night's investigation to the ducal councilors (*Faliero*, pp. 173–175). For this interpretation, he follows the Trevisan and Villani chronicles, which mention no general meeting, and rejects as not contemporary enough the more extensive chronicle tradition which described such a meeting (pp. 174–175, n. 1). When Lazzarini attempts to explain the arrest of the conspirators that night, he relies upon neither Villani nor Trevisan, instead following the chronicle attributed to Zanetti—the chronicle that he rejects in the previous note as too late to be trusted. This might seem a minor discrepancy, but it is a central one, because without Zanetti and the supposed "later tradition" Lazzarini cannot explain how the

"nobili e popolani fedele e ben armati" appeared so quickly to make arrests (p. 175). Zanetti reveals, and the general chronicle tradition supports, the fact that the ducal councilors almost immediately called in the broader group described in the text. The Council of Ten, which by the 1350s was working in close cooperation with the ducal councilors anyway, had a well-organized police force ready to react to the threat of conspiracy. It is most likely that it was the Ten's men who secured the conspirators as they secured the streets of Venice. Unfortunately, the archival records of the Ten provide only a tantalizing uncertainty, reporting suggestively that they were too busy protecting the city to record their actions. A.S.V., Dieci, Miste, Reg. 5, f. 33r (1355). For the tradition that this meeting was held at the Ducal Palace, see Lazzarini, Faliero, p. 174, n. 4 and p. 175. The opposing tradition is represented in Correr, MS. Cicogna 1180, f. 691r, attributed to Barbaro.

3. Lazzarini, Faliero, pp. 177–181.

4. The nature and implications of the Serrata are discussed later in this chapter.

5. Bertaldo, Splendor, pp. 12–13.

6. For a general introduction on the function of the Forty, see Antonio Lombardo, ed., Le deliberazioni del Consiglio dei XL della Repubblica di Venezia, vol. 1, 1342–1344, Deputazione di storia patria per le Venezie, 9: v–xxiv.

7. These remarks are generalized results of research on the Cinque alla Pace and an analysis of the eighteen registers of gratie preserved in the Venetian archives. Gratie were adjustments made to penalties imposed by councils such as the Cinque by the Major Council or the Forty. For the period 1343–1364, in registers 10–15 of the Gratie, there are 1068 petty knifings and quarrels handled by the Cinque. This may reflect only a small proportion of the cases handled by the Cinque in that period.

8. Bertaldo, Splendor, p. 10. Both the Cinque alla Pace and the Signori di Notte are discussed more fully in Chapter 2.

9. Guido Ruggiero, "The Ten," p. 198. This is discussed in Chapter 2.

10. Correr, MS Cicogna 1180, f. 534r.

11. On the opinion that Gradenigo had engineered the Serrata because of hate for the lower classes and had therefore earned their enmity, see Correr, MS Cicogna 1180, f. 534r. The chronicler Nicolo Trevisan describes similar antagonisms in a Guelph–Ghibelline context. Marciana, MS Ital., Cl. VII, 519 (8438), f. 89r.

12. This account, clearly based on an earlier tradition, is found in the Barbaro chronicle and provides considerable additional detail. Correr, MS Cicogna 1180, ff. 534r–541r. Variants consulted in the Marciana report essentially the same events. Marciana, MS Ital., Cl. VII, 92 (8575) beginning f. 242r and MS Ital., Cl. VII, 789 (8425), f. 150r.

13. Although Frederic Lane has attempted to minimize the importance of this conspiracy, it seems evident from the emphasis most chroniclers place on the attempt to gain entrance to the Major Council that it was an early manifestation of dissatisfaction with the Serrata. For Lane's position, see Frederic Lane, "Enlargement of the Great Council of Venice," p. 245.

14. Again implying a reliance on an early tradition, the Barbaro chronicle pro-

vides an unusually long list of forty-one major conspirators. Correr, MS Cicogna 1180, f. 539r.

15. This is not to suggest that the non-nobility of Venice had some sort of proto-democratic sense of participatory government. It is more realistic to assume that the primary danger for the nobility was its self-definition. Animosity is focused on a defined ruling class much more easily than on a nebulous one. Some non-nobles, however, were also concerned by the realization that they were excluded from the power at the heart of the commune. Less abstractly, others were aware that governmental offices meant power and wealth and resented the nobility's monopoly. These tensions are discussed more fully later. A good example of the strategies the nobility eventually used to ameliorate them is their use of the *scuole* to provide the prestige of officeholding for those excluded from government. The Venetian humanist, Gasparo Contarini, pointed this out clearly in the sixteenth century, noting that the officers of the *scuole* "imitate the nobility . . . such honours do the plebians . . . attaine . . . to the end that they should not altogether thinke themselves deprived of publike authority and civil offices, but should also in some sort have their ambition satisfied, without having occasion either to hate or preturbe the estate of nobilitie." The full text can be found in Brian Pullan, *Rich and Poor in Renaissance Venice,* pp. 107–108.

16. Marciana, MS Ital., Cl. VII, 519 (8438), ff. 89r–91r.

17. See Lane, "Enlargement," pp. 240–241. The classic analysis of these animosities remains Giovanni Soranzo, *La Guerra fra Venezia e la S. Sede per il Dominio di Ferrara,* p. 179.

18. For the Paduan connection of the Venetian Guelphs, see John K. Hyde, *Padua in the Age of Dante,* pp. 234, 252–253. Hyde reveals that the Badoer family was closely related to the Guelph da Peraga family of Padua. In addition, the Querini had a long association with the Paduan Pars Marchionis, the local equivalent of the Guelph party. Lane provides additional detail, based primarily on the late but detailed Caroldo chronicle ("Enlargement," p. 240). It provides an unusual amount of information in the guise of fabricated speeches by members of the Querini family. Marciana, MS Ital., Cl. VII, 128A (8639), ff. 136r–137v.

19. Hyde, *Padua,* pp. 252–253. One year after the conspiracy had failed, Tiepolo was still secretly meeting with mainland Guelphs in the hope that he might stir his old allies to support him in another attempt at revolution.

20. Soranza, *Guerra,* p. 179.

21. Although the Serrata, as Lane has argued, did not substantially change the reality of the elite (this is one of the basic theses of "Enlargement"), by 1310 it did meaningfully change the communal perception of that elite. Access to the elite was perceived as closed. The illusion was so significantly changed, in fact, that the Guelph leaders could assume popular dissatisfaction with the Serrata.

22. Most of the documents dealing with the response to the conspiracy are published in the appendix to *Consiglio dei Dieci, Deliberazioni Miste, Registri I–II (1310–1325),* ed. Ferruccio Zago. In references to this legislation in the follow-

ing notes, both the archival references and the references to Zago will be given.

23. A.S.V., M.C., *Presbyter*, f. 20v; Zago, *Dieci*, p. 243. "Reliqui vero nobiles, qui erant de maiori consilio vel esse poterant, debeant ire et stare ad confines."

24. A.S.V., M.C., *Presbyter*, f. 20v.

25. Ibid. The Major Council's offer of lenient treatment to noble conspirators and its crafty promise of pardon to non-nobles does not seem to have met entirely with success. Many did not ask pardon or refused to report to their places of exile or, having reported, broke exile to roam about the mainland stirring up Venetian fears of continuing revolt. These problems were one of the main concerns of the early Council of Ten. Ruggiero, "The Ten," pp. 134–149.

26. A.S.V., M.C., *Presbyter*, f. 21r; Zago, *Dieci*, p. 245.

27. A.S.V., M.C., *Presbyter*, f. 21v; Zago, *Dieci*, p. 247.

28. A.S.V., M.C., *Presbyter*, f. 62v; Zago, *Dieci*, p. 253.

29. For a brief discussion of the birth of the Ten and the relevant texts, see Ruggiero, "The Ten," pp. 27–31.

30. Ibid., pp. 134–198.

31. A.S.V., Adv., *Raspe*, Reg. 1, f. 172v (1336). It is significant for an understanding of the relationship between legislation and practice that the records of the Signori di Notte indicate that returning cases to the Five was already a practice in the 1330s although it was formalized by a law only in 1355. A.S.V., M.C., *Novella*, f. 46r (1355).

32. A.S.V., Adv., *Raspe*, Reg. 1, f. 172v (1336).

33. A.S.V., Dieci, *Liber, Magnus*, f. 6r–v; Zago, *Dieci*, pp. 25–28.

34. A.S.V., Dieci, *Miste*, Reg. 2, f. 89v; Zago, *Dieci*, p. 36.

35. A.S.V., M.C., *Fronesis*, f. 38r–v. These new Capi were elected in the Major Council again for six months. It is significant also that heads of sestiere were forbidden to take on more than eight armed *vardianos*, apparently to prevent them from building their patrols into private armies. Every six months, these Capi were renewed, until 1324 when they were confirmed permanently. A.S.V., M.C., *Fronesis*, f. 144v. That these patrols were to control violence in the city was well understood. In describing the creation of the Capi, the Barbaro chronicle stressed this and observed that much of this violence was associated with foreigners from Tuscany and Lombardy. In that there was considerable migration of perennially disruptive cloth workers from both these regions during the period, Barbaro again seems to be providing accurate detail. Correr, MS Cicogna 1180, f. 630r.

36. A.S.V., Dieci, *Miste*, Reg. 2, f. 153v; Zago, *Dieci*, pp. 182–183.

37. A.S.V., Dieci, *Miste*, Reg. 3, f. 47r; Zago, *Dieci*, pp. 105–106. An attempt to read this text under ultraviolet light in 1970 failed to reveal even as much of the text as Zago read in the mid-1960s.

38. A.S.V., Dieci, *Miste*, Reg. 3, f. 48r; Zago, *Dieci*, p. 107.

39. A.S.V., Dieci, *Miste*, Reg. 3, f. 49r–v; Zago, *Dieci*, pp. 108–110. One head of the *contrata* led one-half the *duodenas* of his *contrata*, reporting to one of the heads of his sestiere; the other led the other half and reported to the other head of the sestiere. Apparently this elaborate set of checks was intended to keep any one individual from gaining too much power.

40. A.S.V., Dieci, *Miste,* Reg. 3, f. 45r–v; Zago, *Dieci,* pp. 100–102. The conspiracy also involved a number of others, including Giacomo Querini, suggesting that there were still some remnants of the Querini–Tiepolo faction active in Venice.

41. A.S.V., Adv., *Raspe,* Reg. 2, ff. 172r–173r (1351). For another example of patrols in action, see Chapter 2, *n.* 33.

42. A.S.V., M.C., *Novella,* f. 84v (1360). The *parte* also specified that these patrollers were to be between twenty-five and fifty years of age and to be armed with at least a sword, a knife, and a helmet.

43. Ibid., f. 197v (1382).

44. Ibid., f. 84v (1360).

45. This figure is based upon an estimate of a population in Venice of about 80,000.

46. A.S.V., Adv., *M.C.,* Reg. 24/7, f. 3v (1349). This right was reaffirmed and extended to *famuli* and scribes of the Cinque alla Pace in 1350. Ibid., f. 6r (1350).

47. On this, see Chapter 9.

48. A.S.V., Archivio Notarile, *Testamenti, Atti Gibellino Giorgio,* 575, 276. Obviously, these ties were not all politically effective; but Giovanni certainly had a wide range of opportunities for influencing the council's activity.

49. Ibid. Examples could be easily multiplied; for a few more, see Ruggiero, "The Ten," pp. 247–252. Familial dominance on the Ten is reflected by the fact that even though there were some vicissitudes within family political fortunes through the fourteenth century 43 percent of the Ten's reported members (1471 of 3454 in the period 1310–1407) were drawn from fifteen families, in order of importance: Contarini, Morosini, Michiel, Dolfin, Loredan, Venier, Marcello, Corner, Trevisan, Foscari, Molin, Soranzo, Zorzi, Falier, Nani. The first ten families controlled more than one third the offices reported, 34 percent to be exact.

Chapter II

1. "Coram popolo (the Doge and through him the whole judicial apparatus of Venice) ostenduntur iuxta racionabilem consuetudinem atque usum et maxime ut populus inde doceatur declinare a malo et facere bonum." Bertaldo, *Splendor,* p. 12.

2. A.S.V., Adv., *Capitulare,* Reg. 3, cap. 100 (1310), n.p.

3. In the late fifteenth and early sixteenth centuries, when the Ten and the Avogadori came into conflict over who would have final control over criminal justice, this was thrown into clear relief; but the power of the Avogadori predates even the trecento. For the Avogadori in the later period, see Gaetano Cozzi, "Authority and the Law in Renaissance Venice."

4. For election procedure, see A.S.V., Adv., *Capitulare,* Reg. 3, cap. 205 (1323); and also ibid., Adv., *M.C.,* Reg. 21/4, f. 204v (1323). For length of term, see Adv., *M.C.,* Reg. 21/4, f. 54r (1318). Here the Major Council ruled that because of the importance of the Avogadori and the need for authority in that office, they were to serve for two years. Previously their terms had been one year. Ibid., Adv., *M.C.,* Reg. 20/3, f. 20v (1300). Da Mosto argues that in 1314

a standard term of one and one-half years was instituted. Andrea Da Mosto, *L'Archivio di Stato di Venezia,* 1: 69. However, the 1318 text refers to the fact that the two-year term replaced a one-year term; the Avogadori "esse debeat per duos annos sicut erant per unum."

5. A.S.V., Adv., *M.C.,* Reg. 20/3, f. 21r (1308), for the 1308 meeting time; ibid., Reg. 21/4, f. 12v (1314), for daily meetings.

6. Antonio Lombardo, ed., *Le deliberazioni del Consiglio dei XL della Repubblica di Venezia,* vols. 1–3. *Deputazione di storia patria per le Venezie,* vols. 9, 12, 20, 1: nn. 256–257.

7. Ibid., *n.* 259.

8. A.S.V., Adv., *Raspe,* Reg. 2, f. 65v (1343).

9. For the consideration of penalties, see Lombardo, *Deliberazioni,* 1: nn. 276–277.

10. A.S.V., Adv., *Capitulare,* Reg. 3. In the opening oath of office, they were required to swear that they would regularly read their capitulary.

11. Ibid., cap. 225 (1308).

12. A.S.V., Adv., *M.C.,* Reg. 21/4, f. 6v (1313). In certain cases of violence, especially the rape of very young girls or serious injury to communal officials, a part of the fine would be reserved for the victim; but this was done only at sentencing. See Chapter 10.

13. Ibid., Reg. 24/7, ff. 78v–79r (1378).

14. A.S.V., Adv., *Raspe,* Reg. 2, f. 183r (1351). There is little reflection of this complex procedure in the primary legal text on *contumacia* from the thirteenth century, the *Promissio Maleficorum.* Marciana, MS Lat., Cl. V, 137 (10453) f. 80r; on the *Promissio,* see Chapter 3.

15. A.S.V., Adv. *Capitulare,* Reg. 3 (1303), n.p. This procedure is similar to the Roman-canon *Inquisitionsprozess.* For the origin and development of this, see Raoul von Caenegem, "The Law of Evidence in the Twelfth Century: European Perspectives and Intellectual Background"; and John W. Baldwin, "The Intellectual Preparation for the Canon of 1215 against Ordeals." It will become apparent, however, that in many specific areas Venetian practice differed from the ideal of the *Inquisitionsprozess.*

16. For example, there are seven reported cases of the torture of accused murderers by the Avogadori; six use a *collegio;* the seventh was a case referred by the Signori di Notte in which the accused had already been tortured. A.S.V., Adv., *Raspe,* Reg. 1, ff. 118v–119r, n.d.

17. The noble, Michaleto Giustinian, for example, was tortured by a *collegio* at the behest of the Avogadori after being accused of poisoning his nephew, Pantalione. He was eventually absolved by the Forty. A.S.V., Adv., *Raspe,* Reg. 3, f. 160r (1371). Another interesting case involved Catarina, slave of Mora Tulon, who was accused of infanticide. She had supposedly thrown her baby into a canal to drown. Her continued denial under torture, however, secured her a narrow acquittal before the Forty. A.S.V., Adv., *Raspe,* Reg. 3, f. 90v (1366).

18. The process of taking testimony and its subjective nature is summed up well in the *Promissio Maleficorum* where it is ruled that if no confession or no clear testimony is secured the matter is to be left to the discretion of the judge. Marciana, MS Lat., Cl. V, 137 (10453), f. 82r. This is discussed more fully in Chapter 3.

19. A.S.V., Adv., *Capitulare*, Reg. 3, cap. 176 (1327). "Ut res equaliter, et juste pro-
cedat ex omni parte."
20. Ibid., cap. 255 (1355).
21. Ibid., cap. 304, n.d.
22. For example, Nicoleto Rosso, a caulker who had attempted to rape Magda-
lena, wife of Geragio di Leonardo, was released by the Forty in 1364 because
he had already spent two months in jail awaiting trial. A.S.V., Adv., *Raspe*,
Reg. 3, f. 67v (1364). This may seem light, but penalties for rapes were generally light, as is discussed later.
23. A.S.V., Adv., *Capitulare*, Reg. 3, cap. 328 (1384).
24. A.S.V., Adv., *M.C.*, Reg. 24/7, f. 10v (1351).
25. Ibid., f. 72v (1367). The swift secret execution of Doge Marin Falier already
discussed and the Ten's secret proceedings against Doge Lorenzo Celsi, falling within a decade of each other, both indicate the profound respect still held
for ducal power. No documents reveal what Celsi was involved in; some later
chronicles suggest that he, like Falier before him, was considering overthrowing the order of the commune. A.S.V., Dieci, *Miste*, Reg. 6, f. 30r (1365).
26. A.S.V., Adv., *M.C.*, Reg. 21/4, f. 157v (1321). This *parte* was actually a mere
clarification of earlier procedure in a particular case involving the noble, Nicoleto Dolfin, son of Paolo, who asked for the clarification because he was
being tried before two courts at once.
27. A.S.V., Adv., *Capitulare*, Reg. 3 (1361), n.p.
28. The main exception to this generalization falls in the area of sexual violence,
where apparently there was often some doubt about the forced nature of a
rape (as might be expected given the male-oriented nature of society) especially when the victim was sexually mature and single. In these cases, even
lower-class defendants regularly received close votes and often acquittals.
29. Andrea da Mosto, *Archivio*, 1: 97; Marco Ferro, *Dizionario del diritto comune e
veneto*, 2: 693; Melchiorre Roberti, *Le Magistrature Giudiziarie Veneziane e i loro
capitolare fino al 1300*, 3: 3–11; and, Pompeo Molmenti, *La storia di Venezia nella
vita privata*, 1: 97.
30. A.S.V., Adv., *M.C.*, Reg. 21/4, f. 17v (1314). That they were receiving a portion of fines collected as salaries their capitulary makes clear in 1278: Mocenigo, *Signori di Notte*, p. 24, n. 19 (1278), where reference is made to their
receiving one-fourth of the penalty. This principle was reaffirmed in 1358 by
the Major Council according to their capitulary: A.S.V., Signori di Notte, *Capitulare*, Reg. 3, f. 14r–v (1358). They were also given the right to keep the
weapons they confiscated: Mocenigo, *Signori di Notte*, pp. 27–28, n. 25.
31. Another serious crime they dealt with was sodomy, defined as both homosexuality and any unnatural sexual act. Such crimes were usually nonviolent,
however, except for the penalty, which was normally death by burning.
32. A fuller discussion of these distinctions is presented in Chapter 11.
33. A.S.V., *Signori di Notte al Criminale* (hereafter cited as Signori di Notte), *Processi*, Reg. 6, f. 14r–v (1348). This case provides another excellent example of
police patrols and citizen cooperation at their best.
34. This precedent was not always followed; see A.S.V., Signori di Notte, *Processi*,
Reg. 11, f. 26v (1395), where the crime was committed in a tavern in the ses-

tiere of San Marco but the Signore di Notte in charge was Johannes Pasquale-gio from Castello.

35. A.S.V., Signori di Notte, *Processi*, Reg. 6, f. 14v (1348). The *Promissio Male-ficorum* clearly stated that testimony without confession was enough to convict for murder. Moreover, even when neither was enough to prove guilt, the judge could punish at his own discretion. Marciana, MS Lat., Cl. V, 137 (10453) f. 80r. This is discussed in Chapter 3.

36. In fact, a few scribal notes on original testimony survive to provide a rough comparison. They run up to forty or fifty folio pages for cases condensed to one or two pages in the *Processi*; in the process, much of the variety of testi-mony must have been lost. For original scribal notes, see A.S.V., Adv., *Misc. Penale*, Buste 108, 111, 114, and 116.

37. A.S.V., Adv., *Raspe*, Reg. 2, f. 127v (1348). The Avogadori occasionally inves-tigated this type of case as part of their responsibility for the lawful operation of other councils of state.

38. For more on this aspect of cooperation between doctors and the law, see Guido Ruggiero, "The Cooperation of Physicians and the State in the Control of Violence in Renaissance Venice."

39. A.S.V., Signori di Notte, *Processi*, Reg. 11, f. 21r–v (1395).

40. Marciana, MS Lat., Cl. V, 137 (10453) f. 80r.

41. A.S.V., Signori di Notte, *Processi*, Reg. 10, ff. 63r–67v (1372). This is merely the final summary of the testimony, representing much more extensive original notes.

42. For Luysio's death, see A.S.V., Signori di Notte, *Processi*, Reg. 6, f. 14r (1348). For further examples, see Ruggiero, "Physicians and the State."

43. A.S.V., Signori di Notte, *Processi*, Reg. 6, f. 14r (1348).

44. For the original *parte*, see Mocenigo, *Signori di Notte*, p. 160, *n.* 206 (n.d.); and A.S.V., Adv., *M.C.*, Reg. 21/4, f. 165r (1322). The 1338 confirmation is found in Mocenigo, *Signori di Notte*, p. 246, *n.* 315 (1338); A.S.V., Adv., *M.C.*, Reg. 22/6, f. 27r–v (1338). This *parte* also reveals that this time on Friday was to be spent both on regular examination and torture.

45. For the *contumacia* procedure, see Mocenigo, *Signori di Notte*, p. 89, *n.* 122 (1303). Significantly, this *parte* also required that the suspect could not intro-duce new evidence if he failed to come in within the time prescribed by the doge. For letters to rectors, see ibid., p. 135, *n.* 179 (1317). Of course, once the suspect left Venetian territory, he was legally beyond the reach of Venetian authority. Occasionally, however, Venice would offer rewards for the death of an especially serious offender even when he was outside of Venetian terri-tory. A prime example of this procedure was the murder of Pietro Querini following the Querini–Tiepolo conspiracy. Baiamonte Tiepolo, in fact, lived out his life with a sizable Venetian reward for his death following him.

46. Ibid., pp. 47–48, n. 50 (1290 and 1291). The right to torture *raubatores* was reasserted in 1307–1308. The reasoning for this *parte* provides a good measure of the ability to forget or more accurately lose track of previously passed pro-cedure: "Cum domini de nocte habeant in suo Capitulari si sunt omnes sex in concordia posse tormentare latrones, et de raubatoribus nullam bayliam ha-beant."

47. Ibid., pp. 138–139, *n.* 184 (1318).
48. A.S.V., Adv., *M.C.,* Reg. 22/5, f. 66v (1327).
49. Mocenigo, *Signori di Notte,* p. 45, *n.* 45 (1290).
50. Ibid., p. 38, *n.* 38 (1287).
51. Ibid., pp. 77–78, *n.* 99 (1299).
52. Ibid.
53. Ibid., p. 179, *n.* 231 (1325).
54. Bertaldo, *Splendor,* pp. 9–14.
55. A.S.V., Dieci, *Miste,* Reg. 6, f. 14v (1364).
56. Ibid., f. 19r.
57. Ibid.
58. Zago, *Dieci,* vol. 1, Reg. 3, docs. 375 and 376 (1329). Another case of referral involved a man from Friuli who had been arrested originally by the Cinque alla Pace for committing "excesses," including speaking against the state. The Ten's investigation revealed no evidence to support the charge, and he was released. A.S.V., Dieci, *Miste,* Reg. 5, f. 30v (1354).
59. Rinaldo Fulin, "Gli Inquisitori dei Dieci," p. 43.
60. A.S.V., Dieci, *Liber Magnus,* f. 11r.
61. Ibid.
62. A.S.V., Dieci, *Miste,* Reg. 5, f. 32v (1355).
63. Ibid., Reg. 8, f. 134v (1406–1407).
64. Ibid., f. 146v (1406–1407). This case had wide ramifications, most of which fall beyond the period of this work. In fact, it may reflect a conflict within the ruling class that had important effects upon the unity of the nobility in the early part of that century.
65. Ibid., f. 135v (1406–1407).
66. Ibid., ff. 141v–142r (1407).
67. Ibid., f. 145r (1407).
68. Ibid., f. 135v (1406–1407).
69. Zago, *Dieci,* vol. 2, Reg. 3, doc. 9 (1325).
70. Ibid., vol. 1, Reg. 2, docs. 112 and 115 (1320).
71. Ibid., vol. 2, Reg. 3, doc. 332 (1328).
72. Ibid., doc. 334 (1328).
73. In the volumes of collected *gratie* covering the period 1329–1392 in fifteen registers, there is not one clear reference to a *gratia* of a case actually tried by the Ten. The same can be said of the *gratie* recorded in the six registers of the Major Council for the period 1310–1415 and in the thirty-two registers of the Senate for the period 1332–1408. Theoretically the collected *gratie* represent all the *gratie* passed in the Major Council and Senate, but the *gratie* do not always successfully do this; it is therefore necessary to check not only the collected *gratie* but also the registers of the Major Council and Senate.

Chapter III

1. Parts of this chapter were originally published as an article, "Law and Punishment in Early Renaissance Venice," *Journal of Criminal Law and Criminology,* 69 (1978): 243–256.

2. On the general problem of just what constituted the law in Late Medieval and Early Renaissance Venice probably the best introduction is now Lamberto Pansolli, *La gerarchia delle fonti di diritto nella legislazione medievale veneziana.* The source for easiest access to Venetian law remains Marco Ferro, *Dizionario del diritto comune e veneto.* For the development of Venetian law and its relationship to other legal traditions, see Enrico Besta, "Il diritto e le leggi di Venezia fino al dogado di Enrico Dandolo."

3. Existing capitularies seem to concentrate primarily on texts from the fifteenth and sixteenth centuries. The main exception to this later orientation is the capitulary for the Signori di Notte published by Nani Mocenigo, *Capitolare dei Signori di Notte esistante nel Civico Museo di Venezia.* The early entries of judicial capitularies were edited by Melchiorre Roberti, *Le magistrature giudiziarie veneziane e i loro capitolare fino al 1300.*

4. Marciana, MS Lat., Cl. V, 137 (10453) f. 78v. Tiepolo's law code was edited by Roberto Cessi, *Gli statuti veneziani di Jacopo Tiepolo del 1242 e le loro glosse.* The *Promissio,* however, is not included although it was published in the eighteenth century.

5. Marciana, MS Lat., Cl. V, 137 (10453) ff. 78v–79v.

6. Ibid., f. 79v.

7. Ibid., f. 80r.

8. Ibid., f. 82r.

9. "Si vero hec manifesta non fuerint nec probari poterit in discretione sit iudicum penam eis talem imponere," Ibid., f. 82r.

10. Ibid., f. 83v. An exemplar of the tradition that names this as part of the Dandolo correction is a manuscript now preserved in the Querini Stampalia: Querini, Cl. IV, Cod. 2 H 7, f. 11r.

11. Marciana, MS Lat., Cl. V, 137 (10453) f. 82r; this section is entitled "De maleficiis variis et diversis specificata sententia sit in discretione iudicium iuxta maleficii qualitatem."

12. Carlo Calisse, *A History of Italian Law,* p. 175.

13. Ibid. Calisse was aware that Venice may have been different in that it used jail sentences for penalties; see ibid., p. 417.

14. A.S.V., M.C., *Novella,* f. 80v (1359), also registered with the Avogadori; Adv., M.C., Reg. 24/7, f. 45r (1359).

15. Ibid.

16. Harry Elmer Barnes, *The Story of Punishment,* p. 114.

17. Ralph B. Pugh, *Imprisonment in Medieval England,* p. 385.

18. For a brief list of *parti* dealing with overcrowded jails, see Ruggiero, "Law and Punishment," p. 248, *n.* 22.

19. For *gratia* procedure, see Ibid., *n.* 23.

20. For a complete breakdown by register of cases, see Ibid., p. 249, *n.* 24.

21. That is 145 cases out of 272 cases where penalties were recorded involved the execution of the culprit. In 155 cases there is no record of the penalties imposed because in Registers 10 and 11 the Signori di Notte failed to record the penalties imposed by the Giudici di Proprio.

22. A.S.V., Adv., *Raspe,* Reg. 2, f. 314r–v (1360).

23. Bertaldo, *Splendor,* pp. 12–13.

24. The distinction between rational manipulation of penalties and ritualistic use of penalties should perhaps be clarified. Essentially, the rational penalty is a calculated force designed to counterbalance violence. Although ritual executions certainly have this element, they are set apart because they operate on another plane as well. They teach not by means of proof but by means of the emotions elicited by ritual.

25. This equivalency is based upon the penalties imposed when judges gave a choice between a fine or a jail sentence. Rough but remarkably consistent, in fifty cases where an option was given there is a deviation between total points for jail sentences and fines of less than 5 percent from the balance that would have obtained if judges had been scientifically consistent. This consistency prevailed over more than eight decades and involved judges who were often little more than amateurs. In fifteen cases, generally the major ones, the equivalency is exact: A.S.V., Adv., *Raspe,* Reg. 1, ff. 168v, 173r, 175v, 175v, 181r (one year equals 200 lire di piccoli), 202v (six months equals 100 lire di piccoli), 203r–203v (one year equals 200 lire di piccoli); Reg. 2, ff. 78r (six months equals 100 lire di piccoli), 84v (one year equals 200 lire di piccoli), 105r (six months equals 100 lire di piccoli), 106v (three months equals 50 lire di piccoli), 145r (six months equals 100 lire di piccoli), 164r (three months equals 50 lire di piccoli), 164r (three months equals 50 lire di piccoli).

26. This conversion of values can become extremely complex. Nicolò Papadopoli outlined the major conversion rates for the period 1345–1353. On the basis of his figures, 10 lire di piccoli equal 3.12 ducats or 12.3 lire a grossi a moneta; .3 lire di grossi a moneta; .3 lire di grossi a oro; 12.3 lire a grossi a oro. To plot continuously the fluctuating rates between these currencies, which are not really adequately worked out, would have been nearly impossible. Instead, these ratios are used for the period under consideration. Fines became more and more standardized in lire di piccoli as the century progressed. A decade-by-decade breakdown shows this pattern: 1320s—nine fines in other currencies; 1330s—twelve; 1340s—eleven; 1350s—twenty-two; 1360s—twelve; 1370s—eleven; 1380s—one; 1390s—one. In fact, most penalties in other monies cluster around the figures presented by Papadopoli. Because 10 lire di piccoli equal 1 point, each amount listed above is worth 1 point. Nicolò Papadopoli-Aldobrandini, *"Sul valore della moneta veneziana,"* p. 17. For a yet more complex vision of Venetian currency, see Frederic Lane, "The First Infidelities of the Venetian Lira."

27. The cost of jails weighed heavily on Venetians because they were maintained from state revenues. For this, see A.S.V., Adv., *M.C.,* Reg. 21/4, f. 148r and Reg. 22/5, f. 45v, both of which refer to adjustments in salaries paid to jailors.

28. As is discussed in detail in Chapter 9, major assault involved the shedding of significant amounts of blood.

Chapter IV

1. For a discussion of the rentier–merchant question, see Cracco, *Società,* p. 64 passim. Cracco also provides the most detailed modern account of the devel-

opment of the pre-Serrata nobility, though he has been seriously attacked for his Marxian approach to the subject.

2. Stanley Chojnacki, "In Search of the Venetian Patriciate," p. 83, n. 49.

3. Ibid. Moreover, Lane's article on the Serrata argues convincingly that there was no absolute reference to earlier membership in the Major Council in the 1297–1298 legislation, beyond a ruling that the previous year's Major Council would be automatically reapproved. The hereditary view only came later, first through the Quarantia and finally specifically through law in 1323. Lane, "Enlargement," pp. 255–256. This means that Chojnacki's lists of members of the Major Council between 1261 and 1297 have, a priori, little relationship to the Major Council that sat in the years immediately following the Serrata.

4. Lane makes reference to a final law of 1328 that required approval of "five out of six ducal councillors, thirty of the Quarantia, including their three Capi, and two-thirds of the great council itself." Lane, "Enlargement," p. 258.

5. For Chojnacki's position, see "Search," p. 73. Note again that this is not 1298 but the whole of the 1290s, which tends to confuse the issue. He categorizes only twenty-six families as from the trecento alone. The archives record the eight families as Adoldo (1310), Barison (1317), Dal Sol (1310), Da Verardo (1312), Dente (1310), Di Pigli (1334), Papacizza (1311), and Stornello (1311). A.S.V., Misc. Cod. I, Storia Veneta, Reg. 44, ff. 1r–2r. This register was originally part of the archive of the Avogaria di Comun, the office responsible for investigation of claims of noble status.

6. The following mainland families were added: Carrara (1326), D'Este (1329), Della Scalla (1329), Gonzago (1332), Visconti (1332), and Da Polenta (1335). Incidentally, this shows a high level of interest in mainland affairs for a society supposedly without interests on the mainland in the trecento.

7. Lane sums this up well: "After the admission of the commoners who were rewarded for their support during the conspiracy of 1310, practically no new families were admitted until the war of Chioggia about seventy years later." Lane, "Enlargement," p. 258. The records of the Avogaria di Comun provide the final proof of this point. Because the Avogadori investigated applications for admission to the Major Council and hence to the elite after 1319, they should give a relatively full accounting of new families added. Their records are fairly complete from 1324 on, but the cases of noble status examined are scarce and deal primarily with cadet branches of older noble families. For some interesting cases see: A.S.V., Adv., Raspe, Reg. 2, f. 317r (1360), Aloysius Cocco; ibid., Reg. 3, f. 8v (1361), Prelatus Mudazzo; ibid., f. 95v (1368), Frangibus da Molin; ibid., Barbus Barbo; ibid., f. 96v (1368), Nicolaus Dandolo; ibid., Nicolaus Corner; ibid., f. 224r, Thomas Querini.

8. This may in fact explain the difference between trecento Florentine protohumanistic literature and Venetian literature of the same period. In Florence, there was concern with questions of elite identification, the essential question being by what right a man of money displaces a man of blood from first place in society. The eventual answer, of course, is by virtù, which transcends blood. In Venice, elite status was defined by law not by literature. Thus Venetian literature seems much more tied up with the myth of the state even in this early period.

9. For a discussion of earlier attitudes toward the nobility, see Cracco, *Società*, pp. 104–132. See also Lane, *Maritime Republic*, pp. 89–90.

10. Lane, *Maritime Republic*, pp. 113–114.

11. A.S.V., M.C., *Presbyter*, f. 20v (17 June 1310), "Primo quod ipse Baiamons et predicti sui seguaces et participes debeant de presenti exire Veneciis et districtum et ipse Baiamons debeat ire et stare per quatuor annos completos ad confines et ad mandata domini ducis in partibus Sclavonie ultra Iadram, exceptis terris et locis nostris et terris nostrorum inimicorum. *Reliqui vero nobiles, qui erant de maiori consilio vel esse poterant,* debeant ire et stare ad confines. . . . Ceteri vero, qui non erant de maiori consilio nec esse poterant, si venerint ad mercedem dominis ducis, dominus dux fatiet eis misericordiam sicut conveniet ad largum." Not only does this text give a specific association of membership in the Major Council and nobility, it also reveals a clear elite mentality with the doge giving mercy to members of the nonelite almost as if they were incapable of actively conspiring against the state. Of course, there were political reasons for such an attitude as well: the Doge Pietro Gradenigo hoped by promising leniency to the non-nobility to strip the conspirators, especially Baiamonte Tiepolo, of popular support.

12. For an analysis of how the Venetian nobility controlled these offices through a process of election in the Senate, see Celestino Piana and Cesare Cenci, *Promozioni agli ordini sacri a Bologna e alle dignità ecclesiastica nel Veneto nei secc. XIV–XV.*

13. Roberto Cessi, *Politica ed economia di Venezia nel Trecento-Saggi*, p. 20. On the galley convoy system in general, see Lane, *Maritime Republic*, pp. 124–131. On maritime law and administration, a fine view of the tight control the state applied (unfortunately with little attempt to analyze the social impact of that control) is again provided by Lane in "Maritime Law and Administration, 1250–1350," reprinted in *Venice and History*, pp. 227–252. Lane provides a more detailed view of merchant galley operation in "Merchant Galleys, 1300–34, Private and Communal Operation," reprinted in ibid., pp. 193–226. For yet another view of the state-controlled merchant economy of trecento Venice, see Gino Luzzatto, *Storia economica di Venezia dall' XI al XVI secolo*, pp. 41–57.

14. Lauro Martines, *Lawyers and Statecraft in Renaissance Florence*. On legislation relating to doctors, see the collection by Ugo Stefanuti, *Documentazioni cronologiche per la storia della medicina chirurgia e farmacia in Venezia dal 1258 al 1332;* and on foreign doctors: Ruggiero, "Physicians and the State," pp. 165–166.

15. For Mapheo's case see: A.S.V., Adv., *Raspe*, Reg. 2, f. 91v (1346). Donald Queller is working on a study of this prevalent form of corruption for the early renaissance period in Venice.

16. If there is any exception to this, it would be the wool guild after mid-century. This guild, though always in the final analysis under state control, gained considerable independence in electing its own officers and running its own business according to Nella Fano, "Ricerche sull'Arte della Lana nel XIII al XIV secolo." Fano suggests cautiously that this independence may have stemmed from the fact that after the plague the guild received important reinforcements from mainland cities. These new arrivals were used to a more independent guild structure than the Venetian (p. 137). Inasmuch as the Major

Council and Senate passed a number of measures aimed at attracting cloth workers to Venice in this period, the suggestion seems logical.

17. For Venetian control of guilds, see Giovanni Monticolo, *I capitolare delle arte veneziane sottoposte alla Giustizia Vecchia dalle origini al MCCCXXX*. See also Lane's highly laudatory view of the Venetian guild system in Lane, *Maritime Republic*, pp. 104–109.

18. Lane, *Maritime Republic*, p. 106.

19. In a short article, Lane argues that in fact seamen did very well on the Venetian fleet. Working from Marin Sanuto Torsello's estimates of pay for his planned crusading fleet, he projects a base pay of 51–52 piccoli per day for the lowest paid oarsmen. He concludes, "If a diet as good as that specified by Sanuto—bread, wine, cheese, meat, and vegetables yielding 3,920 calories a day—could indeed be purchased for 12⅘ piccoli, then the 51 piccoli plus food received by even the lowest-paid seaman could not be called starvation wages." But Lane admits that Sanuto was underestimating food costs to make his crusading plans look more attractive. Moreover, this conclusion is misleading because the "meat" (salt pork was used in preparing a bean soup, the actual staple of Sanuto's proposed diet) was to be distributed only every other day. "Thus," continues Sanuto, "they will each have [*solid*] meat three days a week and share in the broth of the meat on five days." (Italics mine.) The diet seems less attractive when presented in Sanuto's own terms. And Lane is forced to admit Sanuto warned that distributing such meals might be an occasion "for favoritism and brawling." Lane, "Diet and Wages of Seamen in the Early Fourteenth Century," in *Venice and History*, pp. 263–268. Finally, of course, Lane is talking about wages when the fleet was at sea that often had to feed a family back in Venice when jobs were not available.

20. For the growth of the wool industry in the fourteenth century, see Fano, "Lana," pp. 125–246; and for the silk industry, see R. Broglio d'Agano, "L'industria della seta a Venezia." For an analysis of their violence, see Chapter 7.

21. As this group of men presumably were regularly moving in and out of the labor market, especially as seamen and day-laborers in related industries, their position is somewhat confused by the social breakdown used; but they nonetheless reflect a reality of the lowest rung of Venetian society. On the success of the policy of attracting labor to Venice following the plague, see my article on sex crime and its continuity throughout the plague years in Venice, "Sexual Criminality in the Early Renaissance," p. 26.

22. Lane, *Maritime Republic*, p. 18; Karl Julius Beloch, *Bevölkerungsgeschichte Italiens*, 3: 3 gives a figure of about 100,000 for the same period; idem, "La popolazione di Venezia nei secoli XVI e XVII," p. 47, estimates 110,000 for the early trecento; and, Aldo Contento, "Il censimento della popolazione sotto la Repubblica Veneta," p. 20, calculates the population at 133,000. Whichever figure one might choose to accept, each is low in that it leaves out most of the marginal inhabitants of Venice, who would not show up in a census of able-bodied men.

23. For Venetian rapid recovery following the 1347–1348 plague see Ruggiero, "Sexual Criminality," pp. 25–27. On the demographic impact of the plague

in general, see David Herlihy, *Medieval and Renaissance Pistoia*, pp. 102–120. Beloch reports the following losses for plagues: 1382—nineteen thousand; 1397—fifteen thousand; 1400—sixteen thousand; "Popolazione," p. 48.

24. One source gives males between the ages of twenty and sixty as 30,000 (cited by Beloch, *Bevölkerungsgeschichte*, 3: 3) and another 40,100 (cited by Contento, "Censimento," p. 20). The later figure comes from a perhaps more accurate chronicle, though such judgments are hard to make given the paucity of statistical material in Venetian chronicles. The number of men in the Venetian Major Council in the early trecento is estimated by Lane as 1200. (Lane, *Maritime Republic*, p. 20). Though men had to be twenty-five to enter the Major Council, presumably they could serve beyond sixty, and Venetian nobles did live to ripe old ages. Thus by dividing one figure into the other, a rough percentage of noble adult males to total adult males can be found. Then one must assume that nobles in the Major Council had about the same size families as the rest of the population, an unlikely assumption unfortunately, and one has a percentage of nobles to the total population. Still it does not seem that these adjustments could push this figure much above 5 percent or much below 2 percent. In the mid-sixteenth century, when the nobility reached its largest size according to Lane (ibid.) it still constituted only 4 percent of the population according to the much more secure figures presented by Beloch, *Bevölkerungsgeschichte*, 3: 22.

25. Daniele Beltrami, *Storia della popolazione di Venezia dalle fine del secolo XVI alla caduta della Repubblica*, pp. 193–213 and Table 14. This breakdown seems to square roughly with the *estimo* of 1380 according to Gino Luzzatto, *I prestiti della Repubblica di Venezia (sec. XIII–XV) Introduzione Storica e Documenti*, pp. CXLV–CXLVI.

26. Chojnacki, "Crime," pp. 227–228 passim.

Chapter V

1. Marciana, MS Ital., Cl. VII, 128A (8639) f. 309r.

2. A *parte* from 1350 passed by the Major Council, for example, forbade the riding of horses on the main thoroughfares around the Rialto and in San Marco except during jousts and required horses to wear bells. A.S.V., M.C., *Novella*, f. 13r (1350). At this time, most bridges in Venice were without steps, which made them more easily usable by men on horseback.

3. Some have speculated that high levels of noble prosecution also reflect the unique sense of justice of the Venetian system. On this, see Stanley Chojnacki, "Crime," pp. 227–228. The article is provocative, but a closer study of the sources casts some doubt on this thesis.

4. A.S.V., Adv., *Raspe*, Reg. 4, f. 70r–v (1384). Examples of similar behavior can be found at other levels of society. Puzinello Menegi, a merchant from Lucca living in the *contrata* of Santa Sofia, also tortured his servant, Bartolomeo Gamba, believing he had robbed him. Although Bartolomeo had already been questioned by the Signori di Notte and released, Puzinello kept him without food for three days and finally called in a surgeon to torture him when no admission of guilt was forthcoming. Although the surgeon, Francesco da

Firenze, was sentenced to a year in jail and a fine of 50 lire di piccoli, Pu-zinello, who had planned and paid for the whole crime, was sentenced to only three months and a fine of 50 lire di piccoli. A.S.V., Adv., *Raspe*, Reg. 4, f. 67r–v. Even though such examples exist, it is evident that the nobility as-sumed this superiority to the law much more frequently.

5. Ibid., Reg. 2, f. 303v (1359). Nobleman Uberto Querini demonstrated another aspect of this attitude in his attempt to supplement legal penalties with his own sense of vengeance. He attacked a certain Stephano, striking him twice and seriously wounding him because he was unsatisfied with the penalty im-posed on Stephano by the Signori di Notte as a result of a previous quarrel. That penalty had not satisfied his honor. Eventually, his honor cost him a fine of 300 lire di piccoli from the Forty; ibid., Reg. 3, ff. 49v–50r (1363).

6. A.S.V., Adv., *Raspe*, Reg. 4, ff. 115v–116r (1388).

7. See Ruggiero, "Sexual Criminality," pp. 32–33, *n*. 8, last paragraph.

8. A.S.V., Adv., *Raspe*, Reg. 2, f. 204v (1357).

9. Ibid. For a further discussion of this case, see Chapter 10.

10. For the original prosecution, see ibid., f. 191v (1352); the second prosecution is reported in ibid., f. 196v (1352).

11. Ibid., f. 164v (1351) for the first case; and f. 176r–v (1351) for the second. On this see also Ruggiero, "Sexual Criminality," pp. 30–31.

12. A.S.V., Adv., *Raspe*, Reg. 2, ff. 249–250r (1355).

13. Ibid.

14. Ibid., Signori di Notte, *Processi*, Reg. 11, f. 13r (1394).

15. Ibid., Adv., *Raspe*, Reg. 5, ff. 125v–126r (1400).

16. Contributing to the lack of data is the fact that several registers of the Signori di Notte do not report murder penalties imposed by the Giudici di Proprio: 155 out of a total of 427 penalties are not reported. Inasmuch as the Giudici di Proprio tended to simpler executions without as much ritual display, there is an overemphasis on the elaborate executions favored by the Forty.

17. See Ruggiero, "Sexual Criminality," pp. 27 and 36, *n*. 41.

18. A factor here may be that such rapes were hushed up and revenged outside the law, thus allowing the father and family of the damaged merchandise to profit by her marriage with no one presumably the wiser. The noble life style itself, surrounded by servants and retainers, made secrecy unlikely in such matters.

19. A.S.V., Adv., *Raspe*, Reg. 4, f. 171v (1391). This penalty was approximately four times more severe than the average for women prosecuted for adultery. An example of a less severe penalty involved the widow of Nicoleto Bembo, Anna. Anna had sexual relations after her husband's death with a gold worker; her penalty from the Forty was a humiliating and painful beating; ibid., Reg. 3, f. 140r. Though not as severe as Lucia's penalty, it was in terms of the crime unusually severe. Corporal punishment of any type was unusual for a noble and especially unlikely for a noblewoman.

20. Ibid., Reg. 3, f. 98r (1367).

21. For a brief summary of the case between Morosini and Querini see Romanin, *Storia*, 3: 27.

22. A.S.V., Adv., *Raspe*, Reg. 3, f. 97v (1367).

23. Ibid., Reg. 1, f. 171v (1336).
24. Ibid., Reg. 4, f. 82r (1385 m.v.).
25. Ibid., Reg. 2, f. 28v (1341 m.v.).
26. Ibid., Reg. 3, f. 30r (1362).
27. Ibid., Reg. 2, ff. 85v–86r (1345).

Chapter VI

1. A.S.V., Adv., *Raspe,* Reg. 2, f. 292v (1358).
2. Ibid., Reg. 3, f. 257r–v (1378).
3. Ibid., Reg. 4, f. 160v (1391).
4. Ibid., Reg. 3, ff. 19v–20r (1361).
5. Such situations, of course, do not need to be consciously created, and that is not being suggested here. In the area of policing, as noted earlier, it was not so much the desire to create a buffer class as the desire to avoid dangerous and tiresome chores beneath the dignity of important members of the nobility that led to the passing of primary patrolling responsibility to non-noble *custodi.*
6. A.S.V., Signori di Notte, *Processi,* Reg. 10, ff. 40v–41r (1371).
7. Ibid., f. 78r–v (1372).
8. A.S.V., Adv., *Raspe,* Reg. 4, f. 151v (1390).
9. Ibid., Reg. 3, ff. 209v–210r (1374).
10. Ibid., Reg. 2, ff. 255v–256v (1355). Two of their more fortunate compatriots evaded capture and were banned perpetually. As in the case of Nicoleto Damiani, the Forty ruled that if caught in Venice they would receive a full show execution.
11. Ibid., f. 139v (1349).
12. Ibid., Reg. 3, f. 120v (1369).
13. Ibid., Reg. 5, f. 165r (1402).
14. Ibid., Reg. 3, f. 189r (1373).
15. Ibid., Reg. 4, ff. 179v–180r (1392).
16. An important reason to suppress a sexual crime would be that in the case of a single girl it might hurt her marriage chances, but rape whether by noble or commoner presumably would have had a similar effect on prospective husbands and their families.

Chapter VII

1. This point is pursued in greater detail in the chapter on the perception of speech crimes.
2. A.S.V., Dieci, *Miste,* Reg. 5, f. 11v (1350).
3. For the conspiracy, see Zago, *Dieci,* vol. 2. The primary documents are 261, 262, 271, 279–297, 314, 315, 330, 334, 338–352, 364, 379, 395, 406, 413, 448, 472, 473, 510, 511, 577 spanning the period 1328–1330; confiscation and sale of Barozzi property is reported in documents 314, 352, 364, 472, 473; banning of heirs of traitors in 395 and executions and other penalties in 279–297, 338–350. The main conspirators were members of the Barozzi family, led by

Nicolo called Magnus. He was supported by his brothers, Cataldo, Iacabino, and Marino, along with several members of the Querini family, Andreolo and Mafeo being the primary reported leaders. Unfortunately, the records are laconic on the conspiracy, and the chronicle record is equally silent, though the inclusion of the Querini family plus the subsequent strengthening of communal patrols under the centralizing direction of the Ten suggest another attack on the ruling class on the model of the Querini–Tiepolo conspiracy.

4. A.S.V., Dieci, *Miste*, Reg. 5, f. 11v (1350).
5. A.S.V., Adv., *Raspe*, Reg. 5, f. 73v (1397): "Ve lasceva cosi mal menar istis nobilibus, date eis de uno cutello in gulla, quia tantam penam portaretis ad interficiendum unum nobilem quantam portaretis ad interficiendum viliorum hominem Venetis."
6. At first, it might seem anomalous from Table 7.2 that workers' penalties still fall significantly below the mean for all speech crimes. This is caused by the large number of cases where social class is not clear. These figures represent primarily lower-level workers and marginal men. Given the tendency for increasing penalties to accompany decreasing status these penalties were predictably most strict. This group of lower-class unknowns pulls up the average.
7. A.S.V., Adv., *Raspe*, Reg. 3, f. 100r–v (1367).
8. Ibid., Reg. 2, f. 287v (1358).
9. See, for example, Ibid., f. 162r (1350), where a worker named Laurenzo who punched a relative during the course of a family squabble was fined 10 soldi di grossi by the Forty.
10. The average for workers, however, is somewhat below the average for important men (21.8). This is less significant because, as noted above, the worker figure is minimal.
11. A.S.V., Adv., *Raspe*, Reg. 4, f. 155r–v (1390). The requirement of a dowry may seem rather strange in that a dowry was normally paid to the husband. In this case, Guido would in theory have given it to himself. In practice, however, following the husband's death his wife's dowry was returned. Thus this dowry provided a promise of some inheritance for Micola if Guido died before her. A few other marriage examples can be found in ibid., Reg. 1, f. 17v (1325); ibid., Reg. 2, f. 75 (1344); and ibid., f. 105 (1347).
12. A.S.V., Signori di Notte, *Processi*, Reg. 10, f. 60r–v (1371 m.v.).
13. Ibid., f. 35r–v (1370).
14. For each crime, see respectively ibid., Reg. 8, ff. 13v–15r (1361); ibid., Reg. 10, ff. 57v–58r (1371); ibid., Reg. 11, f. 37r (1396); ibid., Reg. 10, f. 54r–v (1371); and ibid., Reg. 11, f. 10 (1394).
15. A.S.V., Adv., *Raspe*, Reg. 4, f. 46v (1382).
16. Ibid., Reg. 5, f. 9v (1393). A more orthodox example would be the case of Antonia, wife of a worker rather than a madam, beaten because of her testimony before the Cinque alla Pace against a carpenter named Bartolomeo, ibid., Reg. 2, f. 180v (1351).
17. Ibid., Reg. 4, f. 177v (1392).
18. Venice was a confined area where much of daily life was carried on in the streets; and there is little evidence of any social segregation in housing pat-

terns. These factors suggest a relatively high level of casual contact between the classes. To the noble for whom violence was a style of life, however, casual contact with a worker would not often have led to murder because it did not have enough dignity or honor involved to warrant a major crime. A bump or cross word from a peer required a serious response; the same from a worker could be handled by the state if it warranted attention at all. The point in essence is that serious contacts between workers and nobles were minimal.

19. It might be argued against this view that nobles, as the entrepreneurs who utilized their labor, did have tense relationships with workers. Venetian nobles, however, were not the entrepreneurs or capitalists of the modern stereotypes. The most powerful were primarily moneylenders, investing now for spice voyages, now for the purchase of cloth or grain, now in shares of the communal debt. They had little business contact with the lower classes.

20. A.S.V., Signori di Notte, *Processi,* Reg. 10, f. 24r–v (1370).

21. Ibid., Reg. 11, f. 10r (1394).

22. A.S.V., Adv., *Raspe,* Reg. 2, f. 152r (1350).

23. A.S.V., Signori di Notte, *Processi,* Reg. 8, ff. 13v–15r (1360).

24. A.S.V., Adv., *Raspe,* Reg. 2, f. 19r (1340).

25. Ibid., Reg. 5, f. 45r (1395).

26. A.S.V., Signori di Notte, *Processi,* Reg. 10, f. 73v (1372).

27. A.S.V., Adv., *Raspe,* Reg. 3, f. 140v (1370). An interesting problem for Venetian penology is also brought out by this case. How does society punish slaves so as not to punish masters as well? One option, mild corporal punishment, was used here. Fines, jail sentences, and serious corporal punishment all decreased the nobles' investment in slaves. This may have indirectly contributed to underreporting of minor crimes; innocent nobles who owned slaves stood to lose more than the criminals themselves.

28. A.S.V., Signori di Notte, *Processi,* Reg. 8, ff. 19v–24v (1362). This case is not quite so long as the folio numbers indicate; folio 21 *recto* and *verso* is missing because of misnumbering.

29. A.S.V., M.C., *Novella,* f. 103r (1364).

30. A.S.V., Adv., *Raspe,* Reg. 2, f. 162r (1350).

31. Ibid., f. 105v (1346).

Chapter VIII

1. Zago, *Dieci,* 1:246.

2. Ibid., p. 247.

3. Ibid., Reg. 2, doc. 56 (1320). The Camera Frumenti was used as a communal treasury at least in the early part of the fourteenth century; on this see Reinhold C. Mueller, "The Procuratori di San Marco and the Venetian Credit Market."

4. Zago, *Dieci,* vol. 1, Reg. 2, doc. 151. This should not be read as quaint or paranoic; it represents instead the perception that such a crime was dangerous, thus warranting careful scrutiny even of public servants such as Donato.

5. The figures for Register 8 have been adjusted because there was a large-scale sodomy case at the end of 1406 involving more than forty people. This greatly

distorts the picture, but the case was an anomaly; the Ten did not normally prosecute sodomy in this period. They were content to let the Signori di Notte handle such matters.

6. Zago, *Dieci,* vol. 1, Reg. 2, doc. 510 (1324).

7. Ibid.

8. Ibid., vol. 2, Reg. 3, docs. 493 and 494 (1329).

9. A.S.V., Adv., *Raspe,* Reg. 2, f. 107r (1347).

10. Ibid., f. 165r–v (1351). Nicolo Orio, also a noble, was absolved of the same crime.

11. Ibid., f. 296v (1358).

12. Ibid., Reg. 3, f. 32v (1362).

13. Ibid., Reg. 4, f. 97r (1386).

14. Zago, *Dieci,* vol. 2, Reg. 3, docs. 375 and 376 (1329).

15. A.S.V., Dieci, *Miste,* Reg. 8, f. 64v (1400 m.v.).

16. Ibid., Reg. 5, f. 11r (1350).

17. A.S.V., Dieci, *Miste,* Reg. 5, f. 112r (1362 m.v.). On the Ten's growing control over the *scuole* following mid-century, see Ruggiero, "The Ten," pp. 177–197.

18. A.S.V., Dieci, *Miste,* Reg. 5, ff. 35r–37r (1355).

19. A.S.V., Adv., *Raspe,* Reg. 4, f. 74v (1385). The Dandolo family ranked fourth in all offices listed in the Segretario alle Voci Registers 1–3 and third in important offices, i.e., the Forty, Senate, Ten, Ducal Councilors, and Avogadori. The Malipiero family ranked thirty-fourth in all offices and thirty-first for important offices. Though this is only a rough measure of family importance, it suggests a significant gap between the two.

20. Ibid., Reg. 2, f. 162r (1350).

21. Ibid., Reg. 3, f. 153v (1371).

22. Ibid., Reg. 4, f. 187v (1392). The Forty tended to deal with both verbal and physical assault on communal officials.

23. Ibid., Reg. 2, f. 63r (1343).

24. Ibid., f. 137r (1349).

25. Ibid., Reg. 4, f. 82r (1385).

26. A.S.V., Dieci, *Miste,* Reg. 5, f. 40r (1355); Reg. 8, f. 80r–v (1402) and f. 85r–v (1403); Zago, *Dieci,* vol. 2, Reg. 3, docs. 375–376 (1329).

27. A.S.V., Dieci, *Miste,* Reg. 6, ff. 21v–22r (1364), 22v (1364); Adv., *Raspe,* Reg. 3, f. 140v (1370).

28. A.S.V., Adv., *Raspe,* Reg. 3, f. 192r (1373); ibid., Dieci, *Miste,* Reg. 5, f. 59r (1357) and f. 35r (1355) respectively.

29. These figures do not total because the courts routinely gave mixed sentences. The validity of the point equivalency scale is verified by the fact that the range of penalty points for each type of punishment is virtually the same. Jail sentences range from 1 to 100. Fines range from 1 to 110.

30. Zago, *Dieci,* vol. 2, Reg. 3, docs. 375–376 (1329 m.v.). This penalty was not pushed through by men unfamiliar with power and politics. It was proposed by the doge, two ducal councilors, two captains of the Ten, and an Avogador.

31. One case involving speech against the commune by a worker carried a penalty of three months in jail followed by life banishment: A.S.V., Adv., *Raspe,*

Reg. 1, f. 40v (1327); and one case involving a servant who threatened his master was penalized by banishment for life: Reg. 1, f. 195r (1339).

Chapter IX

1. A.S.V., M.C., *Novella,* f. 84v (1360).
2. Zago, *Dieci,* vol. 2, Reg. 3, doc. 311 (1328).
3. A.S.V., Adv., *M.C.,* Reg. 24/7, f. 3v (1349); f. 6r (1350).
4. Ibid., *Raspe,* Reg. 3, ff. 30v–31r (1362).
5. Ibid., Reg. 2, f. 303v (1359). The fine for carrying a concealed weapon should have been at least 100 lire di piccoli more.
6. Ibid., Reg. 3, ff. 5v–7r (1361).
7. The total comes to over 122 cases because some cases involved both fines and jail terms.
8. A.S.V., Adv., *Raspe,* Reg. 3, f. 100r–v (1367).
9. Ibid., Reg. 5, f. 58r (1396).
10. Ibid., Reg. 4, f. 8v (1378).
11. Ibid., Reg. 2, f. 108v (1347). Of course, deciding to what extent two crimes are parallel requires a subjective judgment. Such crimes nevertheless provide an important elaboration of the more objective statistics presented earlier.
12. Ibid., Reg. 5, f. 10r (1393).
13. Ibid., Reg. 3, f. 98v (1367).
14. For this insight I am grateful to Reinhold Mueller, who has been working on the grain office and communal policy. It is to be hoped that his work will systematically explain this situation. For an example of the type of problem that led to tensions, see Roberto Cessi, *La regolazione delle entrate e delle spese,* pp. 105–109.
15. A.S.V., Adv., *Raspe,* Reg. 4, ff. 179v–180r (1392). Penalties were not always so severe. In a similar dispute, Simoneto da Vale hit an official with a sword when he tried to collect a payment owed on two *stare* of grain distributed through the grain office. The wound was serious but Simoneto was only sentenced to six months in jail and fined 100 lire di piccoli. He may have feared worse, for he fled the city and was given one month to return or face a doubling of his jail term; Reg. 3, f. 107r (1368).
16. Ibid., f. 155v (1371).
17. Ibid., Reg. 1, f. 172v (1336).
18. Ibid., Reg. 2, f. 67v (1343).
19. Ibid., f. 189r (1351). Another example that included both family troubles and litigation was the dispute discussed earlier between Francescino Sourosin and his mother-in-law, Besina Mare; see Chapter 7, *n.* 17.
20. Ibid., Reg. 1, ff. 204v–205r (1340). A certain continuity in severity is illustrated by a similar case discussed earlier involving the sailor, Zanino da Cimento, who attacked the noble patron of his ship, Marco Venier, slapping him and calling him a "bastarde et multa alia." For this minor violence, the Forty sentenced him to a year in jail; ibid., Reg. 3, f. 30r (1362).
21. An interesting aspect of this case is that one of the mutilated sailors returned

to Venice, breaking his banishment. He was imprisoned until June 8, 1364 when he was released by a *gratia*. It is not clear exactly when he broke his banishment, but because he was serving a life sentence, one assumes that he spent a good portion of the twenty-two years between his original conviction and his eventual release in a Venetian jail; ibid., Reg. 2, ff. 49v–50r (1342).

22. Ibid., ff. 85v–86r (1345).
23. Ibid., Reg. 3, f. 264r (1378).
24. Ibid., Reg. 2, f. 95v (1346).
25. A *parte* from 1342 typifies the troubled rhetoric of such legislation: "Cum multi excesses et percussiones enormes committantur contra clericos et transeant impunita contra deum et iusticiam et in minus honoris domini"; ibid., M.C., Reg. 6, f. 82r (1342). Actually, such rhetoric was routinely used when the Major Council revised its stance on violence between clerics and laymen, a revision that seems to have been based as often on diplomatic relations with the church as on actual levels of violence. For further examples, see ibid., Reg. 4, f. 17r (no date, but probably 1314); ibid., Reg. 5, f. 16r (1324); ibid., f. 104v (1329); ibid., f. 135v (1332); ibid., Reg. 6, ff. 116r–119v (1344)—a typical long report of *sapientes*; ibid., Reg. 7, f. 27r (1355). Regular revisions continued throughout the period.
26. Ibid., *Raspe*, Reg. 2, f. 141r (1349).
27. Ibid., Reg. 1, f. 132v (1333).
28. Ibid., ff. 187v–188r (1339). A less significant incidence of the economic impact of the clergy involved a Hungarian priest who was struck in the face by a boat owner while dickering about the price of a trip to Hungary. The Forty sentenced the owner to three months in jail and fined him 25 lire di piccoli; ibid., Reg. 2, f. 155v (1350).
29. Marciana, MS Lat., Cl. V, 137 (10453), *Liber Statutorum*, f. 79v.
30. Ibid., f. 78v.

Chapter X

1. Parts of this chapter first appeared as an article, "Sexual Criminality in Early Renaissance Venice: 1338–1358," *Journal of Social History* 8 (1974–1975): 18–37.
2. William Bowsky maintains that in Siena rape was one of the "so-called 'enormous crimes' " similar to homicide, treason, arson, kidnapping, and poisoning; William M. Bowsky, "The Medieval Commune and Internal Violence," p. 2. For fourteenth-century Florence, Umberto Dorini, though citing laws that allowed milder penalties and wide judicial latitude, argues that penalties for rape varied between a minimum fine of 500 lire and a maximum of 2000 lire; Umberto Dorini, *Il diritto penale e la delinquenza in Firenze nel sec. XIV*, p. 69. Werner Gundersheimer sees a similar severity in Ferrara: "Under the law, thieves and murderers were hanged or like rapists, decapitated"; Werner L. Gundersheimer, *Ferrara*, p. 140.
3. Chojnacki, "Crime," p. 199.
4. The only exceptions to this generalization occurred in the areas of sexuality that retained a reputation of abnormality. Sodomy remained under a strong taboo, though there is evidence that it was fairly prevalent in the forms both

of homosexuality and of bestiality. The penalty for these crimes remained burning throughout the century. Such strong enforcements of a sexual taboo stand in marked contrast to the lenient—even relaxed—penalties associated with rape and nonviolent fornication and adultery.

5. A.S.V., Adv., *Raspe,* Reg. 5, f. 36v (1395).

6. The statistics for fornication and adultery reveal a similar leniency, indicating that these are more crimes of tradition than real crimes. It is as if they were occasionally prosecuted because of an inertia of ideas that had not kept pace with the social realities of the world in which those ideas existed.

7. In order to have some statistical validity, only cases within two standard deviations of the original mean were used, which meant that in both cases all crimes over 90 points were excluded. A review of these cases revealed that there was little that could be considered normal about them.

8. See, for example, A.S.V., Signori di Notte, *Processi,* Reg. 6, ff. 4v–5v (1354) where graphic descriptions of the following type are repeated several times for one case of homosexuality: "vero post hec sex vel octo diebus iterum duabus vel tribus vicibus hore noctis fuit in lecto cum ipso Jacobello et ascendit super corpus ipsius et ponens suum membrum virile in choxis ipsius."

9. A total penalty of 22.5 points; A.S.V., Adv., *Raspe,* Reg. 3, f. 104r (1368).

10. This in a small way contradicts Phillipe Aries's rather blanket generalization that there was an absence of a sense of childhood in the premodern world; see Phillipe Aries, *Centuries of Childhood.*

11. A.S.V., Adv., *Raspe,* Reg. 2, f. 320v (1360). His penalty was six months in jail.

12. Ibid., Reg. 5, f. 127r (1400). Needless to say, a cry of fire in a medieval city with buildings jumbled closely together and highly flammable was much more likely to bring help than today. It is significant, however, that individual women were aware enough to make use of such a situation. It also reveals indirectly that they understood how unimportant their victimization seemed to society. To secure help, they cried "fire" because fire elicited a concern that their rape did not.

13. Ibid., f. 82v (1398). Mutilation for crimes involving sexuality, as well as such public exposure of criminals, was extremely rare. As noted earlier, it is significant that facial mutilation by the commune was commonly used for serious crimes committed by females when a similar penalty for a man would be the loss of a hand. Apparently a woman's worth in this male-oriented society was seen in her beauty while a man's was seen in his working ability.

14. Ibid., Reg. 3, f. 144r (1370). Nanino served one year in jail and was fined 500 lire di piccoli. His helpers received a three-month jail sentence together with a fine of 100 lire di piccoli and a one-month jail sentence respectively.

15. "Voluisse violare et sibi de nocte in domum intrasse per vim," Ibid., Reg. 1, f. 146r (1334).

16. An unusual instance of this approach involved a slave, neither a neighbor nor a friend, who gained entrance to the house of his victim by imitating the voice of her husband. The lights were out, which aided the culprit; but when discovered he proceeded to rape his victim anyway. Though by this means he avoided the extra crime of breaking and entering, the Forty still penalized him very heavily because he had raped a woman from a higher class, and in a

particularly tricky way at that. Ingenuity of the criminal sort was not appreciated among the lower classes. Ibid., Reg. 4, ff. 7v–8r (1378).

17. Ibid., Reg. 2, f. 322r–v (1360).

18. Ibid., Reg. 3, f. 127r (1369). The Forty gave Bernardo a couple of months in jail, not much of a penalty for a rather sorry attempt.

19. Ibid., f. 90r (1366).

20. Ibid., f. 213r–v (1375). Polani's penalty was a fine of 100 ducats, of which two-thirds went to the girl for her dowry. If caught, the mother was to be whipped from San Marco to the Rialto where her guilt was to be proclaimed; then she was to be placed in jail for six months. Four years later, the girl, Catarucia, using the return on the investment of Polani's fine, married a young worker, "Andream filius Jacobi Vaginarii."

21. Ibid., f. 268r (1378). Leonardo's penalty was three months in jail and a fine of 50 lire di piccoli. Perhaps his penalty was so light because of the "purifying" nature of his rather wild passion. Though not very subtle, it was an instance of pure passion that often elicited the empathetic compassion of the nobility.

22. Ibid., Reg. 4, f. 81v (1385).

23. This figure was reached by multiplying 6.6 points times the number of cases involving breaking and entering, subtracting these points from the total of all points, then dividing by the total number of cases, a method that obviously provides an inexact figure to be taken only as a suggestion of the impact of breaking and entering on the penalty. A subjective reading of the documents suggests that in fact this correction probably errs on the side of conservativeness.

24. A.S.V., Adv., Raspe, Reg. 2, f. 76v (1345).

25. Ibid., f. 160v (1350). The case is repeated, apparently because of a confusion of first names by the scribe, on ff. 162r and 163r.

26. Ibid., ff. 302v–303r (1359).

27. Ibid., Reg. 1, f. 120v (1332).

28. Higher penalties were also prescribed for thieves who fled the city to avoid prosecution, as Bartolomeo had done. Marciana, MS Lat., Cl. V, 137 (10453), Liber Statutorum, f. 79r–v. Later this statute was revised to require only the loss of one eye for crimes in the range of 20 lire to 100 soldi. Querini, Cl. IV, Cod. I H 3, ff. 82v–83r.

29. A.S.V., Adv., Raspe, Reg. 3, ff. 186v–187r (1373). Bartolomeo apparently did not rob his victim because he lacked funds, for he paid his fine immediately after he was apprehended in November 1373.

30. Ibid., Reg. 2, f. 156v (1350).

31. Robbery as a sporting aside rather than a necessity was certainly the case in these crimes. Another typical example involved Alberto Alberto, a noble, who raped Gerita, wife of Jacobello Trevisan, and stole a number of books as well. Books, of course, were valuable commodities, but Alberto hardly appears to have been out to make his fortune with such a robbery, especially as Trevisan, also a noble, probably had considerably richer things to carry off. The fact that Alberto's victim was a noble's wife upped the ante in a way that the theft of the books probably did not. He was fined 200 lire di piccoli, to be paid before his time in jail would count toward his sentence of two years. Still

it was a small penalty in relation to the norms for robbery. Ibid., f. 24v (1341).

32. The convent was to an important degree an outlet especially for the more substantial members of society, for females who could not be fitted into the normal patterns of female life in society.

33. In the case of the rape of Donata, "puellam etatis annorum 10," the Avogadori even mentioned the girl's pain, a type of sentimentality for the victim virtually absent from the records of rape: "posuit suum membrum modicum in orificio suo cum maximo suo dolore"; A.S.V., Adv., *Raspe*, Reg. 3, f. 146r–v (1370).

34. Ibid., Reg. 5, f. 140v (1401).

35. In 1367, a boatman named Bartolomeo was accused of attempting to rape the infant daughter of a neighbor and fellow boatman, but he was absolved by the Forty; ibid., Reg. 3, f. 98r (1367). A certain Matheo was accused of actually raping Francescina, a four-year-old girl, but he too was absolved; ibid., Reg. 2, f. 129r (1348).

36. Ibid., f. 149r (1350).

37. In fact, though dowries were not regularly given to girls of marriageable age when they were raped, many *puellae* were given a portion of the fines imposed by the Forty. See the analysis in the text.

38. A.S.V., Adv., *Raspe*, Reg. 4, f. 119r (1388).

39. A substantial dowry for a girl from the lower classes; ibid., Reg. 2, f. 204v (1353). For more on this case, see Chapter 5, pp. 70–71.

40. Marquis de Sade, *The Complete Justine, Philosophy in the Bedroom and Other Writings*, p. 325.

41. This was a fairly typical provision in such cases; it guaranteed the girl at least some part of her husband's patrimony if he died before her. A.S.V., Adv., *Raspe*, Reg. 2, f. 105r (1346).

42. According to the records, only nine cases spread throughout the period involved marriage. One of these involved a widow rather than an unmarried girl. Agnesina, widow of a builder, was raped violently (her assailant was armed with a knife) by a neighboring worker. The Forty offered him the option of marrying his victim, which he did, escaping all penalties. Ibid., f. 126r (1348).

43. Ibid., f. 145r (1349).

44. Ibid., f. 207r (1353).

45. Fra Paolino Minorita, *De recto regimine*, p. 90.

46. See Phillip Elliot Slater, *The Glory of Hera*, for an analysis of the psychological implications of living in a society where late marriage for males and young marriage of females created a large group of widows who exercised considerable power over the psychological development of their sons and therefore contributed to a deep-seated antipathy in mature males to mature women and a concomitant fear of the sexuality of mature women. There are strong reasons for suspecting that similar fears were operative in at least the upper reaches of Renaissance society. One has merely to sample the misogynist literature of the period to find suggestive instances of a similar fear.

47. A.S.V., Adv., *Raspe*, Reg. 2, ff. 316v–318v (1360).

48. An excellent example of the rhetoric of the Major Council in seeking to elimi-

nate sexual crime in convents can be found in a *parte* of 1349, "Quoniam abhominabilis frequentatis criminum . . . fornicandi in monasteriis . . . continue commituntur. . . . Et considerato et diligentur quod gravius multo sit eternam quam temporalem offendere magestatem. Vadit pars quod statuatur ad laudam et reverentiam Jeshu Christi ac beatissime matris eius." Basically they ruled that the Avogadori were to investigate such cases and the Forty to try them; ibid., *M.C.*, Reg. 7, f. lv (1349).

Chapter XI

1. That only the Signori di Notte were responsible for murder has up till now been the generally accepted scholarly opinion; see Ferro, *Dizionario*, 2:693; Roberti, *Magistrature*, 1:208–209; Chojnacki, "Crime," p. 220. In fact, the records of the Avogadori contain 102 investigations of homicide or attempted homicide for the period from 1324 to 1402, all of which were prosecuted by the Forty. Inasmuch as the total number of prosecutions before the Forty and Giudici di Proprio amounted to only 427 cases, slightly fewer than a quarter of the cases heard were actually handled by the Avogadori and Forty. It is also significant that cases were occasionally handled by the Major Council or the Senate as well. Once again, the law makes things look much more simple and straightforward in theory than they were in fact.

2. Dente may have been related to a minor Venetian noble family. The records of the Avogadori note that after the Querini–Tiepolo conspiracy a Francesco Dente da San Paternian was added to the Major Council along with several other families. A.S.V., Misc. Codici I Storia Veneta 44, f. lr. Before the assassination plot was discovered, Vitiliano also had been living in San Paternian. However, he was living at the Cha Giustinian and was referred to specifically as "de Padua," perhaps to distinguish him from Venetian namesakes or even relatives. A.S.V., Adv., *Raspe*, Reg. 1, ff. 208r–209r (1340).

3. Ibid. This response was typical for those beyond communal authority, whether they were foreigners living abroad or members of the clergy living in Venice. Banishment from Venice was an effective technical punishment apparently acceptable to foreign and ecclesiastical authority. Occasionally, however, the commune took more serious action, with important implications for interstate relations. In 1392, for example, three Florentines were sent to kill two Florentine dyers living in Venice. The Forty's response was as stern as possible. After show mutilations, the captured murderers were drawn and quartered, and their remains were hung up for the view of the populace as a lesson against becoming paid assassins. The Florentines who paid for the crime, Bucello Francesco del Richo and Benghi Thadei, wool merchants, were not only banned but also warned that if caught in Venice they would be subjected to the same penalty as their paid men. Moreover, the Forty took a step with unusual implications for relations with Florence: they offered a reward of 4000 lire di piccoli for the capture of these Florentine citizens alive or 2000 lire di piccoli for their capture dead. Essentially Venice was offering to pay for the murder or kidnapping of foreigners. Such expedients were rarely taken,

but they reveal how seriously the nobility was committed to elimination of such crime. Ibid., Reg. 4, ff. 182r–184r (1392).

4. Ibid., Reg. 2, ff. 58r–59v (1343). A similar case involving important foreigners occurred in 1388 when the Venetian noble Zanino Contarini was implicated in a plot to poison the Count of Vertù, Gian Galeazzo Visconti. This was no ordinary plot, and no ordinary judge was capable of evaluating all the social and political ramifications of the case. As a matter of state and diplomacy, the Forty acted, but their moderation showed more respect for Contarini power in Venice than fear of the rising power of Gian Galeazzo. Contarini was banned from Venice for two years, a penalty stiff enough to show Gian Galeazzo that Venice would not allow its citizens to interfere with its neutrality yet light enough to cause no major hardships for the Contarini family. Ibid., Reg. 4, f. 115r (1388).

5. Ibid., Signori di Notte, *Processi*, Reg. 10, ff. 96v–97v (1373).

6. Ibid., Reg. 11, ff. 25v–26r (1395).

7. Ibid., Adv., *Raspe*, Reg. 4, f. 112r (1387).

8. Only 28 paid assassins were prosecuted in the period, i.e., they account for only 6.6 percent of 427 murderers.

9. A.S.V., Adv., *Raspe*, Reg. 2, ff. 249v–250r (1355).

10. Ibid., f. 246r (1355).

11. Ibid., ff. 308v–309r (1359).

12. Ibid., Reg. 4, ff. 182r–184r (1392); see note three for this case.

13. It is notable that the commune was especially careful to discover motives in cases where the victim was socially superior to his murderer. One reason for this must have been a desire to identify all cases of paid assassination. As a result, there are few questionable cases of such murders; the figure of 6.6 percent cited in note 8 appears to be fairly accurate. It should be noted, however, that there is some likelihood that beyond the prosecuted cases there were a considerable number of such cases where the culprit or culprits escaped and could not be identified.

14. It is somewhat unusual, given the strictness of the penalties for robbery, that murder was not a normal concomitant of robbery. To a degree, this can probably be attributed to the nature of the reports of such crimes by the Signori di Notte. In part, it may also be attributable to the fact that many of the people who robbed in Renaissance society were marginal people, robbing to live, without much criminal intent or understanding of the relative dangers of their crime. To the nobility, robbery might seem the most serious threat to society possible, but to a marginal man robbery was a part of life and murder was still another matter.

15. A.S.V., Adv., *Raspe*, Reg. 3, ff. 143v–144r (1370). The third person involved in this crime, a female servant, had been a party to the plan but had not actually participated in the murder. She escaped with a comparatively light penalty. She was taken along with the other two on their ritual mutilation, but only when she arrived in San Marco was she actually mutilated, first being branded and then having her nose cut off, typical penalties for women. Instead of being executed, she was banished perpetually.

16. Ibid., Reg. 4, ff. 174v–175r (1391). The Forty heard a few lesser cases of robbery and murder as well. One that seemed to attract the judges' attention for sentimental reasons was the murder of an elderly slave named Marte Tartare. A certain Giacomo attacked her one day, beating her and robbing her of 8 lire di piccoli. Several days later he came back, robbed her again, and stabbed her to death, apparently without getting anything. The Forty's penalty, though more restrained, provided that Giacomo be hanged between the columns in San Marco. Ibid., f. 115v (1388).

17. Ibid., Reg. 3, f. 90v (1366).

18. Ibid., Reg. 1, f. 78r (1329).

19. In Venice, the Pietà was the best known early hospital concentrating on foundling care, founded in the mid-trecento. By the sixteenth century, when figures become available, it was responsible at times for more than one thousand foundlings. Pullan, *Rich and Poor*, p. 207. The whole question of the exposure of infants after the classical period warrants careful reexamination.

20. Out of a total 427, 194 murders (45.4 percent of the murders prosecuted in the period) have such factors as their identified motives. Moreover, there is only one such case involving a noble, and only 15 involve important men. Clearly such crimes were the prerogative of the lower classes. There is one qualification, however; crimes committed by nobles were generally more carefully investigated, and apparently superficial motivations such as drunkenness or casual brawls would probably be replaced by more substantial motivations. For the lower classes, the prejudices of the noble investigators were most likely satisfied by an establishment of the surface context of the crime.

21. A.S.V., Signori di Notte, *Processi*, Reg. 10, f. 49r–v (1371).

22. Ibid., Reg. 11, f. 17v (1394). Perhaps the best example of a senseless murder involved Giovanni Faber and Francesco Sartore. The two had been drinking and playing dice with friends at a tavern near the Rialto. When the game broke up, Giovanni began arguing that he had been cheated. Francesco managed to calm him down and started leading him home. On the way, Giovanni began arguing about which was the quickest way home. Apparently fed up, Francesco left Giovanni to take his own path; but as he walked away he expressed his disgust by flipping a stone at Giovanni. A moment later, Giovanni rushed up from behind and stabbed his friend to death with a bread knife. Reg. 10, ff. 108v–109r (1374).

23. In theory, self-defense was grounds for acquittal, but in many cases what constituted sufficient self-defense was difficult to establish in the courtroom. Inasmuch as the *Promissio Maleficorum* allowed judges wide leeway, as noted earlier, in cases where guilt was not completely established, lighter penalties were often used.

24. Of all penalties for murder given by the Forty, 41 were show hangings.

25. A.S.V., Adv., *Raspe*, Reg. 4, f. 25v (1380).

26. "Debeat amputari capud a spaltullis ita quod moriantur sicud observetur per totem orbem." This was part of the Ducal Promissione passed by the Major Council in 1382. A.S.V., M.C., *Novella*, f. 178v (1382).

27. A.S.V., Adv., *Raspe*, Reg. 4, f. 115v (1388); see note 16.

BIBLIOGRAPHY

Archival Sources *

Archivio di Stato, Venice (A.S.V.)

Archivio Notarile

> *Cancelleria Inferiore*
> *Testamenti*
> *Miscellanea Notai Diversi*

Avogaria di Comun (Adv.)

> *Deliberazioni di Maggior Consiglio (M.C.)*
> Reg. 20, 3 December 1294–29 August 1308
> Reg. 21, 6 May 1312–10 April 1324
> Reg. 22, 22 April 1324–11 February 1334
> Reg. 23, 5 March 1335–7 April 1349
> Reg. 24, 26 April 1349–23 January 1379
> *Raspe*
> Reg. 3641, 4 April 1324–28 March 1341
> Reg. 3642, 18 April 1341–10 February 1361
> Reg. 3643, 3 March 1361–28 July 1378
> Reg. 3644, 3 August 1378–28 February 1393
> Reg. 3645, 3 March 1393–26 February 1406
> *Miscellanea Penale*
> Busta 108
> Busta 111
> Busta 114
> Busta 116
> Reg. 4358
> Reg. 4608
> *Parte in Materia Araldica*
> Reg. 14, 10 November 1274–17 February 1728
> *Parti prese nel dare la nobilita veneta a diverse famiglie*
> *(this was originally Cod. Brera 49)*
> Reg. 15, 1304–1686

---

* Where feasible, a more complete reference is given because of the unavailability of an adequate published reference work on the material used.

Sunti di disposizione araldica
   Reg. 16, 26 October 1277–1781
Speculum Venetae Nobilitatis
   Reg. 17, 15 November 1263–1654
Alberi genealogici di alcuni famiglie patrizie Venete
   Busta 184, sec. XIII–XIX
Alberi di famiglie aggregate alle nobilita Veneta e di famiglie Venete non patrizie
   Busta 185, sec. XIV–XIX
Miscellanea Araldica
   Busta 186
Capitulare
   Reg. 3

Cassiere della Bolle Ducale

Grazie del Maggior Consiglio
   Reg. 3, 12 June 1329–4 September 1330
   Reg. 4, 21 August 1331–17 June 1332
   Reg. 5, 27 October 1331–19 May 1335 (note that Reg. 5 both in its dates and contents seems to be incorrectly part of this series. It deals primarily with civil matters.)
   Reg. 6, 9 September 1333–1 October 1335
   Reg. 7, 16 October 1335–12 December 1338
   Reg. 8, 15 November 1338–22 April 1341
   Reg. 9, 2 April 1341–18 July 1343
   Reg. 10, 23 July 1343–27 November 1344
   Reg. 11, March 1345–September 1346
   Reg. 12, April 1348–August 1352
   Reg. 13, September 1352–October 1356
   Reg. 14, September 1356–1360
   Reg. 15, April 1361–1364
   Reg. 16, April 1364–May 1372
   Reg. 17, August 1372–March 1390
   Reg. 18, 1390–1400

Cinque Anziani alla Pace

   Busta 1 Capitulare

Collegio

Lettere segrete 1308–1310; 1354–1363; 1375–1377; 1382–1385
Notatorio 1327–1391
Secrete 1363–1366

Commemoriali

Reg. 1–5

Consiglio dei Dieci

Miste
   Reg. 1, 1310–1340 (fragment)
   Reg. 2, October 1315–18 February 1325 (fragment)
   Reg. 3, May 1325–February 1332 (fragment)
   Reg. 4, 22 May 1334–February 1335 (fragment)
   Reg. 5, 21 January 1349–24 March 1363
   Reg. 6, 19 April 1363–24 June 1374
   Reg. 7, 1374–1392 (lost)
   Reg. 8, 15 May 1392–28 February 1408
Liber Magnus
Miscellanea Consiglio dei Dieci 12A
Miscellanea Consiglio dei Dieci 20
Rubrica 2, 3, 4

Maggior Consiglio (Deliberazione) (M.C.)

   Magnus et Capricornus 1299–1308
   Presbyter 1308–1315
   Clericus Civicus 1315–1318
   Fronesis 1318–1325
   Spiritus 1325–1349
   Novella 1350–1384
   Leona 1384–1415

Miscellanea di Atti Diplomatici e Privati

   Busta 11

Miscellanea Codici I Storia Veneta

   Reg. 44 (originally Avogaria, Reg. 15)
   Reg. 51 and 52, Caroldo, *Cronaca Veneta*
   Reg. 58, Trattati e croniche varie
   Reg. 83, Cronici Veneti; cose appartenanti al Consiglio dei Dieci . . .
   Reg. 84, Raccolta di memorie storice e annedote per formare la storia
      dell' eccelso Consiglio dei Dieci
   Reg. 205, Sommario di leggi del Consiglio dei Dieci XIV–XVIII

Quarantia Criminale

Parti:
   Reg. 15, 1342–1343
   Reg. 16, 1347–1375
   Reg. 17, 1375–1389
Capitulare:
   Reg. 7, Capitulare fino al 1393
   Reg. 8, Sommario del Capitulare . . . fino al 1769
   Reg. 153, Decreti in Materia di Prigioni e Condennati, 1428–1795

Quattro Ministeriali Stride e Chiamori

Reg. 1, n.d.
Reg. 1 bis, 1396–1398
Reg. 2, 1404–1405

Segretario alle Voci

Miste
Reg. 1, 1349–1353
Reg. 2, 1362–1367
Reg. 3, 1383–1388

Senato

Miste
Reg. 1–14, 1293–1322 (lost)
Reg. 15, 1332–1334
Reg. 16, 1334–1335
Reg. 17, 1335–1339
Reg. 18, 1339–1340
Reg. 19, 1340–1342
Reg. 20, 1342–1343
Reg. 21, 1343–1344
Reg. 22, 1344
Reg. 23, 1344–1345
Reg. 24, 1345–1349
Reg. 25, 1349–1353
Reg. 26, 1353–1354
Reg. 27, 1354–1357
Reg. 28, 1357–1359
Reg. 29, 1359–1361
Reg. 30, 1361–1363
Reg. 31, 1363–1366
Reg. 32, 1366–1368
Reg. 33, 1368–1372
Reg. 34, 1372–1374
Reg. 35, 1375–1377
Reg. 36, 1377–1381
Reg. 37, 1381–1382
Reg. 38, 1382–1384
Reg. 39, 1384
Reg. 40, 1385–1389
Reg. 41, 1389–1391
Reg. 42, 1391–1394
Reg. 43, 1394–1397
Reg. 44, 1397–1399
Reg. 45, 1400–1401
Reg. 46, 1402–1405

Reg. 47, 1405–1408

Signori di Notte al Criminale

Processi
    Reg. 5, 1289–1291
    Reg. 6, 1348–1356
    Reg. 7, 1356–1361
    Reg. 8, 1361–1369
    Reg. 9, 1363–1369
    Reg. 10, 1368–1374
    Reg. 11, 1391–1397
    Reg. 12, 1389–1403 (fragment)
Banditi
    Reg. 13, 1370–1395
Capitulare
    Reg. 3

Chronicles and Related Manuscripts*

Biblioteca Nazionale Marciana

Lat. V 137 (10453) *Liber Statutorum*
Lat. X 136 (3026) attributed to Andrea Dandolo (sixteenth century)
    see Carile, pp. 4–5, 27
Lat. X 237 (3659) Anonymous (fourteenth century)
    see Carile, p. 212
Ital. VII 37 (8022) Enrico Dandolo (sixteenth century)
    see Carile, p. 63
Ital. VII 51 (8528) Anonymous (seventeenth century)
    see Carile, pp. 130, 136
Ital. VII 89 (8381) Enrico Dandolo (fifteenth century)
    see Carile, pp. 57, 63
Ital. VII 102 (8142) Enrico Dandolo (seventeenth century)
    see Carile, pp. 61, 63
Ital. VII 127 (8034) Gian Giacomo Caroldo (sixteenth century)
    see Carile, p. 158
Ital. VII 128A (8639) Gian Giacomo Caroldo (sixteenth century)
    see Carile, p. 158
Ital. VII 519 (8438) Pseudo-Trevisan (sixteenth century)
    see Carile, pp. 138–146, 215
Ital. VII 541 (7314) Anonymous (fifteenth century)
    see Carile, pp. 113, 125
Ital. VII 599 (7888) Enrico Dandolo (fifteenth century)
    see Carile, pp. 60, 63

* Where possible in these entries, reference has been made to the attempts made at tracing the origins of these chronicles by Antonio Carile in *La cronachista veneziana (secoli XIII–XVI) di fronte alla spartizione della Romania 1204.*

Ital. VII 788 (7293) Anonymous (sixteenth century)
>see Carile, p. 28

Ital. VII 791 (7589) Enrico Dandolo (sixteenth century)
>see Carile, pp. 70, 75

Ital. VII 800–801 (7151–7152) Marin Sanudo, *Vite dei Doge*
>(autograph)
>see Carile, pp. 156–157

Ital. VII 965–966 (8405–8406) Antonio Muazzo, *Discorso Istorico Politico del Governo Antico della Repubblica Veneta* (seventeenth century)

Ital. VII 2037 (8561) Anonymous (sixteenth century)
>see Carile, pp. 109, 125

Ital. VII 2048–2049 (8331-8332) Antonio Morosini (fifteenth century)
>see Carile, pp. 56, 214

Ital. VII 2051 (8271) Anonymous (fourteenth century)
>see Carile, pp. 17–18, 28

Ital. II 14 (4835) Fiore di Virtù (fourteenth century)

Ital. II 50 (4943) Statuti Veneziani

Ital. IX 28 (6301) *Cronaca in Terza Rime* (Attributed to fifteenth century, but internal evidence indicates it must be after 1500 and hand is quite late.)

Zanetti, Lat. 544 (2050) Poem to Pietro Gradenigo (fourteenth century)

Zanetti, Ital. 18 (4793) Anonymous (fifteenth century)

Museo Civico Correr

Cicogna 592, Pseudo-Zancaruolo (fifteenth century)
>see Carile, pp. 85–87, 106

Cicogna 1180, Pseudo-Barbaro (Daniel)

Cicogna 2831, Enrico Dandolo (seventeenth century)
>see Carile, pp. 61–63

Cicogna 2832, Enrico Dandolo (nineteenth century)
>see Carile, pp. 61–63

Cicogna 3729, *Origine del Consiglio de' Dieci* (seventeenth century)

Correr 1013, Anonymous (fourteenth century)
>see Carile, p. 28

Correr 1499, Anonymous (fourteenth century)
>see Carile, p. 28

Querini Stampalia

Querini IV cod. 2 H 7   Statuti Veneziani

Published Works

Aries, Philippe. *Centuries of Childhood: A Social History of Family Life.* London: Cape, 1962.

Baldwin, John W. "The Intellectual Preparation for the Canon of 1215 against Ordeals." *Speculum,* 36 (1961): 613–636.

Barnes, Harry Elmer. *The Story of Punishment: A Record of Man's Inhumanity to Man.* 2d ed. rev. Montclair, New Jersey: Patterson Smith, 1972.

Beloch, Karl Julius Alwin. *Bevölkerungsgeschichte Italiens.* 3 vols. Berlin and Leipzig: W. De Gruyter and Company, 1937–1961.

————. "La popolazione di Venezia nei secoli XVI e XVII." *Nuovo Archivio Veneto,* n.s. 3 (1902): 5–49.

Beltrami, Daniele. *Storia della popolazione di Venezia dalla fine del secolo XVI alla caduta della Repubblica.* Padua: CEDAM, 1954.

Bertaldo, Jacopo. *Splendor venetorum civitatis consuetudinum.* Edited by F. Schupfer. *Bibliotheca Iuridica Medii Aevi,* vol. 3. Bologna, 1901.

Besta, Enrico. "Il diritto e le leggi di Venezia fino al dogado di Enrico Dandolo." *Ateneo Veneto* anno 20, pt. 2 (1897): 290–320; anno 22, pt. 1 (1899): 145–184, 304–331; anno 22, pt. 2 (1899): 61–93, 202–248.

————. "Jacopo Bertaldo e lo splendor consuetudinum civitatis veneciarum." *Nuovo Archivio Veneto* 13 (1897): 109–133.

————. *Il senato veneziano (origini, costituzione, attribuzione e riti).* Miscellanea di Storia Venezia, ser. 2, vol. 5. Venice, 1899.

Boerio, Giuseppe. *Dizionario del dialetto veneziano di Giuseppe Boerio.* 2d ed. Venice: Giovanni Cecchini edit., 1856.

Bowsky, William M. "The Medieval Commune and Internal Violence: Police Power and Public Safety in Siena, 1287–1355." *American Historical Review* 73 (1967): 1–17.

Caenegem, Raoul Von. "The Law of Evidence in the Twelfth Century: European Perspectives and Intellectual Background." *Proceedings of the Second International Congress of Medieval Canon Law.* The Vatican, 1965.

Calisse, Carlo. *A History of Italian Law.* The Continental Legal History Series, vol. 8. New York: Rothman Reprints, 1969.

Carile, Antonio. *La cronachista veneziana (secoli XIII–XVI) di fronte alla spartizione della Romania nel 1204.* Civiltà Veneziana, Studi, vol. 25. Florence: L. S. Olschki, 1970.

Cessi, Roberto. "L'officium de navigantibus ed i sistemi della politica veneziana nel sec. XIV." *Nuovo Archivio Veneto,* ser. 3 32 (1916): 106–146.

————. *Politica ed economia di Venezia nel Trecento-Saggi.* Storia e Letteratura, no. 40. Rome: Edizioni di Storia e Letteratura, 1952.

————. *La regolazione delle entrate e delle spese.* Padua: A. Dragi, 1925.

————. *Storia della Repubblica di Venezia.* 2nd ed. 2 vols. Milan: G. Principato, 1968.

Cessi, Roberto, ed. *Le deliberazioni del Maggior Consiglio di Venezia.* Bologna: N. Zanichelli, 1950.

————. *Gli statuti veneziani di Jacopo Tiepolo del 1242 e le loro glosse.* Memorie del Reale Istituto Veneto di Scienze, Lettere ed Arti, vol. 30, no. 2. Venice: C. Ferrari, 1938.

Cessi, Roberto, and Bennato, Fanny, eds. *Venetiarum Historia Vulgo Petro Iustiniano Filio Adiudicata.* Deputazione di Storia Patria per le Venezie. Venice: A spese della deputazione, 1964.

Cessi, Roberto, and Brunetti, Mario, eds. *Le Deliberazioni del Consiglio dei Rogati (Senato) serie "mixtorum" 1332–1335,* Libri XV–XVI, vol. 2. Deputazione di Storia Patria per le Venezie, vol. 16. Venice: A spese della deputazione, 1962.

Cessi, Roberto, and Sambin, Paulo, eds. *Le Deliberazioni del Consiglio dei Rogati (Senato) serie "mixtorum,"* Libri I–XIV, vol. 1. *Deputazione di Storia Patria per le Venezie,* vol. 15. Venice: A spese della deputazione, 1960.

Chojnacki, Stanley. "Crime, Punishment, and the Trecento Venetian State." In *Violence and Disorder in Italian Cities, 1200–1500,* edited by Lauro Martines, pp. 184–228. Berkeley and Los Angeles: University of California Press, 1972.

———. "In Search of the Venetian Patriciate: Families and Factions in the Fourteenth Century." In *Renaissance Venice,* edited by John Hale, pp. 47–90. London: Faber and Faber, 1973.

Contento, Aldo. "Censimento della popolazione sotto la Repubblica Veneta." *Nuovo Archivio Veneto* 20 (1900): 5–96.

Cozzi, Gaetano. "Authority and the Law in Renaissance Venice." In *Renaissance Venice,* edited by John Hale, pp. 293–345. London: Faber and Faber, 1973.

Cracco, Giorgio. *Società e stato nel Medioevo Veneziano (secoli XII–XIV). Civiltà Veneziana, Studi.* vol. 22. Florence: L. S. Olschki, 1967.

D'Agano, Romolo Broglio. "L'industria della seta Venezia." In *Storia dell' economia italiana, saggi di storia economica,* vol. 1: *secoli settimo-diciossettesimo,* edited by Carlo M. Cipolla, pp. 209–262. Turin, 1959.

Da Mosto, Andrea. *L'Archivio di Stato di Venezia.* 2 vols. Rome: Biblioteca D'Arte Editrice, 1937–1940.

Dorini, Umberto. *Il diritto penale e la delinquenza in Firenze nel sec. XIV.* Lucca: Domenico Corsi Editore, 1923.

Ercole, Francesco. "La lotta delle classi alla fine del Medio Evo." In *Dal Comune al Principato. Saggi sulla storia del diritto pubblico del Rinascimento italiano,* edited by Francesco Ercole. Florence: Vallecchi, 1929.

Fano, Nella. "Ricerche sull'arte della lana nel XIII al XIV secolo." *Archivio Veneto,* ser. 5 18 (1936): 73–213.

Favaro, Elena, ed. *Cassiere della bolla ducale, grazie-novus liber (1299–1305). Fonti per la Storia di Venezia, sez. 1—Archivi Pubblici.* Venice: Il comitato editore, 1962.

Ferro, Maro. *Dizionario del diritto comune e veneto, . . .* 8 vols. Venice, 1778–1781. 2d ed. Venice, 1845.

Fulin, Rinaldo. "Gli inquisitori dei Dieci." *Archivio Veneto* 1 (1871): 1–64, 357–391.

———. *Studi nell'Archivio degli Inquisitori di Stato.* Venice: Tip. del commercio di M. Visentini, 1868.

Ghinato, Alberto. *Fr. Paolino da Venezia O.F.M. di Pozzuoli (+ 1344).* Rome: Scuola tip. Don Luigi Guanella, 1951.

Giannotti, Donato. *Libro de la Repubblica de Vinitiani.* Rome, 1542.

Griffo, Rizzaro. *Practica sommaria civile et criminale di tutte le leggi, decreti, consegli, et ordini del statuto veneto.* Venice, 1665.

Gundersheimer, Werner L. *Ferrara: The Style of a Renaissance Despotism.* Princeton, N.J.: Princeton University Press, 1972.

Hale, John R., ed. *Renaissance Venice.* London: Rowman and Littlefield, 1973.

Herlihy, David. *Medieval and Renaissance Pistoia: The Social History of an Italian Town, 1200–1430.* New Haven: Yale University Press, 1967.

Hyde, John K. *Padua in the Age of Dante: A Social History of an Italian City-State.* New York: Barnes and Noble, 1966.

Lane, Frederic C. "Enlargement of the Great Council of Venice." In *Florilegium Historiale: Essays Presented to Wallace K. Ferguson*. Edited by J. G. Rowe and W. H. Stockdale. Toronto: University of Toronto Press, 1971.

—. "The First Infidelities of the Venetian Lira." In *The Medieval City*, edited by Harry Miskimin, David Herlihy, and A. L. Udovich, pp. 43–63. New Haven: Yale University Press, 1967.

—. *Venice, a Maritime Republic*. Baltimore: Johns Hopkins Press, 1973.

—. *Venice and History; The Collected Papers of Frederick C. Lane*. Baltimore: Johns Hopkins Press, 1966.

Langbein, John H. *Prosecuting Crime in the Renaissance: England, Germany, France*. Cambridge: Harvard University Press, 1974.

Lazzarini, Lino. *Paolo de Bernardo e i primordi dell' umanesimo in Venezia*. Biblioteca dell'*Archivum Romanicum*, vol. 13. Geneva: L. S. Olschki, 1930.

—. *Marino Faliero*. Florence: G. C. Sansoni Editore, 1963.

Liber Promissione Malefici (ca. 1232). Leggi Criminali del Serenissimo Dominio Veneto in un solo volume raccolte e per pubblico decreto ristampata. Venice, 1751.

Lombardo, Antonio, ed. *Le deliberazione del Consiglio dei XL della Repubblica di Venezia*, vol. 1–3. *Deputazione di Storia Patria per le Venezie*, vols. 9, 12, 20. Venice: A spese della deputazione, 1957–1967.

Luzzatto, Gino. *Il debito pubblico della Repubblica di Venezia degli ultimi decenni del XII secolo alla fine del XV*. Milan: Istituto editoriale cisalpino, 1963.

—. *I prestiti della Repubblica di Venezia (sec. XIII–XV) Introduzione Storica e Documenti*. Padua: A. Dragi, 1929.

—. *Storia economia di Venezia dall' XI al XVI secolo*. Venice: Centro Internazionale delle Arti e del Costume, 1961.

Maranini, Giuseppe. *La costituzione di Venezia dalle origini alla Serrata del Maggior Consiglio*. Venice: La Nuova Italia, 1927.

—. *La costituzione di Venezia dopo la Serrata del Maggior Consiglio*. Venice, Perugia, Florence: La Nuova Italia, 1931.

Martines, Lauro. *Lawyers and Statecraft in Renaissance Florence*. Princeton, N.J.: Princeton University Press, 1968.

—. "Political Conflict in the Italian City States." *Government and Opposition* 3 (1968): 69–91.

Martines, Lauro, ed. *Violence and Civil Disorder in Italian Cities, 1200–1500*. Berkeley and Los Angeles: University of California Press, 1972.

Merores, Margarete. "Der grosse Rat von Venedig und die sogenannte Serrata von Jahre 1297." *Vierteljahrschrift für Sozial- und Wirtschaftsgeschichte* 21 (1928): pp. 33–113.

Minorita, Fra Paulo. *De recto regimine*. Edited by Adolfo Mussafia. Florence, 1868.

Mocenigo, Nani. *Capitolare dei Signori di Notte esistante nel Civico Museo di Venezia*. Venice, 1877.

Molmenti, Pompeo. *La storia di Venezia nella vita privata*. 3 vols. Bergamo: Istituto italiano d'arti grafiche editore, 1906.

Monticolo, Giovanni. *I capitolari delle arte veneziane sottoposte alla Giustizia Vecchia dalle origini al MCCCXXX*. 3 vols. *Fonti per la storia d' Italia*, vols. 26–28. Rome, 1896–1914.

————. L'ufficio della Giustizia Vecchia a Venezia dalle origini sino al 1330. Monumenti della Deputazione Veneta di Storia Venezia, Miscellanea, vol. 12. Venice: A spese della società, 1892.

Mor, Carlo Guido. "Il procedimento per 'Gratiam' nel diritto amministrativo veneziano del sec. XIII." Cassiere della bolla ducale, grazie-novus liber (1299–1305). Edited by Elena Favaro. Fonti per la Storia di Venezia, sez. 1—Archivi Pubblici. Venice: Comitato editore, 1962.

Mueller, Reinhold C. "The Procuratori di San Marco and the Venetian Credit Market: A Study of the Development of Credit and Banking in the Trecento." Ph.D. diss., Johns Hopkins University, 1970.

Pansolli, Lamberto. La gerarchia delle fonti di diritto nella legislazione medievale veneziana. Milan: Dott. A. Giuffrè Editore, 1970.

Paolino Minorita. Trattato de regimine rectoris. Edited by Adolfo Mussafia. Vienna and Florence, 1868.

Papadopoli-Aldobrandini, Nicolò. "Sul valore della moneta veneziana" letto nell' adunanza del R. Istituto di Scienze, Lettere ed Arti di Venezia. Venice, 1885.

Pastorello, Ester, ed. Andrea Dandolo, chronicon per estensum descripta. Rerum italicarum Scriptores. 2d ed., vol. 12, pt. 1. Bologna, 1940.

Piana, Celestino, and Cenci, Cesare, O.F.M. Promozioni agli ordini sacri a Bologna e alle dignità ecclesiastica nel Veneto nei secc. XIV–XV. Spicilegium Bonaventurianum, vol. 3. Florence, 1968.

Pillinini, Giovanni. "Marin Falier e la crisi della metà del' 300 a Venezia." Archivio Veneto, ser. 5 84 (1968): 45–71.

Priori, Lorenzo. Practica criminale secondo le leggi della serenissima Repubblica di Venezia. Venice, 1738.

Prost, August. "Les chroniques vénitiennes." Revue des Questions Historiques 31 (1882): 512–555; 34 (1883): 199–224.

Pugh, Ralph B. Imprisonment in Medieval England. Cambridge: At the University Press, 1968.

Pullan, Brian. Rich and Poor in Renaissance Venice: The Social Institutions of a Catholic State, to 1620. Oxford: Basil Blackwell, 1971.

Queller, Donald E. "The Civic Irresponsibility of the Venetian Nobility." In Economy, Society, and Government in Medieval Italy: Essays in Honor of Robert L. Reynolds, edited by David Herlihy, Robert S. Lopez, and Vsevolod Slessarev. Kent, Ohio: Kent State University Press, 1969.

Roberti, Melchiorre. Le magistrature giudiziarie veneziane e i loro capitolare fino al 1300. 3 vols. Monumenti Storici publicati dalla R. Deputazione Veneta di Storia Patria. Venice: Tip. Emiliana, 1907–1911.

Ruggiero, Guido. "The Cooperation of Physicians and the State in the Control of Violence in Renaissance Venice." Journal of the History of Medicine and Allied Sciences 33 (1978): 156–166.

————. "Law and Punishment in Early Renaissance Venice." Journal of Criminal Law and Criminology 69 (1978): 243–256.

————. "The Ten: Control of Violence and Social Disorder in Trecento Venice." Ph.D. diss., University of California at Los Angeles, 1972.

————. "Sexual Criminality in the Early Renaissance: Venice 1338–1358." Journal of Social History 8 (1974–1975): 18–37.

Sade, Donatien, Marquis de. *The Complete Justine, Philosophy in the Bedroom and Other Writings.* Edited by Richard Seaver and Austryn Wainhouse. New York: Grove Press, 1966.

Sanuto, Marino. *Vita de' duchi di Venezia.* In *Rerum Italicarum Scriptores,* vol. 22, edited by L. A. Muratori. Milan, 1733.

Slater, Phillip Elliot. *The Glory of Hera; Greek Mythology and the Greek Family.* Boston: Beacon Press, 1968.

Soranzo, Giovanni. *La guerra fra Venezia e la S. Sede per il dominio di Ferrara.* Città di Castello: Casa tip. edit. S. Lapi, 1905.

Stefanuti, Ugo, ed. *Documentazioni cronologiche per la storia della medicina chirurgia e farmacia in Venezia dal 1258 al 1332.* Venice: F. Organia, 1961.

Zago, Ferruccio, ed. *Consiglio dei Dieci, Deliberazioni Miste, Registri I–II (1310–1325).* 2 vols. *Fonti per la Storia di Venezia.* Venice: Il comitato editore, 1962 and 1968.

INDEX

A

Abduction, 14, 162–163, 164
Accusations
  anonymous, 35
  false, 70, 166
Adultery, 76, 102, 113, 115, 168
Aries, Phillipe, 165, 205 *n*. 10
Arms. *See* Weapons
Arrengare, 25
Arsenal workers, speech crime and, 130
Assassins, 77, 80, 150, 171, 175
  marginal people as, 115–116, 172
  murder by important people and, 87–88
  murder by nobles and, 72–73, 87, 102
  paid, 175–176
  ritual execution of, 1–2
  See also Murder
Assault
  bloodshed during, 153
  of clerics, 151–153
  confiscation of goods and, 143–144
  context of, an overview, 138–140
  of guild officials, 91–92, 99–100, 106, 140–141, 144–145
  important people and, 82, 83, 85
    penalties for, 84–85
    as victims of, 91–92
  insults (private) and, 132
  legal procedure for cases of, 11–12
  litigation as cause of, 11, 80, 92, 100, 146–148
  lower classes and, 142–143
  marginal people and, 114–115
    as victims of, 116–117
  minor, summary handling of, 96, 98–99
  nobles and, 66, 67, 68–70
    penalties for, 47, 68–69

Assault, nobles and (*continued*)
    as victims of, 79–81, 84
  of officials, 143–146
    communal, 80, 99, 103, 106, 115, 140–141, 188 *n*. 12
    guild, 91–92, 99–100, 106, 140–141, 144–145
  for pay, 149
  penalties for, 41–42, 46, 47, 50–51, 68–69, 84–85, 100–101, 142, 143, 144, 163
  publicly announced, 149
  of police patrols, 83, 87, 88, 89–90, 91, 99, 115, 140–143
  the *Promissio Maleficorum* and, penalties for, 41–42
  significance of, 153–155
  of social superiors, 148–151
  special types of, 148–151
  as street crime—brawls (*brige*) and fights (*rixe*), 138–139
  workers and, 95, 98–101, 140–141
    penalties for, 47, 100–101
    as victims of, 106–108
Avogadori (Avogaria di Comun), 27, 172
  assault and, 11–12, 138, 139, 147, 153
  authority and structure of, 19–21
  codifying the laws and, 40–41
  Falier conspiracy and, 3
  the Forty and, 5
  judicial procedures of, 21–26
  legislation and, 20
  Major Council membership and, 194 *n*. 7
  murder and, 171, 174–175
  penalties and, 20, 21, 26, 30
  ritual execution and, 1
  speech crimes and, 128, 132, 133
  the Ten and, 34–35, 37
  trials and, 19